## Please Note!

Individuals and book stores in Arizona, British Columbia, California, Idaho, Montana, Nevada, New Mexico, Oregon, Utah, Washington and Wyoming will receive shipment more promptly if ordered direct from

WARREN R. GIBBS
Western Representative
109 Windsor Avenue, Berkeley, California

## Removal Notice

On April 1, 1939, I moved my book business from 5494 Cornell Avenue, Chicago, Illinois, to my home in Bowling Green, Kentucky, in order that I may better look after my business of curing and selling Kentucky Hickory-Smoked hams.

# ADVENTURES
## IN
# GOOD COOKING
### *and the*
## ART OF CARVING
## IN THE HOME

A *Duncan Hines* BOOK

## FAMOUS RECIPES

*Published by*
ADVENTURES IN GOOD EATING, INC.
BOWLING GREEN, KY.

Duncan Hines

# INTRODUCTION

THIS book is in answer to the oft-repeated request of friends who have visited so many of the places listed in my book, *Adventures in Good Eating*. Having enjoyed the particular specialties for which many of them are justly famous, these friends have eagerly sought an opportunity to try to prepare these same dishes in the intimate and friendly atmosphere of their own home kitchen. They are intrigued with the pleasant prospect of giving their own personal interpretation to some of these unusual specialties. It is a matter of extreme gratification to me that so many of my friends whose places are mentioned in *Adventures in Good Eating* have consented to release their recipes for publication here.

In their enthusiasm for the cause of gastronomy, other friends have sent me their favorite cookbook. I am deeply appreciative of the thoughts which prompted these gestures of good will and, today, I possess a rather imposing collection of cookery literature.

Frequently during recent years I have been fortunate to be a guest in many homes, where I have enjoyed some unusual dish or portion. Knowing my failing for gastronomic formulas, my hostess has usually been gracious enough to let me have the recipe for the dish in question. Often it is a treasured family recipe for which I am deeply indebted to these friends for their willingness to share their wealth of culinary knowledge.

Obviously, I have not had an opportunity to test all the recipes included in this first edition of ADVENTURES IN GOOD COOKING. However, many of them I can speak of from personal experience, for I have used them in my own experimental kitchen in Bowling Green to the delight of my guests as well as myself.

ADVENTURES IN GOOD COOKING has been compiled for the benefit of those who like to prepare good things to eat as much for the simple enjoyment of concocting them as for the sheer delight of spreading the results of their labors before appreciative guests and hearing their exclamations of gustatory satisfaction.

The modern home kitchen is no longer the exclusive domain of the gentler sex, for it is common knowledge that many a male is also adept with skillet and pan.

It is only fair to say that the recipes presented herewith are not designed for the beginner. There are many excellent cookbooks which have been prepared especially for the young housewife, whose experience does not go beyond the more familiar phases of culinary routine. But for those who have served an adequate apprenticeship, there will be found among these recipes innumerable invitations to new and zestful adventures in the culinary art. To you, my friends, the contents of this book are addressed.

It should hardly be necessary to remind you that all measurements must be made accurately, and oven temperatures observed closely; nor will the successful adventurer tolerate substitutes; and remember, practically all recipes written for restaurant use contemplate substantially larger quantities than is customary for family use. It is a well-known fact that the amount of ingredients designated in quantity recipes cannot often be reduced proportionately and give the same results. Therefore, I would caution you to mix reason and common sense with your measurements in undertaking to follow any quantity recipes contained herein.

No school of cookery makes such unstinted use of fresh eggs, butter and milk as we do in America.

The heart and soul of any dish is its flavor. Therefore, the true disciple of Escoffier uses his seasonings and flavorings with discretion. Use your seasonings as an artist does his pigments. Some colors must be used with great restraint and a "whisper" of garlic is usually more potent than a handful of herbs. It is genuine economy to use only the best and freshest spices and seasonings. Be sure that they are true to taste, for only in that way can you be assured of the same results every time. Quality ingredients combined with skillful preparation can usually be counted on to achieve the desired result. So let's go out into the kitchen now and set forth on a new adventure in good cooking. May we have fun in the doing as well as the eating. Good luck.

DUNCAN HINES

You will find the recipes numbered rather than the pages, and credit for each one is given in the line immediately following the recipe. Inasmuch as I have not been able to test all the recipes, it is my suggestion that you write the individual or institution, if you desire additional information regarding any of the recipes.

*Many recipes were, unfortunately, received too late to be included in this edition. Others did not give sufficient detailed information. Still others too nearly duplicated recipes previously received.*

*Price of this book is $1.50 (postpaid in United States or Canada) upon receipt of a money order or check. (No stamps please.)*

*Photograph by courtesy of Marshall Field & Company, Chicago*

WHITE linen damask cloth and napkins. Entree fork, dinner fork, salad fork, service plate, dinner knife, entree knife, soup spoon (reading left to right). The silverware is of sterling silver in the Etruscan pattern. The service plates are Lenox china in cobalt blue in traditional eighteenth-century English pattern on a lovely lustrous body, scroll worked out in gold. The water goblet, claret and sherry glasses (reading left to right) are the finest rock crystal, Belgium glass, in the Hampton pattern. A silver candelabra, eighteenth-century style, is in the center of the table. The two sauce tureens and two fruit compotiers are part of an old Worcester dessert service decorated in the early Imari.

# EQUIVALENT MEASURES AND WEIGHTS

A few grains = less than 1/8 teaspoon
3 teaspoons = 1 tablespoon
2 tablespoons = 1 oz. liquid or fat
4 tablespoons = 1/4 cup
16 tablespoons = 1 cup
1/2 cup = 1 gill
4 gills = 1 pint
1 cup = 8 oz. or 1/2 lb. liquid or fat
16 ounces = 1 lb.
2 cups = 1 pint
1 pint = 1 lb. liquid or fat
4 cups = 1 quart
2 pints = 1 quart
4 quarts = 1 gallon
8 quarts = 1 peck
4 pecks = 1 bushel

1 dash = 1/4 teaspoon
1 pony = 1/8 oz.
1 wine glass = 2 oz.
1 jigger = 1 1/2 oz.
1 shell = 1 1/2 oz.

# MEASURES OF CANNED FOOD CONTAINERS

| Size Can | |
|---|---|
| Buffet or Picnic | = 1 cup |
| No. 1 | = 1 1/3 cups |
| No. 1 tall | = 2 cups |
| No. 2 | = 2 1/2 cups |
| No. 2 1/2 | = 3 1/2 cups |
| No. 3 | = 4 cups |
| No. 5 | = 7 cups |
| No. 10 | = 13 cups |

# RECOMMENDED TEMPERATURES

| | | |
|---|---|---|
| Simmering water | 180 F | |
| Boiling water | 212 F | |
| Boiled Icings | 238 F—240 F | |
| Jellying stage | 218 F—222 F | |
| Very slow Oven | 250 F | |
| Slow Oven | 300 F | |
| Moderate Oven | 350 F | |
| Hot Oven | 400 F | |
| Very Hot Oven | 450 F or more | |

## DEEP FAT FRYING

| | | |
|---|---|---|
| Croquettes | 370 F—380 F | 4— 7 minutes |
| Fish | 370 F—380 F | 8—10 minutes |
| Fritters, Doughnuts, etc. | 360 F—370 F | 2— 5 minutes |
| Potatoes—raw | 370 F—395 F | 5— 8 minutes |

## BREADS, ETC.

| | | |
|---|---|---|
| Baking Powder Biscuits | 440 F—460 F | 12—15 minutes |
| Baking Powder Loaf Bread | 375 F—400 F | 50—60 minutes |
| Muffins | 400 F—425 F | 18—25 minutes |
| Yeast Breads | 400 F | 15 minutes, then reduce to 375 F for about 45 minutes |
| Yeast Rolls | 400 F—425 F | 20—25 minutes |
| Cup Cakes | 400 F—425 F | 18—25 minutes |
| Layer Cake | 325 F—350 F | 20 minutes |
| Loaf Cake | 350 F | 45—60 minutes |
| Sponge Cake | 325 F—350 F | 40—50 minutes |
| Angel Food Cakes | 300 F—350 F | 35—50 minutes |
| Pie Shells | 425 F—475 F | 20 minutes |
| Double Crusted Pies | 450 F—425 F | 15 minutes, then reduce to 425 F for 30 to 45 minutes |

## MEATS AND FOWL

| | | | |
|---|---|---|---|
| Beef—Rolled Rib—rare | | 350 F—400 F | 15—18 minutes to the pound |
| | medium | 350 F—400 F | 20—22 minutes to the pound |
| | well-done | 350 F—400 F | 23—26 minutes to the pound |
| Standing Rib—rare | | 350 F—400 F | 12—15 minutes to the pound |
| | medium | 350 F—400 F | 18—20 minutes to the pound |
| | well-done | 350 F—400 F | 25—28 minutes to the pound |
| Fresh Ham | | 350 F | 25—30 minutes to the pound |
| Leg of Lamb | | 350 F | 28—30 minutes to the pound |
| Leg of Veal | | 350 F | 28—30 minutes to the pound |
| Pork Loin | | 350 F | 30—35 minutes to the pound |
| Chicken | | 450 F | 20 minutes, then reduce to 300 F 25—28 minutes to the pound |
| Capon | | 450 F | 20 minutes, then reduce to 300 F 18—22 minutes to the pound |
| Duck | | 475 F | 20 minutes, then reduce to 350 F 18—20 minutes to the pound |
| Turkey | | 325 F—350 F | 18—22 minutes to the pound |

# FOOD WEIGHTS AND MEASURES

This table is for approximate weights and measures of various foods and is intended as a handy compilation in estimating quantities. Courtesy of *Restaurant Management Magazine*, 222 East 42d Street, New York City, N. Y.

| *Ingredient* | *Weights* | *Measures* |
| --- | --- | --- |
| Almonds (shelled, chopped) | 1 oz. | ¼ cup |
| Allspice (ground) | 1 oz. | 5 tablespoons |
| Allspice (whole) | 1 oz. | 6 tablespoons |
| Apple (juice) | 8 oz. | 1 cup |
| Apples (dried) | 1 lb. | 5 cups |
| Apricots (dry) | 1 lb. | 3 cups |
| Apricots (soaked and cooked) | 1 lb. | 4 cups and juice |
| Asparagus (fresh) cut in 1-inch pcs. | 1 lb. | 2 cups |
| Baking powder | 1 oz. | 3 tablespoons |
| Bananas (mashed) | 1 lb. | 2 cups |
| Barley (pearl) | 1 lb. | 2 cups |
| Beans (dried) | 1 lb. | 2¼ cups |
| Beans (green or waxed, fresh) (cut in 1-inch pieces) | 1 lb. | 3 cups |
| Beans, lima (shelled, fresh) | 1 lb. | 2 cups |
| Beef (raw, ground) | 1 lb. | 2 cups |
| Beets (cooked, diced) | 1 lb. | 2½ cups |
| Bread | 1 lb. | 12 slices, ½-inch thick |
| Bread crumbs (dried, sifted) | 4 oz. | 1 cup |
| Butter | 1 lb. | 2 cups |
| Butter | 1 oz. | 2 tablespoons |
| Butter | Size of an egg | ¼ cup |
| Cabbage (cooked) | 1 lb. | 2½ cups |
| Carrots (diced, raw) | 1 lb. | 3¼ cups |
| Carrots (diced fine, cooked) | 5 1-3 oz. | 1 cup |
| Cashew nuts | 1 lb. | 4 cups |
| Celery seed | 1 oz. | 4 tablespoons |
| Celery (minced) | 1 stalk | 1½ tablespoons |
| Celery salt | 1 oz. | 2 2-3 tablespoons |
| Cheese (cream) | 1 lb. | 2 cups |
| Cheese (cream, Philadelphia) | 6 oz. | 1 pkg. |
| Cheese (cubed) | 1 lb. | 2 2-3 cups |
| Cherries (candied) | 1 lb. | 3 cups |
| Chestnuts (in shell) | 1 lb. | 2 cups—meats |
| Chicken (cooked, cubed) | 1 lb. | 3 cups |
| Chili powder | 1 oz. | 4 tablespoons |
| Chocolate | 1 lb. | 16 squares |
| Chocolate (grated) | 1 oz. | 4 tablespoons |
| Chocolate (melted) | 1 lb. | 2 cups |
| Cider | 8 oz. | 1 cup |
| Cinnamon (ground) | 1 oz. | 4 tablespoons |
| Cinnamon (stick) | ¾ oz. | 4 (5-inch size) |
| Cloves (ground) | 1 oz. | 4 tablespoons |
| Cloves (whole) | 1 oz. | 6 tablespoons |
| Cocoa (ground) | 1 oz. | 4 tablespoons |
| Cocoanut (shredded) | 1 lb. | 6 cups |
| Coffee (ground fine) | 1 lb. | 5 cups |
| Corn (canned) | 1 lb. | 1¾ cups |

# FOOD WEIGHTS AND MEASURES—Continued

| Ingredient | Weights | Measures |
|---|---|---|
| Corn (fresh, cut off ear) | 3 ears | 1 cup |
| Cornmeal | 1 lb. | 3 cups |
| Cornstarch | 1 oz. | 3 tablespoons |
| Cracker crumbs | 2½ oz. | 1 cup |
| Crackers (graham, crushed) | 1 cup | 12 crackers |
| Cranberries | 1 lb. | 4 cups |
| Cranberry sauce (strained) | 1 lb. | 2 cups |
| Cream of Tartar | 1 oz. | 3 tablespoons |
| Cucumbers (diced) | 1 lb. | 2 cups |
| Currants (dried) | 1 lb. | 3 cups |
| Currants (dried) | 10 oz. | 1 pkg. |
| Curry powder | 1 oz. | 4 2-3 tablespoons |
| Dates (pitted) | 1 lb. | 3 cups |
| Eggs (1 unbeaten) | 1½ oz. | 3 tablespoons |
| Eggs (whole) | 1 cup | 4 to 6 medium |
| Eggs (whites)—1 cup | 8 oz. | 8 to 10 |
| Eggs (yolks)—1 cup | 8 oz. | 12 to 16 |
| Figs (dried, cut-up) | 1 lb. | 2¾ cups |
| Filberts (shelled) | 1 lb. | 3½ cups |
| Fish (fresh, chopped) | 1 lb. | 2 cups |
| Anchovy Paste | 3½ oz. | 4 tablespoons |
| Caviar | 1 oz. | 2 tablespoons |
| Clams (minced) | 7 oz. | 1½ cups |
| Clam Chowder | 11 oz. | 1 cup |
| Crab | 13 oz. | 2½ cups |
| Lobster | 12 oz. | 1 2-3 to 2 cups |
| Oysters | 4 oz. | 1 cup |
| Salmon | 8 oz. | 1 cup |
| Sardines (in oil) | 3½ oz. | 18-25, tiny |
| Flour (bread, sifted) | 1 lb. | 4 cups |
| Flour (graham, sifted) | 1 lb. | 3½ to 3¾ cups |
| Flour (rye, sifted) | 1 lb. | 5½ cups |
| Flour (whole wheat) | 1 lb. | 3¾ cups |
| Flour (bread) | 1 oz. | 3 to 4 tablespoons |
| Flour (pastry, sifted) | 4 oz. | 1 cup |
| Flour (rice) | 1 lb. | 2 cups |
| Gelatine (granulated) | 1 lb. | 4 cups |
| Gelatine (prepared) | 1 lb. | 2½ cups |
| Ginger (ground) | 1 oz. | 6 tablespoons |
| Grapes (cut and seeded) | 1 lb. | 2 to 3 cups |
| Grapefruit juice | 8 oz. | 1 cup |
| Ham (cooked, diced) | 1 lb. | 2 2-3 cups |
| Ham (cooked, ground) | 1 lb. | 2 cups |
| Honey | 11 oz. | 1 cup |
| Lard | 8 oz. | 1 cup |
| Lemons | 1 lb. | 3 to 5 lemons |
| Lemon juice | 1 cup | 4 to 5 lemons |
| Lemon rind | 1 lemon | 2 teaspoons |
| Macaroni (elbow) | 1 lb. | 3 cups |
| Mayonnaise | 1 lb. | 2 cups |
| Meat (chopped, cooked) | 1 lb. | 2 cups |
| Milk (condensed, sweetened) | 11 oz. | 1 cup |
| Milk (evaporated) | 1 lb. | 2 cups |
| Molasses | 12 oz. | 1 cup |
| Mixed spices | 1 lb. | 4 2-3 cups |

# FOOD WEIGHTS AND MEASURES—Continued

| Ingredient | Weights | Measures |
|---|---|---|
| Mushrooms (canned) | 1 lb. | 2 cups |
| Mustard (dried) | 1 oz. | 5 tablespoons |
| Mustard seed | 1 oz. | 3 1-3 tablespoons |
| Nutmeg (ground) | 1 oz. | 4 2-3 tablespoons |
| Oats (rolled, quick-cook) | 2¾ oz. | 1 cup |
| Oatmeal (quick-cook) | 1 lb. | 3 cups |
| Oils | 1 lb. | 2 cups |
| Olives (stuffed, chopped) | 6½ oz. | 1 cup |
| Onions (chopped) | 1 lb. | 2½ to 3 cups |
| Onions (large, minced) | 1 onion | ½ cup |
| Onions (medium, minced) | 1 onion | 5 tablespoons |
| Onions (small, minced) | 1 onion | 3 tablespoons |
| Onions (medium) | 1 lb. | 4 to 5 |
| Orange (rind, grated) | ½ oz. | 2 tablespoons |
| Paprika | 1 oz. | 3¾ tablespoons |
| Parsley (chopped) | 3 oz. | 1 cup |
| Parsnips (cooked, sliced) | 1 lb. | 2½ cups |
| Peaches (dried) | 1 lb. | 3 cups |
| Peaches (fresh, sliced) | 1 lb. | 2 to 2½ cups |
| Peanuts (shelled, Jumbo) | 1 lb. | 3 cups |
| Peanut butter | 1 lb. | 1 2-3 cups |
| Peas (fresh in shells) | 1 lb. | 1 cup shelled |
| Peas (yellow, split) | 1 lb. | 2¼ cups |
| Pecans (shelled) | 1 lb. | 4 cups |
| Pepper (ground, black or white) | 1 oz. | 4 tablespoons |
| Peppercorns | 1 oz. | 6 tablespoons |
| Peppers (green, chopped) | 4 oz. | 1 cup |
| Pickles (chopped) | 6 oz. | 1 cup |
| Pineapple (canned, tidbits) | 1 lb. | 2 cups |
| Pineapple (canned, sliced, and diced) | 3 slices | 1 cup |
| Pineapple (candied) | 1 lb. | 7 rings |
| Pineapple (juice) | 8 oz. | 1 cup |
| Potatoes (cooked, diced) | 1 lb. | 2½ cups |
| Popcorn | 1 lb. | 3 cups |
| Prunes (cooked, pitted) | 1 lb. | 3 cups |
| Raisins (seedless) | 1 lb. | 3 cups |
| Raisins (seeded) | 1 lb. | 2 cups |
| Raisins (seedless) | 5 1-3 oz. | 1 cup |
| Rhubarb (edible part cooked) | 1 lb. | 2¼ cups |
| Rice | 1 lb. | 2 cups |
| Rutabagas (diced and cooked) | 1 lb. | 2 to 2½ cups |
| Rye Meal | 3 1-3 oz. | 1 cup |
| Sage (rubbed, packed) | 2 oz. | 1 cup |
| Salt | 1 oz. | 1¾ tablespoons |
| Soda | 1 oz. | 2½ tablespoons |
| Sauerkraut (packed) | 1 lb. | 3 cups |
| Scallops | 1 lb. | 20 medium |
| Shrimp | 1 lb. | 3¼ cups or 24 medium |
| Spinach (cooked) | 1 lb. | 2 cups |
| Squash (cooked, mashed) | 1 lb. | 2 cups |
| Strawberries (whole) | 1 qt. | 3½ cups |
| String beans (canned) | 1 lb. | 2 cups |
| Suet (chopped) | 1 lb. | 4 to 5 cups |
| Sugar, brown | 1 lb. | 3 cups |

# FOOD WEIGHTS AND MEASURES—Continued

| Ingredient | Weights | Measures |
|---|---|---|
| Sugar, confectioners | 4½ oz. | 1 cup |
| Sugar, granulated | 1 lb. | 2 cups |
| Sugar, powdered | 6½ oz. | 1 cup |
| Tapioca (minute) | 1 lb. | 2½ cups |
| Tapioca (pearl) | 5 oz. | 1 cup |
| Tea (dry) | 2 oz. | 1 cup |
| Tomatoes | 1 lb. | 4 medium |
| Tomatoes (cooked) | 1 lb. | 1¾ cups |
| Tomato juice | 8 oz. | 1 cup |
| Turnips (diced, raw) | 1 lb. | 2 cups |
| Vanilla | 1 oz. | 2 tablespoons |
| Vermicelli | 8 oz. | 2 cups |
| Vinegar | 8 oz. | 1 cup |
| Walnuts (English, shelled) | 4 oz. | 1 cup |
| Water | 8 oz. | 1 cup |
| Yeast | ½ oz. | 1 cake |

*The dishes most popular are not those complicated with a vast number of ingredients. Instead, those remembered with pleasure and desired often are the simple, easily prepared recipes.*

# 1. Artichoke Bottom Stuffed with Crab or Lobster

(Serves 1)

| INGREDIENTS | DIRECTIONS |
|---|---|
| 2½ ozs. crab meat<br>or<br>½ lobster tail from a<br>1½ lb. lobster | Marinate for 2 hours. |
| 1 tablespoon tartar<br>sauce<br>1 dash of Tabasco sauce<br>1 teaspoon chopped<br>anchovies<br>1 teaspoon catsup | Mix together and add to crab meat or lobster. |
| 1 fresh artichoke<br>bottom | Stuff with mixture, decorate with chopped eggs (yolks and whites), slice of stuffed olive and a spot of caviar. |

*Biltmore Hotel, Los Angeles, California*


# 2. Golden Grapefruit

(Serves 1)

| INGREDIENTS | DIRECTIONS |
|---|---|
| ½ grapefruit<br>1 tablespoon brown<br>sugar<br>1 tablespoon sherry | Core grapefruit and fill center with sugar and wine. Heat in 350 F. oven until sugar is melted. |

*Old Spinning Wheel Tea Room, Hinsdale, Illinois*


# 3. Grapefruit Burgundy

(Serves 6)

| INGREDIENTS | DIRECTIONS |
|---|---|
| 1 cup fruit juice<br>½ cup sugar | Simmer fruit juice and sugar until it becomes of medium thickness. |
| ¼ cup wine (either red<br>or white) | After syrup has cooled, add the wine.<br>Cover top of half grapefruit with syrup and decorate with half a cherry or mint leaves. |

*Rustic Tea Room, Evergreen, Colorado*

## 4. Hot Brandied Grapefruit     (Serves 1)

INGREDIENTS

½ grapefruit
2 tablespoons brown
  sugar
1 teaspoon butter
1 tablespoon brandy

DIRECTIONS

Loosen sections of grapefruit and cover with sugar, butter and brandy. Broil slowly until heated through and bubbling. Serve piping hot as an appetizer.

*The Meiringen, Roanoke, Virginia*


## 5. Cheese Hors d'Oeuvres

INGREDIENTS

1 cake snappy cheese
¼ lb. butter
1¼ cups flour
1 dash red pepper

DIRECTIONS

Work all ingredients together and form into a long roll about 1 inch in diameter. Wrap in buttered paper and store in ice box until ready to use. (Will keep for a week or more). Slice in ½-inch rounds and bake in 400 F. oven for 5 minutes.

An almond may be added to top before baking.

*Mrs. E. P. Morrow, Frankfort, Kentucky*


## 6. Hot Toasted Cheese Hors d'Oeuvres     (Serves 25)

INGREDIENTS

2 cups grated cheese
1 egg beaten
10 dashes Tabasco sauce
1 teaspoon Lea &
  Perrins
¼ teaspoon salt

DIRECTIONS

Mix well with a fork.

2 loaves of bread

Remove crusts and cut in 1-inch squares. Place a spoonful of mixture on each piece.

1 lb. bacon

Top with thin strips of bacon.

Toast in 450 F. oven until brown.

*Cathryn's, Portland, Oregon*

# 7.  Jellied Tomato Canape
(Serves 8 to 12)

INGREDIENTS

DIRECTIONS

1 tablespoon gelatin
¼ cup cold water

Dissolve.

2 cups tomato juice
1 teaspoon powdered
   sugar
1 teaspoon salt

Heat and add to gelatin.  Pour into individual molds and let set.

chicken livers—
cooked.
salt and seasoning to
taste

Make a paste of these ingredients and with a small spoon scoop out the center of each mold. Fill the cavity with the liver paste.  Melt the jelly removed from the centers over hot water and pour over the openings.  Chill.

garnishes

Serve on rounds of crisp toast.  Garnish with ½ deviled egg, decorated with sprig of parsley to make a handle for the basket and dab of mayonnaise, 2 stuffed olives and sprigs of parsley.

*Mrs. Louie M. Weathers, Elkton, Kentucky*


# 8.  Mint Leaf Chips

INGREDIENTS

DIRECTIONS

3 cups mint leaves

Wash fresh picked leaves in cold water and dry on a towel.

1 egg white

Dip each leaf in unbeaten egg white and cover with powdered sugar.

powdered sugar

The sugaring is done as follows: Dust powdered sugar on a bread board and lay the mint leaves on the sugar and tamp lightly. Turn them over and tamp again.

Put in a refrigerator on a cookie sheet.  The leaves will become stiff like potato chips and can be eaten in the same manner or may be used to garnish jello, fruit salad, etc.

*Mr. A. E. R. Peterka, Cleveland, Ohio*

## 9.  Spiced Orange Peel

(Makes 3 gallons)

INGREDIENTS

DIRECTIONS

12 quarts orange peel

Peel oranges carefully, so that no fruit is left on the rind.  Cut rind into 2-inch lengths and measure until there are 12 qts.  Soak over night in cold water.  Drain.  Cover with water and bring to a boil, then discard water.  Do this 3 times, cooking the rind until tender in third cooking.  Drain.

5 quarts sugar
2 pints vinegar
1½ oz. whole cloves
1 pkg. stick cinnamon

Make a syrup and add the orange peel.  This may seem a little thick, but after heating you will find it the right consistency.  Cook slightly and bottle while hot, leaving cinnamon and cloves in the syrup.

This same syrup may be used for spicing grapefruit peel, fresh pineapple, or tiny carrots if they are cooked previously in a little water then added to this syrup.

*The Toll House, Whitman, Massachusetts*


## 10.  Fresh Rhubarb Juice

(Makes 2 quarts)

INGREDIENTS

DIRECTIONS

2½ lbs. fresh rhubarb
2 quarts of water

Cut rhubarb in 1-inch pieces and stew until soft.  Strain and sieve.

1½ lbs. sugar
2 lemons—juice

Add to above.

Chill and serve.

*Grace E. Smith Service Restaurant and Cafeteria, Toledo, Ohio*


## 11.  Spiced Tomato Juice

(Serves 5 or 6)

INGREDIENTS

DIRECTIONS

2 cups canned tomato juice
½ cup sugar
¼ teaspoon cinnamon
a pinch of nutmeg
8 whole cloves

Simmer for fifteen minutes.  Chill.

¼ cup lemon juice
1 cup cold water

Add just before serving.

*The Carr House, Wolfboro, New Hampshire*

# 12. Calf's Head Soup

(Serves 12 to 14)

INGREDIENTS

DIRECTIONS

1 calf's head
1 gallon water
1 onion—cut fine
1 dozen allspice
2 dozen whole cloves
3 or 4 pieces mace
1 nutmeg—grated

After removing brains (discard eyes), put calf's head in large kettle with spices and onion. Boil 3 hours, adding water when necessary to keep at 1 gallon. Cook until meat slips from the bones. Let cool for about 1 hour. Strain and pick all the meat from the bones and slice. Also slice tongue. Put soup away until next day.

2 cups flour
½ cup butter
2 cups cold water

Brown the flour and thicken with cold water.

salt and pepper to taste
1 tablespoon sugar
1 tablespoon walnut catsup

An hour before serving, heat the soup, add thickening and seasoning.

2 eggs well beaten

Add to brains, make into small cakes, and fry brown, and add to soup just before serving.

1 cup sherry wine

Also add, just before serving.

Put one slice of lemon and one slice of hard boiled egg in each plate and pour soup over.

*This is an Old Virginia recipe and no Christmas was complete without Calf's Head Soup. It is not as hard to make as it sounds and well repays your efforts, for it is "SO GOOD."*

*Chaya Tea Room, Petersburg, Virginia*

*Some men have an idea that women spend too much time "fussin' with food," yet they keep on trying to please the beast and educate him to enjoy something more than meat, potatoes, and gravy.*

## 13. Chicken Velvet Soup
(Serves 10 to 12)

INGREDIENTS

DIRECTIONS

1 quart chicken stock
2 tablespoons cornstarch
2 tablespoons cold milk

Combine stock with mixture of cornstarch and milk and boil until it tastes cooked.

½ cup cream 20%
½ cup cream 40 %

Add to above mixture and let come to a boil.

4 egg yolks—beaten

Pour mixture slowly over egg yolks, beating constantly. Put in double boiler.

speck curry powder
speck cayenne' pepper
½ teaspoon salt
⅛ teaspoon white pepper
¼ teaspoon celery salt
1 teaspoon onion juice

Add to mixture and cook until eggs are cooked.

Serve with whipped cream.

*Grace E. Smith Service Restaurant and Cafeteria, Toledo, Ohio*

## 14. Clam Chowder
(Serves 12)

INGREDIENTS

DIRECTIONS

2 quarts chicken broth or meat stock—skim fat
2 cups potatoes—diced
1 cup carrots—diced
1 cup celery—cut fine
1 medium sized onion—chopped
1 cup tomatoes—chopped

Cook together until the vegetables are tender.

1 teaspoon salt
⅛ teaspoon pepper

Add to above.

4 strips bacon—diced

Fry until a golden brown.

½ cup flour

Add to bacon and brown slightly. Gradually add the broth mixture and cook until it is thickened.

1 pint of cooked clams —minced

Add to chowder base and let stand for ½ hour.

Serve hot with crackers and butter.

*Chuckanut Shell, South Bellingham, Washington*

# 15. Philadelphia Clam Chowder (Serves 6 to 8)

| INGREDIENTS | DIRECTIONS |
|---|---|
| 1 onion<br>1 green pepper<br>2 leeks<br>½ cup celery<br>4 tablespoons butter | Dice vegetables and saute in butter. |
| 3 tablespoons flour | Add to above mixture. |
| 8 large clams—minced<br>2½ cups water | Scald clams with their juice and water. Gradually add this to the vegetable mixture and let come to a boil. |
| 3 cups diced potatoes | Add to above mixture and simmer for 15 minutes. |
| 2 large fresh tomatoes (or 1 can) | Skin the fresh tomatoes and cut fine, or cut the canned tomato solids into small pieces. Add to mixture. |
| 4 tablespoons catsup<br>pinch crushed black pepper<br>pinch cayenne pepper<br>pinch sweet marjoram<br>pinch thyme<br>1 tablespoon parsley—chopped<br>salt to taste | Add to mixture and bring to a boil. Serve. |

*Kuglers Restaurant, Philadelphia, Pennsylvania*


# 16. Treasure Island Clam Chowder (Serves 6)

| INGREDIENTS | DIRECTIONS |
|---|---|
| ¼ cup olive oil<br>¾ cup onions—chopped<br>¼ cup celery—chopped | Braise until light golden brown. |
| 1 cup solid pack tomatoes<br>1 cup fresh clams—cut | Add to above and cook 5 minutes. |
| 2½ cups diced potatoes<br>5 cups cold or hot water<br>2 teaspoons salt<br>½ teaspoon pepper | Add to mixture and cook until the potatoes are done. |

*Fishermen's Grotto, San Francisco, California*

# 17.   Clear Dinner Soup

(Serves 12 to 14)

INGREDIENTS

DIRECTIONS

5 lbs. beef from middle round
3 quarts cold water
2 lbs. marrowbone

Wipe and cut meat in 1-inch cubes. Put ⅔ of meat in soup kettle and soak in water 30 minutes. Brown the remainder of the meat in a pan with the marrow from the marrowbone. Put browned meat and bone in kettle with the rest of the meat and heat to boiling point, skim and let simmer at temperature below boiling point for 5 hours.

1 teaspoon peppercorns
1 tablespoon salt
⅓ cup carrots—diced
⅓ cup turnips—diced
⅓ cup onions—diced
⅓ cup celery—chopped

Add to soup and cook for 1 hour. Strain and cool.

1 egg white to each quart of stock—beaten slightly
a little lemon peel—shaved

When cool, remove fat. Add 2 teaspoons of cold water to each egg and break shells in pieces and add to the stock. Also the lemon peel. Place on stove and stir constantly until boiling point is reached, boil 2 minutes, and set back and let stand for 20 minutes without stirring. Strain through a fine sieve lined with double thickness of cheese cloth.

*Chaya Tea Room, Petersburg, Virginia*


# 18.   Crab Soup

(Serves 4 to 6)

INGREDIENTS

DIRECTIONS

1½ tablespoons butter
1½ tablespoons flour

Blend into a paste.

3 cups milk

Slowly add the milk, stirring constantly. Cook until thick.

1 cup crab-meat flakes
1 teaspoon dry mustard
1 tablespoon worcestershire
¼ teaspoon paprika
1 teaspoon salt

Add to above and cook until flavored.

1 tablespoon sherry wine

Do not cook after wine is added.

*Chaya Tea Room, Petersburg, Virginia*

# 19.  Cream of Mushroom Soup
(Serves 6 to 8)

INGREDIENTS

DIRECTIONS

¾ lb. fresh mushrooms
1 quart cold water

Wash and grind mushrooms without peeling or stemming.  Soak ground mushrooms in cold water for 1 hour.

1 teaspoon onion juice

Add onion juice and slowly bring to boil. Boil 5 to 10 minutes.  Strain through a fine sieve or cloth.

2 tablespoons butter
3 tablespoons flour

Make a paste and add to mushroom broth, stirring rapidly to blend.  Bring mixture to boil and cook 5 to 7 minutes to get the flavor.

¾ cup cream
¼ cup milk

Heat the cream and milk and add to mixture just before serving.

1½ teaspoons salt
dash of white pepper

Add the seasoning last.

This is an excellent soup for the first course of a dinner, as it is like a broth and not too rich.  Serve with a spoonful of whipped cream.

*Richards Treat Cafeteria, Minneapolis, Minnesota*


# 20.  Creme St. Germaine Pea Soup
(Serves 6)

INGREDIENTS

DIRECTIONS

3 lbs. fresh peas
(shelled)
1½ cups water

Cook peas in double boiler and force through sieve.

3 cups cream
Salt and pepper to
taste

Put cream in pot and when hot, add puree of peas and seasoning.  Cook 5 minutes, stirring vigorously.

3 egg yolks—beaten

Whip into the above.  Remove from fire.

⅛ lb. butter

Add butter and mash in with a fork and fold in until melted.

*Mrs. C. H. Welch, Mitchell Field, Long Island, New York*

## 21.  Cream of Tomato Soup

(Serves 3)

INGREDIENTS | DIRECTIONS

1 can tomato soup
¼ teaspoon soda

As soon as soup boils up, add the soda, a little at a time, stirring constantly.

½ cup milk
⅓ cup cream

Add and cook until thoroughly heated.

parsley

Just before serving, add to each serving another dash of cream and a sprig of crisp parsley.

*Ward G. Foster, Battle Creek, Michigan*


## 22.  Creole Okra Gumbo

(Serves 12 to 14)

INGREDIENTS | DIRECTIONS

3 lbs. okra

Wipe the okra with a damp cloth and cut into round slices.

½ dozen crabs

Immerse crabs in boiling water for a few seconds.  Remove shells and quarter.  Set aside in covered pan until ready to use.  Save shells.

2 lbs. fresh shrimp

Wash shrimp thoroughly, peel and set aside. Save shells.

3 quarts of water

Put shells in pot and cover with water. Boil for 30 minutes.  You use this water for liquid for the gumbo.

1 cup of lard
salt and pepper to taste
2 onions—minced

Heat lard, add okra, seasoning and onion. Cook until okra is browned.

1 tablespoon tomato paste
2 cloves of garlic— minced

Add to okra and onion mixture, then add crabs and brown for five minutes.  Add the water in which the shells were cooked and boil for one hour.

small piece of bay leaf
1 sprig of thyme
2 tablespoons parsley chopped fine
salt and pepper to taste

Add the shrimp and other ingredients and let simmer for 3 hours, stirring occasionally.

Serve with hot steaming rice.

*Corinne Dunbar, New Orleans, Louisiana. (Recipe by Mary Bell, old family cook.)*

## 23.  Jellied Bouillon

(Serves 8)

INGREDIENTS | DIRECTIONS
--- | ---

1 can tomatoes
1 can water
1 onion

Boil for 20 minutes.  Strain.

2 cans beef bouillon

Add bouillon.  Remove from stove.

1½ envelopes gelatin
½ cup cold water

Soak gelatin for five minutes.  Add to bouillon and bring to boiling point.

Pour in cups and chill.  Serve with slice of lemon.

*Althea, Lewisburg, West Virginia*


## 24.  Mushroom Soup

(Serves 6 to 8)

INGREDIENTS | DIRECTIONS
--- | ---

1 quart chicken broth
1 teaspoon onion juice
¼ lb. fresh mushrooms
  —ground

Simmer for 15 minutes.

¼ cup flour
¼ cup butter

Blend and work together.  Gradually add the broth, stirring constantly.

½ cup cream

Add to mixture and let it boil up.

2 teaspoons lemon
  juice
  salt and white pepper
  and paprika, to taste

Add to soup just before serving.

Top with whipped cream.

*Mrs. Louie M. Weathers, Elkton, Kentucky*


*No one yet has made one egg do the work of two.*

## 25. Onion Soup
(Serves 8 to 10)

INGREDIENTS

DIRECTIONS

1 lb. onions
1/8 lb. butter

Slice and cook until brown.

1 tablespoon flour

Sprinkle over onions and stir.

1½ quarts chicken stock
salt and pepper to
taste

Add stock slowly, stirring until smooth. Add seasoning and allow to stand several hours to improve the flavor.

Serve with slice of French bread sprinkled with cheese and toasted in oven the last moment. Serve extra cheese to be sprinkled over top at the table.

*Toll House, Whitman, Massachusetts*


## 26. Philadelphia Pepper Pot
(Serves 6 to 8)

INGREDIENTS

DIRECTIONS

1 onion
1 green pepper
2 leeks
½ cup chopped celery
4 tablespoons butter

Dice vegetables and saute in butter.

3 tablespoons flour

Add to above mixture.

5 cups veal broth

Slowly add the veal broth and stir constantly.

¼ lb. cooked tripe—
diced

Add tripe and let mixture come to a boil.

3 cups diced potatoes
pinch crushed black
pepper
pinch cayenne pepper
pinch sweet marjoram
pinch thyme
1 tablespoon parsley—
chopped
salt to taste

Add to mixture. Bring to a boil and serve.

*Kuglers Restaurant, Philadelphia, Pennsylvania*

## 27.  Potage Billy By

| INGREDIENTS | DIRECTIONS |
|---|---|
| 3 quarts fresh muscles<br>3 onions—minced<br>½ bunch whole parsley<br>2 quarts dry white wine<br>1 pinch crushed whole pepper | Boil for 15 minutes.  Toss several times.  Drain the juice through a fine cheese cloth. |
| 15 egg yolks—beaten<br>1½ quarts cream<br>¼ lb. butter | Blend these together in another pan and add the strained stock.  Stir vigorously over a slow fire until it thickens.  Do not let it boil. |
| salt and pepper to taste | Add seasoning and serve hot. |

*Hotel St. Regis, New York, New York*


## 28.  Poyster Soup

| INGREDIENTS | DIRECTIONS |
|---|---|
| 1½ lbs. blackeyed peas | Soak in cold water for 2 hours.  Drain. |
| 3 quarts unsalted chicken broth<br>1 knuckle of smoked ham | Add to peas. |
| ½ onion—diced<br>1 tablespoon butter | Saute and add to peas.  Place over a slow fire and let gently boil for 2 hours. |
| salt and pepper to taste | When done, force through a fine sieve and add seasoning. |
| ¼ lb. butter | Put back on the stove and add the butter and bring to just the boiling point, then remove from fire. |
| 18 freshly opened juicy oysters<br>2 tablespoons butter | Heat oysters in butter for not more than one minute.  Place 3 oysters in each plate and pour soup over them and serve. |

*Stirrup-Cup Castle, Oakdale, Long Island, New York*

## 29. Split Pea Soup

(Serves 4 to 6)

### INGREDIENTS

- 2 quarts water
- 2 cups peas
- 4 branches of celery
- 2 carrots
- 1 onion
- 1/4 teaspoon thyme
- 1 pinch cayenne pepper
- 1 bay leaf
- salt and pepper to taste

### DIRECTIONS

Boil hard for 20 minutes, then slowly until the peas are done. Strain through a collander.

*Bueltmore Hotel, Buellton, California*

## 30. Split Pea Soup

(Serves 4)

### INGREDIENTS

- 1 cup green split peas
- 8 cups of water
- 1/2 small onion—chopped fine
- 2 teaspoons salt
- 1/2 teaspoon black pepper
- 1/4 teaspoon celery salt
- 1/4 teaspoon garlic salt
- a small piece of ham hock

### DIRECTIONS

Put in soup kettle and boil slowly until the peas are done. Strain through a wire strainer.

1 can milk

Add enough milk to mixture to make it nice and creamy.

1 tablespoon chopped parsley

Sprinkle each serving with parsley and serve *very* hot.

*Manning's, Trinidad, California*

*A word to dinner givers. PLEASE have ashtrays larger than thimbles.*

# 31.  Tomato Corn Bisque Soup

(Serves 8)

### INGREDIENTS

1 quart milk

1 can corn
1 slice onion

3 tablespoons flour
¼ cup cold water

½ can condensed
tomato soup
¼ teaspoon soda

⅓ cup butter
salt and pepper to
taste

### DIRECTIONS

Scald.

Add to scalded milk.

Mix together and add to the above.  Cook 20 minutes and rub through a sieve.

Cook together and combine with strained mixture.

Add to soup.  Serve with whipped cream.

*Sawyer Tavern, Keene, New Hampshire*


# 32.  Soup Vichyssoise

(Serves 10)

### INGREDIENTS

1⅓ lbs. butter
2 onions—sliced

2 carrots—sliced
½ stalk celery cut fine
¼ lb. string beans—sliced

6 sorrel leaves or
spinach
1 quart chicken broth

2 quarts hot cream
salt and pepper to
taste

1 tablespoon arrowroot

1 teaspoon chopped
chives

### DIRECTIONS

Saute in a 1-½ gallon pot.

Add to the above and let simmer slowly for 30 minutes.

Add to mixture and boil until tender.

Add to mixture.

Thicken mixture.  Strain and chill.

Serve ice cold with chives.

*The Huntington, Pasadena, California*

## 33. Summer Night Soup—Cold Bortch (Serves 6)

| INGREDIENTS | DIRECTIONS |
|---|---|
| 1 can jellied consomme | Put into a mixing bowl. |
| 2 fresh ripe tomatoes | Rub through a sieve and add to the above. |
| 4 green onions—cut fine<br>1 teaspoon parsley—chopped | Add to the above. |
| 2 cups cold beets—cut fine<br>salt to taste | Stir into the above thoroughly with a fork. Let stand in refrigerator for 1 hour.<br>Pour into cups. |
| ½ cup sour cream<br>fresh ground black pepper to taste | 1 teaspoon to each cup. |

*Mrs. A. D. Brooks, Cleveland, Ohio*


## 34. Sunday Night Special (Serves 4)

| INGREDIENTS | DIRECTIONS |
|---|---|
| 1 can tomato soup<br>½ onion—minced<br>½ lb. cheese | Cook in iron skillet until the cheese is melted. Stir frequently. |
| 4 eggs | When ready to serve, turn down heat, break in eggs and cook lightly. |
| 4 slices toast | Pour over toast and serve. |

*Terraza Verde "The Gorham Ranch," Ojai, California*


## 35. Vegetable Soup (Serves 6)

| INGREDIENTS | DIRECTIONS |
|---|---|
| 4 leeks—diced<br>4 carrots—diced<br>3 tablespoons butter<br>½ cup water | Put in saucepan and stir until the vegetables are well coated. Add enough water to keep from burning and cook until tender. |
| 3 cups potatoes—diced | Add to mixture and cook until tender. Mash to a smooth mixture. |
| 4 cups milk<br>salt and pepper to taste | Add enough milk to make the soup of desired thickness. |

*Mildred Poole, Palo Alto, California*

## 36. Avocado Salad (Serves 8)

**INGREDIENTS**

**DIRECTIONS**

1 pkg. lime gelatin
2 cups of water

Dissolve.

1 avocado—mashed
1 pkg. cream cheese—
mashed
½ cup mayonnaise
¼ cup celery—cut fine
½ green pepper—
chopped
a few drops of onion
juice
1 pinch of salt

When nearly set, add these ingredients and place in a shallow pan until completely set. Cut in squares for serving, or it could be poured into individual molds.

*The Anna Maude, Oklahoma City, Oklahoma*


## 37. Black Cherry Gelatin Salad (Serves 24)

**INGREDIENTS**

**DIRECTIONS**

¼ pint lemon jello
1 pint water—boiling
½ lemon—juice
1¼ pints cherry juice

Dissolve jello in liquid and let cool.

¼ cup stuffed olives—
sliced
¼ of No. 2½ can black
cherries—pitted
1 cup almonds—broken

When jello begins to set, add these ingredients and pour into molds. Serve with mayonnaise.

*The Anna Maude, Oklahoma City, Oklahoma*


## 38. Chef's Special Salad Dressing (Makes 1 quart)

**INGREDIENTS**

**DIRECTIONS**

1½ cups chili sauce
¼ cup celery—finely cut
1 cup sour pickles (cut
fine)
2 cups mayonnaise
1 teaspoon lemon juice
½ teaspoon
Worcestershire sauce
1 teaspoon horseradish

Put all ingredients into a bowl and mix together until well blended.

Do not put in refrigerator, but it will keep indefinitely in a cool place.

Excellent dressing for any seafood salad.

*The Fishermen's Grotto, San Francisco, California*

## 39.  Coleslaw with Sour Cream Dressing  (Serves 8)

INGREDIENTS

3½ lbs. cabbage

2 tablespoons salt
2 tablespoons sugar

2 tablespoons vinegar
2 tablespoons lemon
juice
½ onion—grated

1 pint sour cream 18%

DIRECTIONS

Cabbage should be crispy.  Shred edible portion very fine and dry as much as possible. Set in refrigerator to chill.

Put dry ingredients in a bowl.

Mix into dry ingredients.

Stir in sour cream until mixture is thoroughly blended.

Just before serving, pour over chilled cabbage and toss lightly until the cabbage and dressing are thoroughly mixed.  Serve at once.

*Jane Davis Restaurant, New York City, N. Y.*


## 40.  Coleslaw  (Serves 16 to 18)

INGREDIENTS

2 lbs. of white cabbage
—shredded
⅔ cup sour cream
⅔ cup vinegar
⅓ cup sugar
1 tablespoon salt
1½ tablespoons raw
carrots—chopped

DIRECTIONS

Mix all together and chill.

Serve with fish or sea food dishes.

*Post Street Cafeteria, San Francisco, California*


*Dinners are cooked in the kitchen, served
in the dining room, but digested at home.*

# 41.  Fruit Salad

INGREDIENTS

DIRECTIONS

4 large grapefruit

Remove all membrane and break into lumps.

1 can pineapple

Drain pineapple and cut into pieces. (Do not use juice.)

½ lb. blanched almonds
1 small bottle
   Marachino cherries

Mix with grapefruit and pineapple.

4 tablespoons cooked
   dressing

Stir in dressing and serve in grapefruit baskets made of the rinds.

### COOKED DRESSING

2 egg yolks
4 tablespoons Tarragon
   vinegar

Cook in small pan until thick, stirring all the while. Remove from fire.

2 tablespoons butter
1 teaspoon salt
1 teaspoon sugar
1 teaspoon paprika
½ teaspoon dry mustard

Cream butter and other ingredients and add to mixture. Put in ice box and let get cold and stiff.

1 cup whipping cream

Whip and add to the above mixture.

*Chaya Tea Room, Petersburg, Virginia*


# 42.  Frozen Fruit Salad

INGREDIENTS

DIRECTIONS

1 large can fruit salad
3 bananas
1 box pitted dates
¼ lb. marshmallows

Cut in pieces and mix together.

1 cup mayonnaise
1 cup whipping cream –
   whipped

Mix together and blend with fruits. Pour in refrigerator trays and freeze.

*Chaya Tea Room, Petersburg, Virginia*

## 43.  Garden Club Salad

INGREDIENTS

DIRECTIONS

1 can tomato soup
3 pkgs. cream cheese

Bring soup to a boil and add the cheese.  Stir until smooth.

2 tablespoons gelatin
½ cup cold water

Dissolve gelatin and add to mixture.  Set aside to cool.

½ cup chopped celery
½ cup chopped green pepper
½ cup chopped onion

When mixture is partly cooled, add vegetables. (Olives and nuts may also be added.)  Chill in molds.

Serve on lettuce leaves and garnish with olives and mayonnaise.

*Mrs. Ben Poor, Bardstown, Kentucky*


## 44.  Gingerale Aspic Salad

INGREDIENTS

DIRECTIONS

1 tablespoon Knox gelatin
2 tablespoons cold water
¼ cup heated gingerale

Soak gelatin in cold water and dissolve in gingerale.

¼ cup lemon juice
1½ cups gingerale

Stir into above, and put in refrigerator to set.

½ cup seedless grapes
¼ cup celery—chopped
½ cup crushed pineapple
½ cup chopped preserved ginger

When gelatin begins to set, add the ingredients and put back in refrigerator to set.

Serve on lettuce with mayonnaise to which whipped cream has been added.

*The Carr House, Wolfboro, New Hampshire*

## 45.  Jellied Cherry Sherry Salad     (Serves 20)

INGREDIENTS

DIRECTIONS

1 cup wild cherry jello
1½ cups boiling water

Dissolve jello in water.

2 cups juice from
   canned cherries
½ cup sherry wine

Add to jello and stir.

3 Bing black cherries
3 Royal Anne cherries
3 pecan halves

Place these ingredients in each individual mold
and fill with liquid.

Put in refrigerator to set.

*Devon Gables Tea Room, Bloomfield Hills, Detroit, Michigan*


## 46.  Mushroom Supreme Salad     (Serves 12)

INGREDIENTS

DIRECTIONS

1 can condensed
   mushroom soup
2 egg yolks—beaten

Put in double boiler and cook 3 or 4 minutes.

2 tablespoons gelatin
½ cup cold water

Remove soup from fire.  Soak gelatin and add
to soup.

1 can Tuna fish
1 tablespoon lemon
   juice
salt, pepper, and
paprika to taste

When soup begins to thicken, add these ingredients.

2 egg whites—beaten

Fold in egg whites and mold.  Serve with mayonnaise.

*Chaya Tea Room, Petersburg, Virginia*


*When you have to scrape the sauce off the meat what
you find under it is usually not worth the effort.*

## 47. "My Salad" (Called this by Mr. Edgar Guest)

(Serves 6)

### INGREDIENTS

2 heads lettuce (large)
1 head chicory or romaine

6 ozs. julienned chicken or turkey
4 ozs. Roquefort cheese —crumbled
½ teaspoon celery salt
1 cup Thousand Island dressing
2 tablespoons Tarragon vinegar

12 pieces crisp bacon

### DIRECTIONS

Pull lettuce apart in small pieces and cut chicory very fine.

Mix all these ingredients with the lettuce and chicory and serve in 6 bowls on inner leaves of lettuce.

Garnish top with two pieces of bacon and serve at once.

*Wrigley Building Restaurant, Chicago, Illinois*


## 48. Pineapple Salad

(Serves 6)

### INGREDIENTS

1 cup crushed pineapple
½ lemon—juice
¼ cup sugar

1 tablespoon gelatin
½ cup cold water

1 cup grated cheese
½ cup whipped cream

½ cup mayonnaise
1 tablespoon pineapple juice

1 tablespoon pimiento— chopped
1 stalk celery—cut fine
1 tablespoon crushed pineapple

### DIRECTIONS

Heat.

Soak and add to hot mixture. Let cool.

When mixture begins to congeal add these ingredients. Serve with pine-dressing.

*PINE-DRESSING*

Thin the mayonnaise.

Fold into mayonnaise.

*Tick Tock Tea Room, Los Angeles, California*

## 49.   French Cream Potato Salad

**INGREDIENTS**

**DIRECTIONS**

| | |
|---|---|
| 4 cups cooked potatoes —diced | Mix all together. |
| 3 stalks of celery | |
| 3 tablespoons grated onion | |
| 2 teaspoons salt | |
| ⅛ teaspoon pepper | |
| ⅛ teaspoon paprika | |
| ¼ cup white vinegar | Add vinegar and let stand for 15 minutes. |
| ½ pint heavy cream | Heat cream and butter until butter is melted. |
| 2 tablespoons butter | |

Pour over potato mixture and toss with fork until well mixed. Let stand a few minutes. Chill.

Just before serving toss again and serve very cold on lettuce bed and garnish.

*San Carlos French Cafe, Phoenix, Arizona*

## 50.   German Style Potato Salad Dressing

**INGREDIENTS**

**DIRECTIONS**

| | |
|---|---|
| ¾ cup bacon—diced | Fry to a golden brown. |
| ¾ cup (90 grain) vinegar | Add to the above. |
| ¾ cup flour | Make into a paste and add to the boiling mixture. |
| 1¼ cups water | |
| ¾ cup sugar | Add to mixture and boil for 5 minutes. |
| ¼ cup salt | |
| 1 cup water | |

Sprinkle cold potatoes liberally with chopped onions. Pour hot dressing over them and set on the warming shelf to allow the flavor to penetrate into the potatoes.

*Smith Brothers Restaurant, Port Washington, Wisconsin*

## 51.   Potato Salad     (Serves 8)

| INGREDIENTS | DIRECTIONS |
|---|---|
| 4 slices bacon—chopped | Fry. |
| 1 tablespoon flour | Add to bacon and blend. |
| ½ cup vinegar<br>¼ cup water<br>¼ cup sugar<br>2 teaspoons salt<br>⅓ teaspoon dry mustard<br>¼ teaspoon pepper | Blend together and add to the above.  Cook until it thickens. |
| 5 large potatoes | Boil with jackets.  Peel and slice. |
| 1 onion—chopped | Mix into potatoes and add to sauce.  Serve hot. |

*Viola A. Brehmer, Elmwood, Fond du Lac, Wisconsin*


## 52.   Salade Biltmore     (Serves 10 to 12)

INGREDIENTS

DIRECTIONS

3 or 4 heads of lettuce
4 bunches of watercress
1 quart special dressing

Cut each head crosswise into 3 or 4 slices about 1 inch thick and 2½ inches in diameter. Place sprays of watercress on top.  Serve special dressing on the side.

*SPECIAL DRESSING*

1 quart tart French dressing (omit paprika)
1 pint grapefruit juice
½ pint sliced radishes
½ pint parsley—chopped fine
½ cup scallions—sliced fine
½ cup carrots—diced
salt to taste

Mix well and serve.

*Hotel Biltmore, Los Angeles, California*

## 53.  Sea Dream Salad (Serves 6)

INGREDIENTS

DIRECTIONS

1 package lime jello
1 cup boiling water

Dissolve in the water.

1 cup grated cucumber
1 tablespoon vinegar
¼ teaspoon onion juice
a dash of cayenne
½ teaspoon salt

Add to jello and stir.  Turn into individual molds and set in refrigerator.
Serve on lettuce with mayonnaise.

*The Carr House, Wolfboro, New Hampshire*


## 54.  Shower Salad (Serves 12)

INGREDIENTS

DIRECTIONS

2 packages strawberry
gelatin
2 cups boiling water

Dissolve gelatin.

1 No. 2 can crushed
pineapple

Drain the juice off the pineapple and add enough cold water to make 2 cups of liquid. Add to gelatin and let get very cold.

4 tart apples—cubed
1 pinch of salt

Mix the apples and pineapple and add to gelatin.

½ pint whipping cream
—whipped

Fold in whipped cream and pour into molds.

When firm serve on lettuce leaves with mayonnaise and a Maraschino cherry.

*Park View Inn, Berkeley Springs, West Virginia*


## 55.  Stuffed Lettuce

INGREDIENTS

DIRECTIONS

1 package cream cheese
2 tablespoons Roquefort
2 tablespoons raw
carrot—chopped fine
1 tablespoon green
pepper
2 tablespoons raw
tomato—chopped fine
1 teaspoon onion juice
salt to taste

Blend these ingredients.

1 head of lettuce

Hollow out the lettuce and stuff with the mixture.

Wrap in waxed paper and place in refrigerator until ready to serve. Slice in desired thickness.

*Mrs. Louie M. Weathers, Elkton, Kentucky*

## 56.  Raw Spinach Salad

INGREDIENTS | DIRECTIONS
--- | ---
1 lb. spinach | Wash well to remove sand.
1 teaspoon baking soda | Add to spinach and chop in 1-inch lengths.
2 tablespoons olive oil<br>1 tablespoon lemon juice | Season spinach.
1 hard boiled egg—chopped | Add to spinach.
  | Garnish with tomato and asparagus and dressing.

*DRESSING*

INGREDIENTS | DIRECTIONS
--- | ---
1 egg<br>⅓ teaspoon mustard<br>⅓ teaspoon white pepper<br>2 tablespoons salt<br>3 tablespoons paprika<br>1 cup tomato sauce or puree<br>2 tablespoons sugar<br>1 tablespoon Lea & Perrins sauce | Mix into a paste.
1 pint oil | Add to paste slowly.
1 cup vinegar | Add to dressing alternately with the oil.
½ pint warm water | Add to dressing.
  | Keep in a cool place.

*Omar Khayyam's, San Francisco, California*


## 57.  French Dressing   (Makes 1 pint)

INGREDIENTS | DIRECTIONS
--- | ---
1 cup olive oil—warmed<br>1 cup vinegar | Beaten well
⅓ cup catsup<br>½ cup sugar<br>1 teaspoon paprika<br>1 teaspoon salt<br>1 lemon—juice<br>⅓ onion—grated | Mix these ingredients together and add to above, and beat well.<br><br>Shake well before using.

*Roy C. Neuhaus, Evanston, Illinois*

## 58.  French Dressing

(Makes 1½ pints)

INGREDIENTS

DIRECTIONS

4 teaspoons sugar
1 teaspoon salt
1 teaspoon dry mustard
½ teaspoon pakrika
¼ teaspoon pepper

Mix dry ingredients.

1½ cups olive oil

Beat into dry ingredients slowly.

8 tablespoons lemon
    juice

Add to mixture slowly, beating all the time.

4 teaspoons
    Worcestershire sauce
5 teaspoons chili sauce
1 teaspoon chopped
    onion
1 clove garlic

Add to mixture and beat well.

This dressing keeps, but do not put in refrigerator.  Shake well before using.

*Emelie Tolman, Chicago, Illinois*


## 59.  French Dressing

(Makes 1 gallon)

INGREDIENTS

DIRECTIONS

1 quart vinegar
1 quart catsup
2 quarts salad oil
2 cups sugar
⅔ cup salt
    grated garlic and
    onion to taste

Blend all together and mix well.

Shake well before using.

*Pine Tavern, Bend, Oregon*


## 60.  Fruit Salad Dressing

(Serves 6 to 8)

INGREDIENTS

DIRECTIONS

2 eggs—beaten
½ cup honey
1 lemon—juice

Place in double boiler and cook until thick, stirring constantly.  Remove from stove and allow to cool.

½ pint whipping cream
    —whipped

When ready to serve, add whipped cream.

Crushed pineapple may also be added to this dressing.

*Mrs. H. G. Beebe, Chicago, Illinois*

# 61.  Fruit Salad Dressing with Maple Syrup

### INGREDIENTS

2 egg yolks—beaten
1/2 cup maple syrup

1/2 cup whipping cream
—whipped
2 lemons—juice

### DIRECTIONS

Put in double boiler and cook 2 minutes, or until thick.  Set aside to cool.

Fold into mixture and serve with any mixed fruits.

*Maple Cabin, St. Johnsbury, Vermont*


# 62.  Salad Dressing                    (Makes 1 pint)

### INGREDIENTS

1 cup salad oil
1/2 cup tomato catsup
1/3 cup vinegar
1/3 cup honey
1 teaspoon
Worcestershire sauce
pinch ground cloves
1 onion—grated

### DIRECTIONS

Mix all ingredients together, stirring all the while.

*Columbia Gorge Hotel, Hood River, Oregon*


# 63.  Banana Bread

### INGREDIENTS

1/2 cup shortening
1 cup sugar

2 eggs—beaten

1/2 cup sour milk
1 teaspoon soda

2 cups flour
1 pinch of salt
3 crushed ripe bananas

### DIRECTIONS

Cream together.

Stir into mixture.

Mix soda into milk and add to mixture.

Stir into mixture and pour into loaf tins. Bake in 350 F. oven for 1 hour.

*Green Shutters, Whitewater, Wisconsin*

## 64.  Cinnamon Bread

| INGREDIENTS | DIRECTIONS |
|---|---|
| 2 egg whites—beaten<br>½ cup milk | Mix together. |
| ½ cup butter<br>1 cup sugar<br>2 egg yolks—beaten | Cream together and add the above mixture. |
| 1¼ cups flour<br>2½ teaspoons baking powder<br>1 teaspoon cinnamon | Sift together and add to the above mixture. |
| 1 tablespoon butter—melted | Bake in 300 F. oven for 30 minutes. When done pour melted butter over top and sprinkle with mixture of sugar and cinnamon. |

*Mrs. W. B. Taylor, Bowling Green, Kentucky*


## 65.  Cornbread Truett  (Serves 8 to 10)

| INGREDIENTS | DIRECTIONS |
|---|---|
| 3 oz. butter or lard<br>½ cup sugar<br>2 cups corn meal<br>1¼ teaspoons salt | Cream. |
| 2½ cups boiled rice | Work in lightly. |
| 2 eggs beaten<br>2 cups milk | Mix together and add to mixture. |
| 1 cup flour<br>6 teaspoons baking powder | Sift together and add to mixture. |
| | Pour in buttered pan and bake in 375 F. oven for 30 to 35 minutes. |

*Post Street Cafeteria, San Francisco, California*


*I have enjoyed fruit cake in various parts of America but none has
pleased me more than that made by the Post Street Cafeteria.*

## 66.  Spoon Bread

| INGREDIENTS | DIRECTIONS |
|---|---|
| 3 eggs—beaten<br>1 pint buttermilk | Stir eggs into buttermilk. |
| ⅔ cup corn meal<br>   (water ground)<br>1 tablespoon flour<br>1 teaspoon salt<br>1 teaspoon soda<br>1 teaspoon baking<br>   powder | Sift these ingredients and stir into above mixture. |
| 2 tablespoons<br>   shortening | Melt shortening and pour into batter.<br><br>Pour batter into sizzling hot greased pan and bake in 350 F. oven for 30 to 35 minutes. |

*Mrs. Ben Poor, Bardstown, Kentucky*


## 67.  Spoon Bread                                    (Serves 10)

| INGREDIENTS | DIRECTIONS |
|---|---|
| 1½ cups water-ground<br>   corn meal<br>1⅓ teaspoons salt<br>1 teaspoon sugar | Mix together. |
| 1½ cups boiling water | Scald the above ingredients. |
| ⅛ lb. butter—melted | Add to mixture. |
| 5 eggs—beaten<br>2 cups milk | Stir these together.<br><br>Put the two mixtures into baking pan. |
| 1 teaspoon baking<br>   powder | Add and stir enough to get an even mixture.<br><br>Bake in 350 F. oven for 30 to 35 minutes. |

*Hotel Roanoke, Roanoke, Virginia*

## 68.  Spoon Bread
(Serves 4)

INGREDIENTS

DIRECTIONS

2 cups milk
1 cup corn meal
½ teaspoon salt
3 tablespoons butter

Scald together and stir until thick. Remove from stove.

2 egg yolks—beaten
1 teaspoon baking powder

Add to above mixture and set aside to cool.

2 egg whites—beaten stiff

Just before putting into oven, fold in egg whites. Put in buttered baking pan and cook in 300 F. oven for about 20 minutes.

*Valley View Inn, Hot Springs, Virginia*


## 69.  Batter or Spoon Bread
(Serves 8)

INGREDIENTS

DIRECTIONS

1 cup corn meal
2 cups boiling water

Pour boiling water over the meal.

1 cup milk
1 tablespoon melted butter
1 teaspoon salt
2 teaspoons baking powder

Add to mixture.

2 egg yolks—beaten

Add to mixture.

2 egg whites—beaten

Fold into mixture and bake in 350 F. oven for 30 minutes.

*Althea, Lewisburg, West Virginia*


*Some say the best housekeeping in the world
is done by men. Witness the U. S. army.*

## 70. Virginia Batter Bread

INGREDIENTS | DIRECTIONS

2 cups buttermilk
2 eggs
1 teaspoon salt
2 cups cold water

Mix together.

1 cup corn meal

Add to above mixture. Let stand for 10 minutes, stirring at intervals to allow cornmeal to mix well.

1/4 teaspoon baking powder

Add just before cooking.

Bake in 300 F. oven for 40 minutes.

*Mrs. William Rogers Clay, Frankfort, Kentucky*


## 71. Corn Dodger                                    (Serves 6)

INGREDIENTS | DIRECTIONS

1 pint water-ground corn meal
1 teaspoon salt
1 tablespoon lard

Work together.

little milk

Add milk to have consistency to mold by hand. Make size of lady-finger and not over 1/2-inch thick. Bake to golden brown.

*Mrs. A. Scott Hines, Bowling Green, Kentucky*


*The only reason that French cuisine ever overshadows American cooking is because it is more liable to be edible. But when one finds REAL oyster stew, roasted turkey, blueberry pie, ice cream, clam chowder, and many others the "a la" folds up.*

## 72. Corn Muffins

INGREDIENTS

DIRECTIONS

1 pint white corn meal
1 teaspoon salt

Sift together.

1 pint boiling water

Pour over corn meal.

½ pint cold milk

Pour immediately after addition of boiling water to prevent corn meal from lumping.

2 eggs

Add to mixture and beat well.

4 teaspoons baking powder
1 tablespoon melted butter

Add to mixture. Pour into greased and floured individual glass molds and bake in 475 to 500 F. oven for 30 minutes.

*McDonald Tea Room, Gallatin, Mo.*

## 73. Corn Pones

(Makes 12 servings)

INGREDIENTS

DIRECTIONS

2 cups corn meal (must be water ground)
1 teaspoon salt
1 tablespoon fat (half lard, half butter)
1 cup of milk

Form by hand into ovals 1x3 inches and pat on top with fingers. (True Virginia Corn Pones always have the imprint of three fingers on them.)

Bake in 400 F. oven until a rich brown or about 25 minutes.

Serve very hot.

*Forest Tavern, Natural Bridge, Virginia*

## 74. Corn Pones

(Makes 80)

INGREDIENTS

DIRECTIONS

3 lbs. corn meal (water ground)
1 lb. cake flour
1 teaspoon soda
1 teaspoon salt
1¼ lbs. lard—half melted
3 pints buttermilk
4 eggs

Mix lightly, all ingredients into a stiff dough. Form in shape of egg and flatten slightly on a greased paper in a baking sheet. Bake in 450 F. oven for 15 minutes.

*The Brown Hotel, Louisville, Kentucky*

## 75.   Corn Meal Puffs

INGREDIENTS | DIRECTIONS

4 egg whites—beaten
1 teaspoon salt

Beat together.

5 tablespoons corn meal
boiling water

Scald with just enough water to make a paste. When the mixture is warm (not hot), fold in the egg whites. Drop from a spoon onto a baking sheet and bake in 300 F. to 325 F. oven for 30 minutes.

*Mrs. Voijt F. Mashek, Chicago, Illinois*


## 76.   Corn Meal Puffs                    (Serves 6)

INGREDIENTS | DIRECTIONS

5 tablespoons white
corn meal

Scalded with enough boiling water to make mixture, but not too soft.

4 egg whites—beaten
1 teaspoon salt

When corn meal has cooled to a lukewarm temperature, fold in egg whites and drop from spoon onto baking sheet and bake in 350 F. oven for 12 to 15 minutes.

*Old Spinning Wheel Tea Room, Hinsdale, Illinois*


## 77.   Corn Pocket Rolls                  (Serves 6)

INGREDIENTS | DIRECTIONS

1½ cups flour
½ cup corn meal
2 tablespoons baking powder
½ teaspoon salt
2 tablespoons sugar

Mix these ingredients together.

1 egg—beaten
¾ cup sour cream

Combine egg and cream and mix with dry ingredients. Put on floured board and roll out rather thin.

1 tablespoon melted butter

Brush dough with butter and cut in rounds and fold over. Bake in 350 F. oven 12 to 15 minutes.

*Old Spinning Wheel Tea Room, Hinsdale, Illinois*

## 78. Raisin Puffs

(Serves 8 to 10)

INGREDIENTS | DIRECTIONS

½ cup butter
1 cup sugar

Cream together.

2 eggs—beaten

Add to above.

2 cups flour
2 teaspoons baking
   powder

Sift together and add to mixture, alternately with milk.

1 cup milk

1 cup raisins—cut up

Flour raisins and add to mixture. Steam in cups ¾ of hour.

Serve with whipped cream.

*Sawyer Tavern, Keene, New Hampshire*


## 79. Fluffy Rolls

INGREDIENTS | DIRECTIONS

1 cup shortening
¾ cup sugar

Cream and blend together.

1 cup boiling water

Add to the above and let cool until lukewarm.

2 eggs—beaten

Add to mixture.

2 cakes yeast
1 cup lukewarm water

Dissolve, and add to the mixture.

7½ to 8 cups flour
1 teaspoon salt

Sift together and add 4 cups to the mixture and blend thoroughly until the dough is smooth. Then gradually add the balance of the flour.

2 tablespoons melted
   butter

Place the dough in a greased bowl, brush with melted butter and cover the bowl tightly with waxed paper and place in the refrigerator. Use as needed. When made into rolls, let the dough rise for 2 hours before baking. Bake in 450 F. oven for 15 to 20 minutes.

*Mrs. Louie M. Weathers, Elkton, Kentucky*

# 80. Orange Rolls

| INGREDIENTS | DIRECTIONS |
|---|---|
| 1 cake compressed yeast<br>1 pint lukewarm milk | Make sponge. |
| ½ cup orange juice<br>2 orange rinds—grated<br>1 teaspoon salt<br>⅓ cup sugar | Mix with sponge. |
| ¼ cup butter—melted<br>1 egg | Add to above. |
| 3¾ cups flour—sifted | Thicken sponge with enough to knead, or about 1½ cups. |
| 2 or more cups flour<br>(stiff) | Knead until soft. Let rise until double in bulk. Knead again and double in bulk. |
| | Shape into Parker House rolls, very thin. |
| ½ teaspoon orange rind<br>—finely ground<br>1 tablespoon butter<br>½ cup brown sugar | Cook and place under flap of each roll. Close flap tightly and let rise very light. Bake in 425 F. oven for 15 to 20 minutes. |
| | Spread with orange icing when cool. |

### ORANGE ICING

| | |
|---|---|
| ¼ cup orange juice<br>1 teaspoon lemon juice<br>¼ cup melted butter<br>1 orange rind—grated<br>enough powdered<br>sugar to spread well | Mix well. |

*Rustic Tea Room, Evergreen, Colorado*

*There is no true economy in "substitutes."*

# 81. Orange Rolls

INGREDIENTS

DIRECTIONS

1 cup hot water
1 teaspoon salt
1½ tablespoons shortening
¼ cup sugar

Combine these ingredients.

1 cake of yeast
2 tablespoons warm water

Dissolve and add when the above mixture is lukewarm.

1 egg—beaten
2 cups of flour

Add to the mixture. Beat well.

2 to 2½ cups flour

Stir into the mixture and knead until elastic. Grease top of the dough and let rise. Cut down and roll out in long strip about 1 inch thick.

½ cup butter—melted

Spread on dough.

2 orange rinds—grated
2 cups sugar

Mix together and spread on the dough. Roll and cut in 1-inch slices.

Put into greased muffin tins and let rise. Bake in 425 F. oven for 12 to 15 minutes.

*Quaker Bonnet, Orchard Park, New York*


# 82. Butter Horn Rolls

INGREDIENTS

DIRECTIONS

¾ cup butter
½ cup sugar

Cream together.

4 cups flour
1½ teaspoons salt

Sift and add to above.

1 cake yeast
1 cup scalded milk

Mix together and add to mixture.

3 eggs—beaten

Stir into mixture. Let raise light. Put the dough on a towel, fold over and knead.

Cover top of dough with butter and cover with wax paper. Set in refrigerator overnight. Roll out the size of large pie and cut in 6 or 8 pieces. Grease top with butter, then roll. Let get very light and bake in 425 F. oven for 15 minutes. The sponge will keep 3 to 5 days in the refrigerator.

*Emelie Tolman, Chicago, Illinois*

## 83. Buttermilk Rolls

(Makes 24)

INGREDIENTS

2 cups buttermilk
1 cake yeast

½ teaspoon soda
2 tablespoons sugar
2 teaspoons salt
4 cups flour
2 tablespoons
  shortening

DIRECTIONS

Have buttermilk at room temperature. Add yeast and allow it to soften.

Mix these ingredients using only a part of the flour. Beat well into yeast mixture, then add balance of the flour, until the dough forms a stiff ball. Knead quickly until smooth. Roll out to ¾ inch thickness and cut with biscuit cutter. Let rise in a warm place for 1 hour.

Bake in 450 F. oven for 15 minutes. When done, brush over lightly with milk sweetened with a little sugar.

*Marshlands Inn, Sackville, N. B., Canada.*

## 84. Bran Muffins

(Makes 36 muffins)

INGREDIENTS

1⅓ cups brown sugar
1 cup shortening

1 teaspoon soda
2⅔ cups flour
½ teaspoon salt
1⅓ cups bran

½ pint sour milk

⅔ teaspoon vanilla
1 cup raisins

DIRECTIONS

Cream together.

Blend together.

Add to cream mixture alternately with the blended dry ingredients.

Add to mixture. Pour into greased muffin tins and bake in 350 F. oven for 15 minutes.

*Tally-Ho Tea Room, Park Ridge, Illinois*

## 85.  Gingerbread Muffins  (Serves 18)

INGREDIENTS

DIRECTIONS

1 cup butter
1 cup sugar
1 cup molasses
1 cup boiling water

Mix together.

2½ cups flour
2½ teaspoons soda
1 teaspoon salt
1 teaspoon cinnamon
1 teaspoon ginger

Sift together and add to the above.  Mix well.

2 eggs—beaten

Add to mixture.  Pour into greased muffin tins and bake in 350 F. oven for 30 to 40 minutes.

*Cock O' The Walk, Oakland, California*


## 86.  Maple Muffins  (Makes 8 muffins)

INGREDIENTS

DIRECTIONS

1 egg—beaten lightly
¼ cup milk

Whip into beaten egg, the milk, using egg beater.

1¾ cups flour
2½ teaspoons baking powder
¼ teaspoon salt

Sift together and add to mixture a little at a time, alternating with

½ cup maple syrup

Syrup.

¼ cup melted butter

Fold into mixture.  Bake in buttered floured muffin pan in 325 F. oven for about 25 minutes.

*Maple Cabin, St. Johnsbury, Vermont*

# 87.  Orange Muffins

| INGREDIENTS | DIRECTIONS |
| --- | --- |
| 2 tablespoons shortening<br>1 cup sugar | Rub together. |
| 2 eggs—beaten lightly<br>2 oranges—juice | Add to mixture. |
| 3 cups flour<br>1 tablespoon baking powder<br>½ teaspoon salt | Sift together and stir into mixture.  Leave a little of the flour to stir in later. |
| ½ cup milk | Add to mixture. |
| 2 orange rinds—grated | Add to mixture with the balance of the flour. |
| | Pour into muffin pan and bake in 250 F. oven for 30 minutes. |

*Mission Inn, Riverside, California*


# 88.  Spiced Pecan Muffins

| INGREDIENTS | DIRECTIONS |
| --- | --- |
| 2 cups flour<br>3 teaspoons baking powder<br>½ teaspoon nutmeg<br>½ teaspoon cinnamon<br>¼ teaspoon ground cloves<br>¼ cup sugar<br>½ teaspoon salt | Sift dry ingredients together. |
| ½ cup pecans—chopped | Stir in nuts. |
| 1 cup milk<br>1 egg—beaten | Mix milk and egg and stir into mixture. |
| ¼ cup melted shortening | Add the shortening. |
| | Pour into greased muffin pans and bake in 425 F. oven for 25 minutes. |

*The Carr House, Wolfboro, New Hampshire*

## 89.   Potato Flour Muffins

(Makes 8 muffins)

INGREDIENTS

DIRECTIONS

5 egg whites—beaten
2½ teaspoons sugar
½ teaspoon salt

Beat into egg whites until stiff but not dry.

2½ tablespoons ice water

Add gradually to the above.

5 egg yolks—beaten
slightly

Add to mixture.

1 cup potato flour
2 teaspoons baking
powder

Sift together and add to mixture.   Mix thoroughly and place in greased muffin tins immediately.   Bake in 400 F. oven for 20 minutes.   Best results obtained when an electric mixer is used.

*Marshall Field & Company, Tea and Grill Rooms, Chicago, Illinois*

## 90.   Cheese Biscuits

(Makes about 60)

INGREDIENTS

DIRECTIONS

1 lb. cheese—grated
2 cups flour
½ cup butter
2 tablespoons cream
½ teaspoon red pepper
pinch of salt

Mix all together.   Cut with small biscuit cutter.

60 pecans

Place a pecan in the center of each and bake in 350 F. oven for 20 minutes.

*Althea, Lewisburg, West Virginia*

## 91.   Cheese Straws

(Makes 48)

INGREDIENTS

DIRECTIONS

1 cup grated cheese
½ cup butter
1 cup flour
½ teaspoon baking
powder
1 pinch red pepper
½ teaspoon paprika
1 teaspoon curry powder  (optional)
1 egg yolk
2 tablespoons milk or water

Mix and knead well.   Roll thin and cut in strips.   Bake in 375 F. oven for 15 minutes.

*Mrs. Otto J. Sieplein, Miami, Florida*

# 92. Kentucky Egg Bread Chicken Sandwich

INGREDIENTS

DIRECTIONS

### BREAD

1 pint corn meal
½ teaspoon soda
1 cup buttermilk
2 eggs—beaten
1 teaspoon baking powder

Make a batter and thin with sweet milk.

6 tablespoons melted lard
1 teaspoon salt

Add to batter and bake in a thick iron pan (hot and greased) and bake in 400 F. oven for 20 minutes.

Cut in squares.

1 thick slice cooked breast of chicken for a sandwich

Place between squares of buttered bread and cover with sauce.

### SAUCE

2 tablespoons onion—minced
2 tablespoons celery—minced
½ cup butter

Brown until a light golden color.

4 tablespoons flour
1½ pint strong chicken broth
¾ cup cream
salt and pepper to taste

Add to the above and cook until it thickens.

*Mrs. A. Scott Hines, Bowling Green, Kentucky*

*This is my sister. (No, she did not change her name, as she married a Hines.) She is not only delightfully entertaining and handsome but can bring forth many original creations that are superb.*

## 93. Sweet Bread

INGREDIENTS

DIRECTIONS

1 pint milk (fresh or canned)
½ lb. butter
1 teaspoon salt

Scald milk, add butter and salt. Let cool.

1 cake yeast
½ cup warm water
1 teaspoon sugar
2 tablespoons flour

Dissolve yeast in water mixed with sugar and flour. Combine the two mixtures.

4 cups flour—stirred in

Let rise in warm place for several hours.

2 eggs—beaten
1¼ cups sugar

Blend together and add to sponge.

½ lb. currants
1 teaspoon ginger
½ teaspoon mace
3¾ cups flour

Mix into the sponge which will be very thick. Let rise again. Then put into buttered and floured bread pans and let rise briefly again. Bake in 400 F. oven for 10 minutes. Then in 325 F. oven until it is done. Makes a delicious bread for toast and will keep indefinitely.

*Julia S. Wheeler, Berkeley, California*


## 94. Toasty Loaf

(Serves 6)

INGREDIENTS

DIRECTIONS

1 large loaf white bread

Cut all crust from bread except the lower crust. Cut bread in 1-inch slices down to lower crust, but not through the crust; then cut the center of the loaf lengthwise to the crust.

½ lb. snappy cheese
¼ lb. butter

Cream together and spread between slices and all over the outside of the loaf, except the lower crust. Tie string around the loaf and place on pan. Cook in 400 F. oven for 30 minutes, or until well heated through and a crispy golden brown.

Place on platter and remove string. Surround with bacon and sliced tomatoes, which make an attractive-looking, as well as delicious dish.

*Mrs. Mathew Jackson, Chicago, Illinois*

## 95. Sour Cream Maple Gingerbread (Serves 9)

| INGREDIENTS | DIRECTIONS |
|---|---|
| 1 egg—beaten<br>½ cup maple syrup<br>½ cup sugar<br>1 teaspoon ginger | Mix all together. |
| 1 cup sour cream<br>1 teaspoon soda | Mix together. |
| 1 tablespoon butter | To be used if the cream is not very thick. |
| 2 cups flour | Add flour and cream alternately to the egg mixture. |
| | Pour into deep pan and bake in 300 F. oven for 20 minutes. Should be about 1½ inches thick when done. |

*Maple Cabin, Johnsbury, Vermont*


## 96. Sour Milk Gingerbread (Serves 15)

| INGREDIENTS | DIRECTIONS |
|---|---|
| ½ cup butter<br>½ cup granulated sugar | Cream together. |
| 2 eggs | Add to above and mix well. |
| ½ cup molasses | Add to mixture and stir well. |
| ½ cup sour milk<br>1 teaspoon soda | Mix soda and milk and add to mixture. |
| 2 cups flour<br>¼ teaspoon salt<br>½ teaspoon ginger<br>1 teaspoon cinnamon | Mix dry ingredients and add to mixture. |
| | Pour into square cake pan and bake in 350 F. oven for 45 minutes. Has to be watched as molasses cakes are liable to burn quickly. |

*Miss Katharine L. Little, Chicago, Illinois*

## 97.  Gingerbread

INGREDIENTS | DIRECTIONS

1 cup boiling water
1 cup shortening

Pour water over shortening.

1 cup brown sugar
1 cup molasses
3 eggs—beaten

Add to the above.

3 cups flour
1 teaspoon baking powder
1 teaspoon soda
1 teaspoon salt
1½ teaspoons ginger
1½ teaspoons cinnamon

Sift together and add to the mixture.  Beat with an egg beater until smooth.

Bake in 350 F. oven for 30 to 40 minutes.

*Houghtaling's Woahink Lake Resort, Glenada, Oregon*


## 98.  Hot Graham Bread          (Serves 12 to 15)

INGREDIENTS | DIRECTIONS

1 egg
1 cup milk
¼ cup sugar
¼ cup shortening

Beat together quickly.

1 cup flour
1 cup graham flour
1 teaspoon salt
3 teaspoons baking powder

Sift together and mix into the above.

Pour in buttered 9-inch square pan and bake in 325 F. to 350 F. oven for 20 to 30 minutes.

Cut in squares and serve hot with butter.

*Marshlands Inn, Sackville, N. B., Canada*


## 99.  Health Bread

INGREDIENTS | DIRECTIONS

1 beaten egg
3 cups buttermilk
½ cup molasses
1 teaspoon salt
2 teaspoons soda
1 cup walnuts—chopped
1 cup raisins
2 cups flour
4 cups bran

Mix ingredients together in the order given. Pour in a greased pan and bake in 325 F. oven for from 45 to 60 minutes.

This recipe takes only 5 minutes to put together.

*Pacific Beach Hotel, Pacific Beach, Washington*

## 100. Short Bread

INGREDIENTS

DIRECTIONS

1 lb. butter—soft, but
not melted
8 cups flour

Cut in until like coarse sand, as for a pie crust.

1½ cups sugar
1 egg

Mix all ingredients together and roll or knead into large cakes about ½-inch thick and cut with a cookie cutter. Prick each piece several times with a fork.

Bake in 300 F. oven for 20 to 30 minutes.

*Mrs. David Donald, Pittsfield, Massachusetts*


## 101. Orange Bread

INGREDIENTS

DIRECTIONS

2 cups flour
2 teaspoons baking
powder
½ cup sugar
¼ teaspoon salt

Sift these ingredients together.

1 cup candied orange
peel—cut in pieces

Add to the above.

1 egg—beaten
1 cup of milk

Stir well into the dry ingredients.

Put in pan and sprinkle with sugar. Let stand 20 minutes before baking. Bake in 325 F. oven for 30 minutes.

*Grace E. Smith Service Restaurant and Cafeteria, Toledo, Ohio*

*I never pass up an opportunity to eat at Grace Smith's—especially her unexcelled lemon pie.*

## 102. Orange Bread

INGREDIENTS

DIRECTIONS

1 orange—juice
enough boiling water
to make 1 cup

Do not strain juice. Put juice and water in mixing bowl.

1 orange rind—grated
1 cup pitted dates
½ cup pecans

Stir into liquid.

2 tablespoons melted
butter
1 egg
1 teaspoon vanilla

Blend these ingredients together and add to above mixture.

2 cups flour
1 teaspoon baking
powder
½ teaspoon salt
½ teaspoon baking soda
¾ cup sugar

Sift together and fold into mixture.

Bake in bread pan well greased in 350 F. oven for 1 hour, then reduce heat to 300 F. and bake for 30 minutes longer.

This makes a delicious moist bread that keeps fresh a long time.

*Mrs. Alonzo Newton Benn, Chicago, Illinois*


## 103. Orange Toast

INGREDIENTS

DIRECTIONS

2 tablespoons orange
juice
1 orange rind—grated
½ cup sugar
⅛ teaspoon cinnamon
6 slices buttered toast

Spread this mixture on buttered toast and put in oven or under the broiler for 2 or 3 minutes.

*The Nut Tree, Vacaville, California*

## 104.  Orange Toast

INGREDIENTS

½ cup orange rind—
   grated
1 cup sugar
1 tablespoon orange
   juice

DIRECTIONS

Mix together and spread on buttered toast.
Put in oven a few minutes until heated.

*Grace E. Smith Service Restaurant and Cafeteria, Toledo, Ohio*


## 105.  Miniature Cinnamon Rolls

INGREDIENTS

1 tablespoon butter
3 tablespoons brown
   sugar

small amount of
bread dough

melted butter

2 tablespoons sugar
¼ teaspoon cinnamon

DIRECTIONS

Dot bottom of baking pan with butter.  Cover
evenly with the sugar.

Roll out to about ⅛ inch thick and brush
with melted butter.

Mix together and sprinkle over dough.  Roll
and cut in pieces ½ inch thick.  Place in
baking pan 6x6 inches and allow to rise.

Bake in 400 F. oven for 10 to 12 minutes.
After baking, brush the top of rolls with
melted butter and turn upside down to remove rolls from pan.  Serve hot.

*Crane's Canary Cottage, Chagrin Falls, Ohio*

*These cinnamon rolls are outstanding and
I hope those you make turn out as well.*

# 106. Raised Cinnamon Rolls

INGREDIENTS

DIRECTIONS

1 pint milk
1 tablespoon sugar

Bring to a boil and let cool.

1 cake yeast
¼ cup water

Dissolve and add to above.

1 cup flour—sifted

Add to mixture and make into a soft batter. Let rise in a warm place.

1 egg—beaten
1 cup flour—sifted

When mixture has risen, stir in the egg. Add flour and let rise again.

butter
cinnamon
brown sugar

Turn onto a floured board, roll to about 1 inch thickness. Spread well with soft butter, sprinkle with cinnamon and brown sugar.

Roll whole sheet of dough into a long roll and cut into pieces. Place in greased muffin tin and set to rise again. Put into a 350 F. oven and bake 20 to 25 minutes.

*Mrs. E. H. Singmaster, Germantown, Pennsylvania*


# 107. Peter Pan Rolls                   (Makes 20 rolls)

INGREDIENTS

DIRECTIONS

1 cake of yeast
¼ cup warm water

Dissolve yeast.

3 eggs—beaten
3 tablespoons melted butter
1 tablespoon sugar
1 teaspoon salt

Blend together. Then add the yeast and water mixture.

3 cups of flour

Gradually add to mixture beating all the while. Tie mixture in muslin bag or in a towel and tie the ends together to form a bag, and hang in container ¾ full of warm water. Allow to rise until the bag comes to the top, or about 2 hours. Then take from the bag and place on floured board. Pat out to 1-inch thickness, cut with a biscuit cutter, roll in melted butter and then crumbled corn flakes or chopped blanched almonds.

3 tablespoons melted butter

Twist and place on a cookie sheet. Let rise for 1 hour and bake in 450 F. oven for 12 to 15 minutes.

*Peter Pan Lodge, Carmel, California*

## 108.  Pop-Overs

**INGREDIENTS**

1 cup flour
1 teaspoon salt

1 cup sweet milk
1 egg
1 tablespoon melted
shortening

*Miss Laura Pepper*

**DIRECTIONS**

Sift together.

Blend and add to the above, beat with an egg beater or a mixer.  Pour into hot molds about ⅔ full.  Bake in 425 F. oven for 15 minutes, then reduce heat to 375 F. for 20 minutes. Cook in iron pop-over rings.


## 109.  Popovers

**INGREDIENTS**

2 eggs
2 cups flour—sifted
2 cups thin milk

*Santa Maria Inn, Santa Maria, California*

**DIRECTIONS**

Blend into a smooth batter.  Half fill well-greased muffin pans and bake in 400 F. oven for 10 or 12 minutes, or until they have raised ½ inch above the top of pan.  Turn down the fire and continue baking for about 30 minutes until they are nice and brown.


## 110.  Sally Lunn

**INGREDIENTS**

½ cup butter
1 tablespoon sugar
½ teaspoon salt

2 eggs

1 cake yeast
1 cup milk

3 cups flour

*Althea, Lewisburg, West Virginia*

**DIRECTIONS**

Cream together.

Add to above and beat.

Dissolve yeast in lukewarm milk and add to mixture.

Add to mixture and pour into buttered tube cake pan.

Let rise 1½ hours.  Bake in 300 F. oven for 45 minutes.

# 111. Batter Cakes

(Makes 12 to 18 cakes)

**INGREDIENTS**

**DIRECTIONS**

3 egg yolks—beaten
¼ cup maple syrup
1⅛ cups milk

Mix well.

3 cups cake flour
2 tablespoons baking powder
1½ teaspoons salt
1⅛ cups milk

Sift together. Add to mixture, alternately with the milk. Beat well.

¼ cup melted shortening

Should not be hot when added to mixture. This mixture will be very thin when first made, but should be allowed to stand for 30 minutes before using, to thicken.

Make cakes on a griddle that has been rubbed over with a piece of salt pork.

*Williamsburg Inn, Williamsburg, Virginia*


# 112. Old Fashioned Overnite Raised Buckwheat Cakes

(Serves 7)

**INGREDIENTS**

**DIRECTIONS**

½ cake yeast
1 quart lukewarm water

Dissolve yeast in water.

2 cups old-fashioned buckwheat flour
1 cup white flour
½ cup sugar
3 teaspoons salt

Stir into yeast mixture until a smooth batter and let set overnight in the refrigerator. (If in a hurry to use, it may be set a couple of hours in kitchen temperature, and they will be just as good.)

1 pinch of soda

Before using, add pinch of soda.

If thinner cakes are desired, add cold water.

Serve with sausages.

*Lee Hoffman Hotel, Cresson, Pennsylvania*

## 113. Buckwheat Cakes

(Serves 6)

| INGREDIENTS | DIRECTIONS |
|---|---|
| 1 cake yeast<br>2 cups warm water | Mix together. |
| 1 cup buckwheat flour<br>1 cup flour | Add to yeast mixture and let stand overnight in a large bowl. |
| 2 tablespoons molasses<br>1 teaspoon salt<br>4 tablespoons melted butter<br>1 teaspoon soda | Add to sponge and beat into a batter. |

*Mrs. Voijt Frank Mashek, Chicago, Illinois*


## 114. Buckwheat Cakes

| INGREDIENTS | DIRECTIONS |
|---|---|
| 2 cups buckwheat<br>¾ cup flour<br>1 teaspoon salt<br>buttermilk | Mix to a batter and let stand overnight. |
| 1 teaspoon soda<br>little warm water | Dissolve in water and when ready to fry cakes, add to batter. Add enough more buttermilk so that batter will pour off spoon onto hot griddle. |

Use piece of salt pork to grease the griddle.

Make cakes and serve with maple syrup.

*Marshlands Inn, Sackville, N. B., Canada*


*Few are the cooks who can view their results impersonally.*

## 115. French Pancakes or Crepe Suzette with Southern Comfort Sauce

(Makes 5 to 6 cakes)

| INGREDIENTS | DIRECTIONS |
|---|---|
| 3 eggs—beaten<br>1 cup milk<br>⅓ cup water | Mix together. |
| 1 cup flour<br>¼ teaspoon baking powder<br>½ teaspoon salt<br>3 tablespoons sugar | Sift together and add to mixture.<br><br>The batter should be very thin. Take about ½ cup to a griddle. Turn carefully and when done, put on a dinner plate, sprinkle with powdered sugar and jelly and roll. |
| 1 jigger Southern Comfort to a cake | Pour over pancake and light with a match. |

*Mr. Francis E. Fowler, Jr., St. Louis, Missouri*


## 116. Corn Meal and Rice Griddle Cakes

| INGREDIENTS | DIRECTIONS |
|---|---|
| ½ cup corn meal<br>½ cup flour<br>½ teaspoon soda<br>1 teaspoon salt | Mix and sift. |
| 2 egg yolks—beaten<br>1 cup sour milk<br>1 cup cold cooked rice | Mix up together and add to dry ingredients. |
| 2 egg whites—beaten | Fold in egg whites. Fry on hot griddle.<br><br>Serve with maple syrup. |

*Sawyer Tavern, Keene, New Hampshire*

## 117. German Pancake

INGREDIENTS

3 eggs—beaten
½ teaspoon salt
½ cup flour

½ cup milk

2 tablespoons butter

DIRECTIONS

Mix all together.

Add and beat constantly.

Spread bottom and sides of 10-inch cold frying pan with butter. Pour in the batter. Put in 450 F. oven and bake 20 to 25 minutes, gradually reducing the heat. Place on a hot plate and serve with lemon juice, cinnamon, sugar, and hot apple sauce.

*Roy C. Neuhaus, Evanston, Illinois*


## 118. Special Hot Cakes        (Serves 8)

INGREDIENTS

2 cups flour
1 cup corn meal
1 teaspoon salt
½ teaspoon soda
4 teaspoons baking
  powder

1 cup whole wheat flour
1 cup bran flakes

2 eggs—beaten
1 quart buttermilk

DIRECTIONS

Sift together.

Add to the above.

Beat together and mix with the dry ingredients. Thin with a little sweet milk to desired consistency. Bake on ungreased griddle slowly, allowing 2 minutes for each side of cake.

*Big Sur Lodge, Big Sur, California*


## 119. Potato Pancakes        (Serves 8)

INGREDIENTS

4 large potatoes—grated
2 eggs—beaten
1 tablespoon flour
1 onion—grated
  (optional)
salt and pepper to
  taste

DIRECTIONS

Mix thoroughly.

Bake on a hot griddle. Bacon grease griddle is the best.

*Viola A. Brehmer, Elmwood, Fond du Lac, Wisconsin*

## 120.  Waffles

INGREDIENTS | DIRECTIONS

2 egg yolks
1 cup milk
1½ cups cake flour—sifted
2 teaspoons sugar
1 teaspoon salt
¼ cup butter—melted

Stir to a smooth batter.

2 egg whites—beaten stiff
2 teaspoons baking powder

Fold in eggs and baking powder.

*The House by the Road, Ashburn, Georgia*


## 121.  Wheat Cakes                    (Serves 6)

INGREDIENTS | DIRECTIONS

2 egg yolks
2 cups milk
2 cups flour
1 tablespoon sugar
1 teaspoon salt
4 tablespoons melted butter
2 teaspoons baking powder

Beat all together with an egg beater until a smooth batter.

2 egg whites—beaten

Fold in egg whites.

(If sour milk or buttermilk is used, substitute soda for baking powder and do not separate the eggs.  If sour cream is used, put in only 2 table-spoons.)

*Mrs. Voijt F. Mashek, Chicago, Illinois*


## 122.  Corn Meal Scrapple

INGREDIENTS | DIRECTIONS

1¼ cups corn meal
4 cups water

Add corn meal slowly to boiling water, stirring constantly.  Cool for 2 or 3 minutes.

1 lb. pork sausage
1½ teaspoons salt
dash of pepper

Add to mixture and cook in double boiler for 1½ to 2 hours.

Mold in bread tins which have been dipped in cold water.  Let stand overnight.  Cut in slices, dip in flour and fry brown.

*Mrs. Gertrude Spiro, Michigan City, Indiana*

## 123.   Philadelphia Scrapple

INGREDIENTS

2½ lbs. fresh pork
    shoulder
 2 quarts cold water
 1 teaspoon salt
½ teaspoon pepper

2¼ cups corn meal
¾ cups flour
 4 teaspoons summer
    savory
 1 teaspoon salt
½ teaspoon black pepper

DIRECTIONS

Simmer slowly for 2 hours adding seasoning when nearly done. Remove meat from stock and shred with a fork. The longer the meat fibers the better. Strain stock and let 2 cups cool. Should have 5 cups left, which keep boiling.

Blend these ingredients. Add 2 cups of cooled stock slowly, stirring constantly to prevent lumping. This will make a paste. Slowly add this to boiling stock and keep stirring. Add shredded meat and cook slowly 2 hours, constantly stirring to prevent burning.

More seasoning can be added to suit taste.

When done, put in *enamel* pans. Slice very thin and fry on dry griddle until browned on each side. Serve with maple syrup. This will keep in refrigerator about 3 weeks.

*Dr. John A. Flanders, Chicago, Illinois*


## 124.   Philadelphia Scrapple

INGREDIENTS

1 pig's head—remove
  eyes

2 lbs. corn meal to every
  3 lbs. of meat

½ tablespoon salt
¼ teaspoon black
  pepper
1 teaspoon onion juice

DIRECTIONS

Cook slowly in boiling water to barely cover until meat comes off bones. Remove meat from stock and let meat and stock cool.

Weigh meat after removed from bones. Remove fat from stock and strain. Bring stock to boil and slowly add corn meal. Cook to a mush, adding hot water to thin a little, if necessary.

Mix this into each pound of meat. Add to mush and cook in double boiler for 1 hour. Place in pans and when ready to serve, cut in ¼-inch slices and brown in a little fat. Serve piping hot.

*Waldorf Astoria Hotel, New York City, New York*

# 125. Baked Clams au gratin

INGREDIENTS

DIRECTIONS

2 cups coarsely ground clams
2 eggs
½ cup grated cheese
1 teaspoon salt
½ teaspoon white pepper

Mix all these ingredients together. Set aside until needed.

¼ lb. butter
3 strips diced bacon
⅓ cup chopped celery, green pepper, and green onion

Braise in a pan, but do not brown.

1 cup flour

Add the flour and cook well.

1 pint of boiling milk

Gradually add the boiling milk and let cook until thick. Stir in the first mixture and place in buttered dish, sprinkle with grated cheese, melted butter and dust with paprika and bake in 350 F. oven for 10 to 15 minutes. (Clam shells or individual molds may also be used.) Serve immediately, piping hot.

If clams are not available, shrimp, crab, or lobster may be used, adding 3 or 4 oz. of dry sherry wine.

*Plessas Tavern, Pismo Beach, California*

*Something I have never figured out is why most of the food we like best is not good for us.*

# 126.  Minced Clam Souffle

| INGREDIENTS | DIRECTIONS |
|---|---|
| 6 tablespoons butter<br>3 tablespoons onion—chopped | Saute until a light brown color. |
| 5 tablespoons flour | Blend into above. |
| ½ green pepper—chopped<br>2 pimientos—cut fine | Add to mixture. |
| 2 cups milk<br>clam juice from 2 cans | Mix liquids and slowly add to mixture, stirring until smooth.  Bring to a boil and remove from the fire. |
| 6 egg yolks—beaten<br>2 cans clams—minced<br>2 teaspoons Worcestershire sauce<br>2 pimientos—cut fine<br>salt and pepper to taste | Stir into mixture. |
| 6 egg whites—beaten | Fold into mixture.  Pour into individual casseroles. |
| buttered bread crumbs<br>grated cheese | Top casseroles with a little of each and place in pan of hot water and bake in 325 F. oven for 30 minutes.<br><br>A small piece of garlic may be used, but care should be taken as it is easily ruined. |

*Cafe Del Rey Moro, San Diego, California*

*Dining was a pleasure in B.C.   (Before Calories.)*

# 127.   Crab Custard en Casserole   (Serves 6)

INGREDIENTS

DIRECTIONS

4 tablespoons butter
1 teaspoon grated onion

Cook in top of double boiler, but do not brown.

4 tablespoons flour
salt and pepper to taste

Blend and add to the above.   Cook and stir until smooth.

1 cup milk
½ cup cream
1 dash of Tabasco sauce
1 teaspoon A-1 sauce

Blend and add to mixture slowly, stirring constantly until thick.   Cover and keep hot.

4 eggs—beaten
1 tablespoon sherry

Blend.   Strain sauce and add to combination.

3 cups crab meat

Into individual (pint size) casseroles, put ½ cup crab meat.   Pour sauce over each.

½ cup buttered bread crumbs

Sprinkle over each casserole.   Bake in 325 F. oven for 1 hour, or until a silver knife comes out clean.

*Valley Green Lodge, Orick, California*


# 128.   Crab Meat Souffle a la Rene   (Serves 6)

INGREDIENTS

DIRECTIONS

3 tablespoons butter
4 tablespoons flour
¼ teaspoon salt
pepper to taste
1 cup milk

Make a white sauce and let cool.

3 egg yolks

Stir into sauce.

1 cup cooked crab meat
—flaked
1 teaspoon lemon juice

Mix with the sauce.

3 egg whites—beaten

Fold into mixture.

Place in baking dish and bake in 350 F. oven for 40 minutes, or until a silver knife comes out clean when thrust into center.

Served with a tossed salad and dessert, this makes an ideal luncheon.

*Phil Libby, Radio Food Commentator, Chicago, Illinois*

# 129. Crab Stew

(Serves 4)

INGREDIENTS | DIRECTIONS

4 tablespoons butter
3 tablespoons flour
1 piece red pepper to taste

Cream together until smooth. Cook in double boiler.

2 cups milk

Gradually add to mixture and cook slowly until thick.

½ cup cream
3 tablespoons Worcestershire sauce
1 teaspoon celery salt

Blend these ingredients and add to mixture.

4 cups shredded crab meat
segments of lemon

Add to sauce and keep hot in double boiler. Do not boil.

4 tablespoons sherry

At the last moment add the wine and serve.

*This recipe is given as a one dish meal. If used as an entering soup, use less crab meat so the consistency of the finished dish meets the requirements of the server.*

*Dr. T. J. LeBlanc, Cincinnati, Ohio*


# 130. Deviled Crab

(Serves 6)

INGREDIENTS | DIRECTIONS

1 tablespoon butter
2 tablespoons flour
⅔ cup white stock
2 egg yolks—beaten
salt and pepper to taste

Make a cream sauce. Chill for 2 hours.

1 cup chopped crab meat
1 cup chopped mushrooms
2 tablespoons sherry wine
1 teaspoon chopped parsley
salt and pepper to taste

Blend together and mix into sauce.

6 crab shell backs

Fill shells with mixture.

5 tablespoons bread crumbs
4 tablespoons melted butter

Mix together and sprinkle over top.

Bake in 400 F. oven for 10 to 12 minutes.

*Tarpon Inn, Port Aransas, Texas*

## 131.  Imperial Crab

| INGREDIENTS | DIRECTIONS |
| --- | --- |
| 1 quart crab meat<br>½ cup mayonnaise<br>1 teaspoon dry mustard<br>½ green pepper—cut fine<br>1 pimiento—cut fine | Mix all these ingredients together. |
| 4 crab shells | Fill shells and pile high.  Brown in 400 F. oven for about 20 minutes, or until nice and brown.  Serve hot. |

*The Chaya, Petersburg, Virginia*


## 132.  Spaghetti and Crab

| INGREDIENTS | DIRECTIONS |
| --- | --- |
| ½ cup chopped onions<br>1 teaspoon chopped garlic<br>1 teaspoon chopped parsley<br>1 teaspoon chopped celery<br>¼ cup olive oil | Braise vegetables in oil, until a golden brown. |
| 1 cup solid pack tomatoes<br>1 cup tomato sauce<br>1½ cups water<br>2 teaspoons salt<br>1 teaspoon black pepper<br>½ teaspoon paprika | Mix together and add to the above ingredients and let simmer for 1 hour. |
| 1 lb. fresh crab meat<br>¼ lb. sherry wine | Add and simmer for a few minutes. |
| 1 lb. spaghetti<br>grated cheese to taste | Cook and drain spaghetti.  Put on platter and pour sauce over it and mix well.  Sprinkle with cheese.  Serve immediately. |

*Fishermen's Grotto, San Francisco, California*

## 133.  Lincklaen Famous Fish Balls  (Makes 36 small balls)

INGREDIENTS

½ lb. salt codfish—cut in pieces
1 quart raw potatoes—diced
2 quarts cold water

4 tablespoons butter
black pepper to taste
2 eggs—beaten

DIRECTIONS

Cover with cold water and soak overnight. Pour off half the water and add hot water. Boil until the potatoes are done. Mash thoroughly.

Stir into mixture. Flour the hands and roll into small round balls. Fry in a good grade of hot lard.

Serve with bacon curls and tartar sauce.

*Lincklaen House, Casenovia, New York*


## 134.  Danish Fish Pudding  (Serves 10 to 12)

INGREDIENTS

1½ lbs. fish pulp

4 egg yolks

1 thick slice of bread (remove crusts)
1½ cups milk

¼ lb. butter
3 teaspoons salt
½ teaspoon pepper
1 teaspoon nutmeg

4 egg whites—beaten

DIRECTIONS

To be either flounder, halibut, or red snapper. Scrape into a pulp.

Add to pulp, one at a time. Stir in well.

Soak bread in milk and add to mixture.

Add to mixture and stir well.

Fold into mixture. Pour into a 2-quart mold that has been greased and crumbed and boil 3 hours.

Serve with drawn butter, lime juice, and parsley, or with sauce.

### SAUCE

1 pint fresh shrimps
1 lb. fresh mushrooms
½ lb. butter

Chop shrimps and mushrooms and saute in butter.

½ pint cream
¾ tablespoon cornstarch
1 teaspoon salt
½ teaspoon pepper

Make a smooth paste of these ingredients. Put all together into a double boiler and cook until smooth and done. With this sauce, the recipe will serve 12 to 15.

*LaChaumiere, Palm Beach, Florida*

## 135.  Golden Creamed Fish
(Serves 4)

**INGREDIENTS**

**DIRECTIONS**

1 onion—chopped
12 peppercorns
   (whole black pepper
   spice)
1 sprig of chopped
   parsley
1 cup water

Boil for 5 minutes.

2 lbs. fish (Sand-pike,
   fresh Cod, Whitefish,
   Lakefront, etc.)

Cut into 4 pieces.  Add to the above sauce
and simmer gently for about 5 minutes, until
the fish is cooked.

salt to taste

Season the fish.

1 tablespoon flour
6 tablespoons cold milk

Blend together and add to the fish.  Simmer
gently for a few minutes.

½ cup cream

Add to the fish and heat, but do not boil.

2 egg yolks—beaten

Beat in earthen bowl from which the fish will
be served until a nice lemon color.  Slowly
add the hot fish and sauce.  Serve with boiled
potatoes.

*Mrs. A. E. R. Peterka, Cleveland, Ohio*


## 136.  Lobster a la Newburg
(Serves 6)

**INGREDIENTS**

**DIRECTIONS**

6 tablespoons butter

Melt in double boiler.

3 cups fresh cooked
   lobster—diced

Add to butter and cook directly over low fire
for 3 minutes.

2 tablespoons sherry
1 dash paprika
1 dash nutmeg

Add to the above and put over hot water.

6 egg yolks—beaten
1½ cups cream

Blend eggs and cream and add to mixture,
gradually.  Stir until smooth and thick.

toast points

Serve at once on toast points.

For a lobster Thermidor, this mixture may be returned to lobster shells
sprinkled with fine buttered bread crumbs and put under low broiler heat
to brown.

*Jordan Pond House, Seal Harbor, Maine*

## 137.  Seafood Newburg

(Serves 2)

| INGREDIENTS | DIRECTIONS |
|---|---|
| 2 Littleneck clams<br>¼ cup lobster meat<br>¼ cup crab flakes<br>¼ cup shrimp<br>1 dash paprika<br>2 tablespoons butter | Saute for a few minutes. |
| 1 tablespoon sherry wine | Add to mixture and toss over the fire for a few minutes more. |
| ¾ cup cream | Add to mixture and let come to a boil. |
| 3 egg yolks—beaten<br>¼ cup cream | Blend together and add to mixture, stirring constantly until thick.  (Do not allow to boil, after eggs are in.)   Remove from the fire. |
| 1 tablespoon lemon juice<br>salt and pepper to taste<br>2 tablespoons butter | Stir into mixture and serve hot on toast or in a chafing dish. |

*Majorie Mills, Boston, Massachusetts*


## 138.  Baked Scallops

(Serves 12)

| INGREDIENTS | DIRECTIONS |
|---|---|
| 36 scallops<br>12 shells | Put 3 scallops in each shell (deep side of shell is best).  Sprinkle with salt. |
| 3 cups bread crumbs | Cover scallops. |
| ¾ cup butter | Dot top of scallops. |
| ¾ cup cream—<br>1 tablespoon to each shell | Add to scallops. |
| pepper to taste | Add to scallops. |
|  | Bake in 400 F. oven for 5 minutes.  Baste and continue baking for 5 minutes, if necessary. |

Serve immediately.  Decorate with parsley and serve with tartar sauce.

*Hackmatack Inn, Chester, N. S., Canada*

# 139. Baked Sea Food

INGREDIENTS

DIRECTIONS

1 green pepper—
  chopped
1 onion—chopped
1 cup celery—chopped
1 cup fresh or canned
  crab meat
1 can shrimp
1 cup mayonnaise
½ teaspoon salt
¼ teaspoon pepper
1 teaspoon
  Worcestershire sauce

buttered and toasted
bread crumbs

Combine and blend ingredients.

Place mixture in individual shells or a shallow
pan.

Top each shell, or sprinkle over all.

Bake in 350 F. oven for 30 minutes.

Serve with sections of lemon.

*Mrs. Gertrude Spiro, Michigan City, Indiana*

# 140. Baked Noodles and Shrimp          (Serves 6)

INGREDIENTS

DIRECTIONS

3 cups noodles

Cook, wash, and drain.

2½ cups milk
2 tablespoons butter
1 tablespoon flour
½ cup cream
  salt and pepper to
  taste

Combine and cook into a well blended smooth
sauce.

1 lb. fresh shrimp

In a buttered casserole put a layer of noodles,
then white sauce, then shrimp, until the dish
is filled. Top with cracker crumbs and dots
of butter. Bake in 350 F. oven, until the
crumbs are well browned.

*Allenwood, Burlington, Vermont*

# 141. Delicious Shrimp Dish
(Serves 6)

| INGREDIENTS | DIRECTIONS |
|---|---|
| 2 tablespoons flour<br>2 tablespoons butter | Blend together in a double boiler. |
| 1 cup milk | Gradually add to the above, stirring constantly and cook until smooth and thick. |
| ¾ cup condensed tomato soup<br>2 cups grated nippy cheese<br>salt to taste | Add to mixture and cook until cheese dissolves. |
| 1 can shrimp | Add to mixture. |
| 1 egg—beaten | When shrimp gets hot, add the egg and serve on toast. |
| buttered toast | |

*Miss Bell Clay, Frankfort, Kentucky*


# 142. Shrimp and Mushroom Luncheon Dish
(Serves 3)

| INGREDIENTS | DIRECTIONS |
|---|---|
| 1 can shrimp | Wash shrimp and drain. |
| 1 can condensed mushroom soup<br>½ teaspoon curry powder | Put soup in double boiler and when hot, add shrimp. |
| | Serve on baked toast.  Also good on waffles. |

*Mrs. A. Scott Hines, Bowling Green, Kentucky*


*This is a good recipe when unexpected guests arrive.*

## 143. Oysters a la Carnival

(Serves 12)

| INGREDIENTS | DIRECTIONS |
|---|---|
| 50 oysters | Chop and let drain. |
| 3 onions—minced<br>1 clove of garlic—minced<br>1 shallot<br>1 bay leaf<br>1 sprig of thyme<br>1 tablespoon lard | Put in iron skillet and fry until onions are a light brown color. Add the oysters. |
| 1 cup toasted bread crumbs | Moisten with water from the oysters and add to mixture. Fry for about 30 minutes, or until the oysters have stopped drawing water. |
| 1/8 lb. butter | Add to mixture and let it cook until the butter is melted. |
| 1 doz. oyster shells<br><br>1/2 cup bread crumbs<br>1/8 lb. butter | Boil and scrub, then fill with mixture. Sprinkle with dry toasted bread crumbs and dots of butter. |
| | When ready to serve, put in 425 F. oven for a few minutes until thoroughly heated and serve at once. |

*This recipe by Mary Bell, an old family cook for Corinne Dunbar, New Orleans, Louisiana*


## 144. Creamed Oysters

(Serves 4)

| INGREDIENTS | DIRECTIONS |
|---|---|
| 1 pint oysters | Scald in their own liquor until the edges curl. Drain and save the liquor. |
| 2 tablespoons butter | Cook until it bubbles. |
| 3 tablespoons flour | Add to butter and stir until it is well blended |
| 1 cup milk to which is added the oyster liquor | Add to the above and cook until it is thick, lower heat. |
| 2 egg yolks—beaten<br>salt and pepper to taste<br>1 dash nutmeg | Add to mixture and stir until thick. Add the oysters and serve. |

*Mrs. William Rogers Clay, Frankfort, Kentucky*

# 145.  Pickled Oysters

INGREDIENTS

1 gallon large oysters
½ cup salt

1 pint vinegar
1 teaspoon black pepper
—whole
1 teaspoon allspice
1 teaspoon cloves
2 or 3 pieces of mace
½ red pepper cut in
rings
½ orange peel—cut fine

DIRECTIONS

Cook until well done as for a stew.  Remove from fire and drain.  Drop oysters in ice cold water and save liquor.

Bring these ingredients to a boil.

When the oysters are thoroughly cold, wipe with a towel and put in a stone jar.  Pour hot vinegar mixture over them.  Skim the oyster liquor and add enough to cover the oysters.

6 lemons—juice

Pour over the oysters, and let stand until the next day before using.  Serve in a large bowl with a few raw cranberries and sliced lemon for a garnish.

*This is a most popular dish at Christmas time for buffet suppers.*

*The Chaya, Petersburg, Virginia*


# 146.  Poached Fish with Oysters          (Serves 4)

INGREDIENTS

1 pint oysters

2 tablespoons catsup

1 lb. Halibut steak

3 tablespoons butter
3 tablespoons flour
½ teaspoon salt
¼ teaspoon pepper

1 cup cream

DIRECTIONS

Drain the oysters.

Heat oyster liquor in an enamel pan with catsup.

Remove skin and brush underside with melted butter.  Put in hot oyster liquor and cover tightly.  Reduce heat to under boiling and cook 20 to 30 minutes until the fish is done.

Blend these ingredients in a small saucepan.

Gradually add to the above paste and stir until it boils.

Put the cooked fish on a platter and pour into the liquor, the cream sauce. Stir well together and add the oysters.  Cook until the gills separate and pour over the fish.  Garnish with sliced hard-cooked egg and lemon slices.

*Sawyer Tavern, Keene, New Hampshire*

# 147. Sea Bass with Almond Butter

INGREDIENTS

DIRECTIONS

1 sea bass

Remove fillets from fish and bones.

salt to taste
2 tablespoons butter

Season fillets

2 tablespoons olive oil

Saturate fillets and broil over slow fire. Do not brown.

fresh boiled
Parisienne potatoes
1 tablespoon chopped
parsley

Dress on a large platter. Surround with potatoes and parsley.

1 tablespoon grated
almonds—browned in
butter
1 dash lemon juice

Cover surface of fish.

Decorate with whole parsley and lemon, cut fancy.

*Hotel St. Regis, New York City*

# 148. Tuna Fish and Noodles

(Serves 5)

INGREDIENTS

DIRECTIONS

½ can tuna fish
½ package pimiento
cheese
1 can mushrooms

Cut in pieces and mix with a white sauce.

1 package noodles

Cook and drain and add to the above mixture, tossing so it is well blended. Put into a baking dish and cover with bread crumbs. Bake in 350 F. oven for 25 minutes.

*Mrs. Voijt Frank Mashek, Chicago, Illinois*

# 149.  Baked White Fish with Ham Sauce    (Serves 6)

INGREDIENTS

DIRECTIONS

2 lbs. white fish fillet
salt and pepper to
taste

Put fish in buttered baking dish and season.
Cover with sauce.

*SAUCE*

2 tablespoons melted
butter
2 tablespoons flour
½ teaspoon salt
¼ teaspoon pepper
1 teaspoon mustard

Blend all ingredients into a paste.

1¼ cups boiling water
1½ tablespoons lemon
juice

Gradually add to the paste and cook over slow
flame until it thickens.

1 cup minced cooked
ham

Fold in ham, pour over fish and sprinkle top
with bread crumbs.  Bake in 350 F. to 375 F.
oven for 30 minutes, basting frequently.

Serve with a garnish of lemon slices and slices
of hard boiled egg.

*The Carr House, Wolfboro, New Hampshire*


# 150.  Baked Red Flannel Hash    (Serves 10)

INGREDIENTS

DIRECTIONS

2 cups cooked corn beef
—chopped
2 cups boiled beets—
chopped
4 cups boiled potatoes—
chopped
salt and pepper to
taste
½ cup milk

Mix all ingredients together and enough milk
to moisten.

1 cup thick cream

Butter a casserole and place a layer of hash
mixture and a thin layer of cream until the
dish is filled.

2 tablespoons butter

Cover top with cream and dabs of butter and
bake in 350 F. oven for 20 to 30 minutes, or
until the cream on top is well browned.

*Allenwood, Burlington, Vermont*

# 151. Chop Suey

(Serves 10)

INGREDIENTS | DIRECTIONS

8 onions—sliced
1 green pepper—sliced
4 tablespoons butter

Saute in Dutch oven.

1 lb. veal
1 lb. round steak
¼ lb. pork

Cut in small pieces or grind up. Add to the above, stirring constantly until most of the juice from the meat disappears.

1 can mushrooms
1 can chop suey sprouts and vegetables

Strain off the juice and add to the meat mixture. Save juices.

2 stalks celery—cut in ½ inch pieces
2 fresh tomatoes—ripe
1 tablespoon catsup
1 tablespoon Worcestershire sauce
3 tablespoons LaSoy sauce
1 dash red pepper

Add to mixture and stir. Cover and let simmer 10 minutes. When celery is tender add sauce.

### SAUCE

mushroom and sprout and vegetable juice
3 tablespoons bean molasses
3 tablespoons flour

Blend together and mix well. Pour over the other ingredients. Place in 400 F. oven for 10 minutes.

Serve with heated crisp noodles over top. Steamed rice balls, a stuffed tomato salad of cucumbers, celery, onions, green pepper, and hard cooked eggs and the Chop Suey, makes a delicious quick meal.

*Charlot C. Moore, Owensboro, Kentucky*


# 152. Doodlebuck

(Serves 6)

INGREDIENTS | DIRECTIONS

2 onions—sliced thin
1 green pepper—sliced

Saute in olive oil.

1 can mushrooms
1 can stuffed olives
1 can tomatoes
1 can corn
1 can Tamale beef
1 pkg. noodles—cooked

Mix all ingredients with above and put in baking dish in 350 F. oven and bake for 1 hour.

*Mrs. W. R. (Irene) Gibbs, Berkeley, California*

## 153. English Steak and Kidney Pie (Serves 12)

INGREDIENTS

DIRECTIONS

3 lbs. round steak—
   diced
1 onion—chopped
2 tablespoons butter

Saute until brown.

1 lb. lamb kidneys

Parboil and add to the above mixture.

1 lb. fresh mushrooms
salt and pepper to
   taste
2 tablespoons butter

Saute until done.  Add to the above mixture
and let simmer until the steak is tender.

2 tablespoons flour

Thicken the mixture and let stand to cool.

Put all ingredients in a half-lined baking dish and cover with a rich
pastry.  Glaze top of pie with white of egg and a little milk.  Bake in
350 F. oven for 30 minutes.  Serve with fresh horse-radish sauce.

*San Ysidro Ranch, Montecito, Santa Barbara, California*


## 154. Steak and Kidney Pudding (Serves 6 to 8)

INGREDIENTS

DIRECTIONS

1 cup grated or
   chopped suet
2 cups flour
1 teaspoon baking
   powder
1 pinch of salt
   enough cold water to
   make a stiff paste

Make a stiff paste.  Roll out thin and line a
pudding dish.  Leave enough dough for a
top on the pudding.

2 lbs. round steak
1 ox kidney

Cut into 2-inch squares.

¼ cup flour
1 teaspoon salt
1 pinch of mace
1 pinch of pepper

Mix these ingredients together and dip the
pieces of meat and kidney into it and place
in the lined pudding dish.

½ cup cold water

Pour over the meat and put on top crust.
Join crusts together by pinching all around.

Steam for 3½ hours.  Serve in the same dish it was baked in, using a linen
serviette wrapped around the outside.  Never use onion in this pudding.

*The Elk, Comox Bay, Vancouver Island, B. C., Canada*

## 155.  Pot Roast

INGREDIENTS

DIRECTIONS

1 quart of water
½ tablespoon mixed
  spices
1 tablespoon salt
1 tablespoon sugar
1 stalk celery—diced
2 onions—sliced
1 teaspoon pepper
½ teaspoon curry
  powder

Mix all together.

5 lbs. beef

Let stand in mixture for 24 hours.  Remove
and sear in 425 F. oven for 20 minutes.  Pour
the spiced liquid over the meat, cover and
bake in 300 F. to 350 F. oven for 2 or 3 hours
until tender.  Remove meat.

2 tablespoons butter—
  melted
2 tablespoons flour

Mix together and add to gravy.  Cook until
thick.  Strain and pour over the meat.

Serve with noodles or pineapple fritters.

*Parry Lodge, Kanab, Utah*


## 156.  Roast Beef Tenderloin

INGREDIENTS

DIRECTIONS

3 lbs. beef tenderloin

Lard with bits of bacon.

salt and pepper to
taste

Rub into meat.

1 carrot—chopped
1 slice of bacon
1 bay leaf
2 whole cloves
1 pinch of allspice

Put into pan with meat, cover and bake in
450 F. oven for 30 minutes, basting often
Serve with mushroom sauce.

*MUSHROOM SAUCE*

¼ can mushrooms
1 tablespoon lemon
  juice

Add to the brown gravy.

*Pilot Butt Inn, Bend, Oregon*

# 157.  Round Steak with Sour Cabbage  (Serves 5 to 8)

INGREDIENTS

DIRECTIONS

4 to 5 lbs. beef (round steak, rump, or sirloin butt)

If round steak is used, cut in 1½-inch pieces, otherwise leave meat in one piece.  Sear meat.

3 onions—diced
1 clove minced garlic
2 tablespoons butter

Brown and add to the meat.

1 head cabbage—shredded
2 cans tomato paste—diluted with a little water
salt and pepper to taste
½ cup vinegar
2 tablespoons sugar

Add to other ingredients.  Cover and cook slowly for 1½ hours.  If too sour, add a little more sugar.

2 tablespoons cornstarch
1 cup water

Make into a paste and add to mixture, stirring to prevent lumping.

Green beans may be used instead of cabbage, in which case, do not use tomato paste.

*Roy C. Neuhaus, Evanston, Illinois*

*Blueberries in milk.  Popped corn in milk.  "Floating" oyster*

*Warren Rockwood Gibbs' boyhood memories:*
*crackers with a dab of butter on them in oyster soup.*

*Okay fellow, but I continue to enjoy these things I liked so well as a boy: fried chicken, country ham, hot biscuit, corn pone, chess pie, and jersey milk.*

## 158.  Sauerbraten                    (Serves 6 to 8)

INGREDIENTS | DIRECTIONS
--- | ---

4 lbs. beef—rump,
chuck, or sirloin
2 quarts vinegar
1 quart water
1 onion—cut in slices
3 bay leaves
3 cloves
1 teaspoon salt

Mix liquids and spices and let meat stand in it for 4 days.  Turn it over once in a while.  Save the vinegar bath.

2½ tablespoons lard

Heat and fry the meat brown on both sides.  Set the meat aside on a platter.

2 tablespoons flour

Brown in the same pan the meat was browned in.  Add the vinegar bath.

2 ginger snaps
½ tablespoon sugar

Add to gravy and boil until thick.  Add the meat to this gravy.  Cover the pan and bake in 325 F. oven for 2½ to 3 hours, turning and basting the meat frequently.

½ glass red wine

About 30 minutes before it is done, add the red wine.  When the roast is tender, finish the gravy.  If too thick, add water, if not sour enough, add vinegar.  Take all grease off the gravy and strain.

Potato dumplings or noodles are good with this roast.

*Mader's Restaurant, Milwaukee, Wisconsin*


## 159.  Straganoff                    (Serves 4)

INGREDIENTS | DIRECTIONS
--- | ---

1½ lbs. round steak—cut
in cubes
⅛ lb. butter

Saute the steak.

¾ lb. fresh mushrooms
⅛ lb. butter
1 onion—minced

Saute in another pan.  Do not let get too brown.  Add to the steak and blend the two.

1 tablespoon tomato
juice
1 tablespoon vinegar
½ pint sour cream
season to taste

Add to the mixture and let simmer for 20 to 30 minutes, or until it tastes done.

Serve with rice and buttered melba toast.

*Emelie Tolman, Chicago, Illinois*

## 160. Tamale Pie

(Serves 6 to 8)

INGREDIENTS

DIRECTIONS

½ cup olive oil
1 onion—chopped
1 clove garlic

Cook until onions are tenderized.

1 green pepper—
  chopped
1 lb. round steak—
  ground
¼ lb. ground pork

Add to the above and brown the meat.

1 can tomatoes (2½
  size)
½ cup ripe olives—pitted
2 chili peppers—cut fine
  salt and pepper and
  cayenne to taste

Add to the mixture and cook slowly for 1 hour. Add a little water from time to time, if it is a little dry.

½ cup grated cheese
2 tablespoons corn meal
1 teaspoon chili powder

When the mixture is soft and mushy, add these ingredients. Stir in well and cook for just a few minutes longer. The mixture should be the consistency of baked hash.

1 cup corn meal
3 cups water

Make a corn meal mush. Place the meat mixture in a pan and cover with corn meal mush. Garnish with ripe olives.

*LaPalma Cafeteria, Los Angeles, California*


## 161. Tongue with Tomato Sauce

(Serves 6 to 8)

INGREDIENTS

DIRECTIONS

1 beef tongue

Boil slowly until tender, or about 3 hours. Peal and put into a baking dish.

1 can tomatoes
1 onion—sliced
1½ cups vinegar
1 cup of stock from the
  tongue
⅓ cup sugar
¼ cup butter
½ teaspoon cinnamon
⅛ teaspoon allspice
¼ teaspoon cloves
1 teaspoon salt

Mix these ingredients and pour over tongue. Bake in 325 F. oven for 3 hours.

Serve with baked or mashed potatoes.

*Pelican Cafe, Klamath Falls, Oregon*

## 162. Berzola Fooroun (Baked Lamb Chops)

(Serves 4)

INGREDIENTS

DIRECTIONS

8 lamb chops

Put in the bottom of a pan.

1 lb. tomatoes—sliced
1 onion—sliced
3 tablespoons parsley—
    chopped
    salt and pepper to
    taste
    Oregoni for seasoning

Mix together and put over the lamb chops.

Cover with water and bake in 375 F. oven for 1½ hours. Then turn the chops and bake for another 20 minutes. The juice is served as gravy.

*Omar Khayyam's, San Francisco, California*


## 163. Haigagan Kebab

(Serves 1)

INGREDIENTS

DIRECTIONS

½ lb. lamb shoulder
½ pepper
½ tomato
¼ onion
¼ egg plant
    salt and pepper to
    taste

Wrap in patapar paper and place in roasting pan. Bake in 350 F. oven for 2½ hours.

Do not turn package or cover pan, or use any water as there is enough moisture in the vegetables and meat to make a natural gravy in the package.

*Omar Khayyam's, San Francisco, California*


## 164. Lahana Sarma

(Makes 20 rolls)

INGREDIENTS

DIRECTIONS

20 cabbage leaves

Boil until half cooked.

1 lb. shoulder lamb—
    ground
½ lb. onions—chopped
2 tablespoons chopped
    parsley
¼ cup rice—washed
1 teaspoon salt
    black pepper to taste
½ lemon juice
⅓ cup tomato puree

Mix all ingredients together and roll in each cabbage leaf.

Place in rotation in cooking pot and fill with water. Cover top.

Cook on top of stove for 1 hour, or bake in 375 F. oven for 1½ hours.

*Omar Khayyam's, San Francisco, California*

# 165. Individual Lamb Roasts with Dressing

(Serves 6)

INGREDIENTS

DIRECTIONS

6 six ounce slices of breast of lamb, after it has been boned and trimmed, about ¾ inch thick

Spread each slice of lamb with dressing, roll and fasten with a tooth pick.

*DRESSING*

2 ozs. chopped onion
2 ozs. chopped celery
2 fresh mushrooms—chopped
1 tablespoon butter

Saute for about 20 minutes.

3 ozs. soft diced bread
1 teaspoon salt
1 teaspoon poultry seasoning

Add to the above mixture. Spread on the slices of lamb.

½ lb. chopped carrots and celery—cut fine
3 onions—chopped

Place in bottom of a roaster and lay the lamb rolls on top. Brown in 350 F. oven for 10 minutes. Turn the rolls and brown the other side.

2 cups of stock

Add to the browned rolls. Cover roaster, turn the oven down to 300 F. and bake for 1½ hours. Additional stock may be added if necessary.

*Jane Davis, New York City, N. Y.*

# 166. Lamb Chops

(Serves 1)

INGREDIENTS

DIRECTIONS

1 lamb chop—2 inches thick

Broil on one side.

1 tablespoon minced chicken spread

Spread on cooked side of chop. Lay in pan, raw side down and bake in 325 F. oven for 30 minutes.

Serve with rich chicken gravy.

*Pilot Butt Inn, Bend, Oregon*

## 167. Lamb Roast

**INGREDIENTS**

1 leg of lamb
salt and cayenne
pepper—to taste

1 bottle tomato catsup
1 cup vinegar
1 clove garlic
1 cup water

**DIRECTIONS**

Rub lamb well with salt and cayenne pepper.

Pour over the roast and bake in 350 F. oven for 1½ to 2 hours. Add water as needed to keep the gravy at the right consistency.

Thicken the gravy with flour before serving, if necessary.

*Mrs. A. Scott Hines, Bowling Green, Kentucky*

## 168. Lamb Roast

**INGREDIENTS**

1 leg of lamb

1 teaspoon dry mustard
2 tablespoons blackberry jam
1 celery stalk cut in pieces or celery seed
4 teaspoons mint jelly or mint leaves
1 cup blackberry wine
½ cup buttered bread crumbs

**DIRECTIONS**

Cook until tender.

Cover the roast with these ingredients, the bread crumbs being last. Brown in 350 F. oven and baste often.

*This is a very, very old Kentucky recipe of my mother's and copied from her book. It is perfectly delicious and different.*

*Althea, Lewisburg, West Virginia*

## 169.  Patlijan a la Naz    (Serves 5)

**INGREDIENTS**

10 slices of egg plant
1½ teaspoons salt

1 lb. lamb shoulder—
   ground
1 onion—sliced
⅓ cup parsley—chopped
   salt and pepper to
   taste

10 slices of bacon

1 cup water
½ cup tomato sauce

**DIRECTIONS**

Salt egg plant and let stand until soft.

Mix and spread on egg plant.

Put on top of meat.  Set in a pan.

Mix together and pour over all.

Bake in 375 F. oven for 1½ hours.

*Omar Khayyam's, San Francisco, California*


## 170.  Turlu Dolma (Stuffed Tomatoes, Peppers and Squash)    (Serves 4)

**INGREDIENTS**

1 lb. lamb shoulder—
   ground
½ cup rice—washed
½ lb. onions—chopped
½ can tomatoes—or fresh
   —chopped
3 teaspoons parsley—
   chopped
1½ teaspoons salt
¼ teaspoon pepper
   a few leaves of fresh
   mint (optional)

4 tomatoes
4 peppers
4 squash

**DIRECTIONS**

Mix all ingredients together.

Stuff with the above mixture.  Place in a baking pan and cover with water.

Cover the pan and cook on top of stove for 1 hour, or in a 375 F. oven for 1½ hours.

Serve 1 of each to a person.  The sauce will serve as gravy.

*Omar Khayyam's, San Francisco, California*

## 171. Baked Slice of Ham (Serves 4)

INGREDIENTS

DIRECTIONS

1 slice of ham an inch
or more thick

Cut off the fat and put fat through a grinder.
Spread it over the slice of ham.

2 tablespoons brown
sugar
1 teaspoon dry mustard

Sprinkle over the top of the fat and place in
pan about half covered with water. Bake in
350 F. oven for 1 hour.

*Miss Katharine L. Little, Chicago, Illinois*


## 172. Duncan Hines Kentucky Ham

INGREDIENTS

DIRECTIONS

1 Duncan Hines hickory
smoked ham

Soak overnight in enough water to cover.
Drain off. Use fresh cold water in starting
to cook.

6 onions
2 bay leaves
2 cups brown sugar
24 whole cloves
1 pint cider, vinegar, or
white wine

Add to above and cover the boiler and let
simmer for 20 to 25 minutes to the pound
until done. Be sure the ham does not boil.
You will know it is done when the small bone
at the hock end can be twisted and pulled out.
Let the ham cool in this mixture. Then peel
off the skin, cut off some of the fat on the
flat side. Cube and decorate with whole
cloves (if desired).

3/4 cup brown sugar
2 teaspoons dry mustard
1 teaspoon pulverized
cloves
1 cup bread crumbs

Mix all together and spread over the ham
while it is still moist. Bake in a 400 F. oven
for a few minutes, until it is glazed or brown.

*There are times when soaking a ham overnight is not con-
venient. In this case simmer the ham in fresh water for 1 to
1½ hours. Drain off and start with fresh water and proceed as
outlined above.*

*Duncan Hines, Bowling Green, Kentucky*

# 173.  Ham Mousse

INGREDIENTS

DIRECTIONS

1 package gelatin
2 cups soup stock—
  highly seasoned

Dissolve gelatin in stock and let cool.

2 cups ground ham
2 cups whipped cream

When gelatin begins to congeal, add ham and cream.  Pour into molds and serve with spiced peaches or pears.

*Mrs. W. H. Taylor, Bowling Green, Kentucky*


# 174.  Hot Baked Ham with Raisin Sauce

INGREDIENTS

DIRECTIONS

1 12- to 14-lb. ham
enough hot water to
cover

Bring to a boil and let simmer 20 minutes to the pound.  When done, remove from the water and skin.  Score, by cutting through the fat diagonally.

½ cup vinegar
2 cups brown sugar
2 tablespoons dry
  mustard

Make a paste and spread evenly over the surface, fatty side up.  Bake uncovered in 350 F. oven for 15 minutes, until nicely browned.  To serve, slice and cover with raisin sauce.

### RAISIN SAUCE

1 lb. seedless raisins
2 cups brown sugar
3 pints  water

Cook together for about 30 minutes, until raisins are soft.

2 tablespoons cornstarch
1 tablespoon cold water

Mix together and add to raisins.

1 lemon—juice

Add to mixture, and bring to a boil.

*Park View Inn, Berkeley Springs, West Virginia*

# 175. Sugar Ham

| INGREDIENTS | DIRECTIONS |
|---|---|
| 1 12-lb. ham<br>enough water to cover | Boil the ham until tender. Remove from water. |
| 3/4 lb. brown sugar | Cover ham. |
| 1/2 cup prepared mustard<br>1/2 cup water | Mix together and pour over the ham. Bake in 425 F. oven for 15 minutes. |

### SAUCE

| | |
|---|---|
| 3 lbs. sugar<br>1 pint water | Let come to a boil. |
| 1 1/2 cups red cinnamon candies | Add to above and cook until they are dissolved. |
| 1/2 cup raisins | These are optional and can be omitted. If desired, add to sauce. Let cool. |
| 1/2 cup sherry | When cooled add to sauce. |

Cut the cooled ham in 1/4-inch slices and heat in sauce. Best results are obtained when the ham is allowed to cool for 24 hours before serving.

*Crane's Canary Cottage, Chagrin Falls, Ohio*


# 176. Barbecued Spare Ribs   (Serves 6)

| INGREDIENTS | DIRECTIONS |
|---|---|
| 4 lbs. of spareribs | Crack and cut in portions. |
| salt and pepper to taste | Season and put in roaster. |
| 2 onions—sliced | Place slice on each portion. |
| 4 tablespoons barbecue sauce<br>3/4 cup water<br>3/4 cup catsup<br>2 tablespoons Worcestershire<br>2 tablespoons vinegar<br>3 drops Tabasco<br>salt and pepper to taste | Mix thoroughly and pour over the ribs.<br><br>Cover the roaster and bake in 350 F. oven for 2 hours. Remove cover and brown the last 30 minutes. |

*Esther Brehmer Orr, Elmwood, Fond du Lac, Wisconsin*

## 177.  Diddleheimer
(Serves 6)

INGREDIENTS

1 lb. pork sausage
3 potatoes—diced
1 onion—sliced
1 can string beans
2 cans tomato soup
1 can hot sauce
½ cup grated cheese
1 pkg. fine noodles—cooked

DIRECTIONS

Mix all ingredients together and put in baking dish in 350 F. oven and bake for 1 hour.

*Mrs. W. R. (Irene)  Gibbs, Berkeley, California*


## 178.  Fried Pork with Vinegar Sauce
(Serves 2)

INGREDIENTS

1 lb. pork—cut in small pieces
3 tablespoons fat

DIRECTIONS

Fry until very brown.


1 cup vinegar
2 tablespoons sugar
¼ teaspoon salt
½ cup water

Cook until it forms a syrup.


1 tablespoon cornstarch
1 tablespoon mixed ginger
3 tablespoons soya bean sauce

Add to the syrup and pour over the meat.


a few ginger grains

Sprinkle on top of meat and serve with rice.

*Madeleine  H.  Normand, Berkeley, California*

## 179. Johnnie Mazotta

INGREDIENTS

DIRECTIONS

1 package broad noodles

Cook noodles in boiling water 12 minutes. Put in colander and let cold water run over them. Drain. Put into a buttered baking dish.

¾ lb. pork shoulder—ground
1 onion—cut fine

Fry together until pork is done. Drain off the grease. Add to noodles.

1 can condensed tomato soup
½ lb. cheese—grated (hold out enough to sprinkle on top)
1 teaspoon sugar
½ cup water
salt and pepper to taste

Mix all ingredients together in baking dish. Dot plentifully with butter and sprinkle top with cheese.

Bake in 350 F. oven for about 30 minutes.

*Mrs. Mathew Jackson, Chicago, Illinois*


## 180. Pork Chops, Spanish

(Serves 6)

INGREDIENTS

DIRECTIONS

6 loin pork chops 1½ inches thick
1 tablespoon fat

Brown the pork chops in a pan and place in a casserole.

2 onions—sliced thin
1 green pepper—chopped
1 can pimiento—with juice
½ can tomatoes
½ teaspoon Worcestershire sauce
salt and pepper to taste

Mix these ingredients together and put over the chops.

1 cup rice—measured and then cooked

Place cooked rice over all and simmer on top of stove for 2 hours, or place in 300 F. to 325 F. oven and bake for 2 hours.

When ready to serve, lift each chop out with a spatula, leaving the rice on top of each chop.

*Hotel Leopold, Bellingham, Washington*

# 181. Sweetbread Braise, Financiere  (Serves 1)

INGREDIENTS

DIRECTIONS

| | |
|---|---|
| 1 pair sweetbreads<br>4 tablespoons salt | Add enough cold water to cover sweetbreads and let stand for 12 hours. Wash thoroughly. |
| whole spice and salt —to taste | Parboil in enough water to cover with these ingredients for about 5 minutes. Dry off and place in a roasting pan. |
| 3 tablespoons butter | Saute for about 10 minutes, or until brown. |
| 1 jigger or more white wine | Add to sweetbreads and bake in 350 F. oven for 30 minutes. |
| ½ cup fresh mushrooms<br>¼ cup olives<br>¼ cup shallots<br>3 tablespoons butter | Dice and place in a separate pan and cook until the mushrooms are done. |
| 1 jigger or more white wine | Add this, and sauce from the sweetbreads. |
| Fines Herbes and butter—to taste | Mix sweetbreads and mushrooms together and add seasoning just before serving. |

*The Monument Inn, Bennington, Vermont*


# 182. Creamed Kidneys  (Serves 4)

INGREDIENTS

DIRECTIONS

| | |
|---|---|
| 1 lb. veal kidneys— sliced thin<br>2 tablespoons butter<br>salt and pepper to taste | Saute quickly on both sides. |
| 1½ cups thin white sauce<br>4 tablespoons red wine<br>½ tablespoon horseradish<br>a dash of cayenne pepper | While the white sauce is still hot, add the other ingredients and mix into the kidneys.<br><br>Serve on toast. |

*Mrs. Edwin P. Morrow, Frankfort, Kentucky*

## 183. Sweetbreads Supreme (Serves 8 to 12)

INGREDIENTS | DIRECTIONS

1½ cups cooked
sweetbreads

To cook sweetbreads. Let stand for 1 hour in cold water. Cook slowly in boiling salted water for 20 minutes, adding the vinegar. Blanch in cold water.

2 tablespoons vinegar to each quart of water used

4 eggs—slightly beaten

Mix with sweetbreads.

2 cups cream
salt and pepper to taste

Add to sweetbreads and place in buttered molds. Bake in pan of water in 350 F. oven for about 20 minutes, or until firm.

individual slices of tenderized ham—lightly browned

Serve on ham slices and cover with a cream sauce.

*CREAM SAUCE*

2 tablespoons butter

Melt.

2 tablespoons flour
¼ teaspoon salt
a few grains of pepper
⅓ cup minced pimiento

Blend into the butter, making a smooth paste.

1 cup milk

Add slowly to the paste and stir until the sauce thickens. Boil 3 minutes.

*The Farm Kitchen, Baraboo, Wisconsin*


## 184. Paprica Schnitzel Hongroise (Serves 1)

INGREDIENTS | DIRECTIONS

1 veal cutlet
salt and pepper to taste
1 teaspoon paprika
1 tablespoon flour
2 tablespoons butter

Pound the veal and season. Dredge in flour and saute in butter. When lightly fried on both sides, remove the steak from the pan.

2 dry shallots—chopped
½ lemon
1 cup tomato sauce

Put shallots in pan, moisten with lemon, add the tomato sauce and boil thoroughly. Replace the veal steak.

½ cup sour cream

Add the cream to veal and mixture and simmer in covered casserole for 25 to 30 minutes.

Serve with french friend onions and noodles.

*The Brown Hotel, Louisville, Kentucky*

# 185. Roast Veal and Kidney with Rice

INGREDIENTS

DIRECTIONS

5 lbs veal—see that the kidney and suet are left in
salt and pepper to taste

Season the meat. Sprinkle the bottom of the roaster with a little flour. Put the meat on top of this and place in 400 F. oven until the flour browns. Reduce the oven to 300 F. Add a small amount of water, cover the pan and bake 2⅓ to 3 hours, basting frequently and adding water as needed.

1 cup washed rice

Add to the roast and cook for 1 hour. Add only a little water at a time as it is needed. The juices should be dark brown, which will make the rice a rich brown color when done and the water has been absorbed.

Serve the meat on a platter surrounded with the rice. A tossed salad, julienne green beans or peas and a light dessert makes an excellent dinner.

*Mrs. H. A. Resener, Huntington, West Virginia*


# 186. Rovellina

INGREDIENTS

DIRECTIONS

2 lbs. sliced scalloped veal

Pound lightly.

2 egg yolks—beaten
⅓ cup milk

Mix together and pass meat through.

½ cup cracker meal

Dip meat and fry in hot oil. Brown on both sides.

1 No. 2 can tomatoes

Pour over fried meat and slowly simmer for 15 minutes.

To be served with any vegetables in season.

*Amelio's, San Francisco, California*

## 187.  Veal Chops Cooked in Wine  (Serves 4)

INGREDIENTS

DIRECTIONS

4 veal chops with
  kidney at least 2
  inches or more thick
1/8 lb. butter
3 tablespoons flour .

Dip chops lightly in flour and saute in butter
until a golden brown.  Remove chops and
place in a casserole.

1 cup white wine

Add wine to drippings the chops were cooked
in and simmer until syrupy.  Pour over the
chops.

1/4 lb. fresh mushrooms
  —chopped
1 grated onion
1/8 lb. butter

Saute slowly for 5 minutes.  Pour around the
chops.  Cover the baking dish with buttered
heavy paper tied tight and bake in 350 F.
oven for 30 minutes.

*Emelie Tolman, Chicago, Illinois*


## 188.  Veal—Pork Roast  (Serves 10)

INGREDIENTS

DIRECTIONS

3 to 5 lbs. veal shoulder
3 to 5 lbs. pork shoulder
  or loin

Have the butcher bone both pieces of meat
and roll and tie it together, having the pork
fat outside.

3 tablespoons flour
salt and pepper to
taste

Roll the roast in dry ingredients and place in
roasting pan, veal side down.

1 cup of water

Add to roast and cover.  Bake in 300 F. to 325
F. oven for 4 hours.  Remove the cover and
brown the top under the broiler for 15 to
20 minutes before serving.  Remove strings
and serve with apple sauce or fresh sliced
mangoes.

*Mrs. Otto J. Sieplein, Miami, Florida*

## 189. Veal Roll with Sausage Stuffing (Serves 6)

INGREDIENTS

DIRECTIONS

2 veal steaks—cut in 2x4 inch pieces

Wipe off each piece of meat.

2 teaspoons chopped onion
1 tablespoon butter

Saute until brown.

½ lb. pork sausage
1½ cups bread crumbs— softened with milk

Add the browned onion to these ingredients and mix together. Spread over each piece of veal and roll. Fasten with skewers or toothpicks.

3 tablespoons flour
salt and pepper to taste

Mix together and dredge each roll. Place in pan.

2 tablespoons fat

Brown the rolls in the fat.

1 can mushroom soup

Pour over the meat and cover the pan and cook in 350 F. oven for 25 minutes or until done.

*The Meiringen, Roanoke, Virginia*


## 190. Aunt Ella's Fried Chicken

INGREDIENTS

DIRECTIONS

1 chicken

Disjoint.

2 cups milk
1 teaspoon salt

Salt chicken down in the milk.

2 tablespoons flour

Dredge in flour and fry until a golden brown

Serve with corn pone.

*The Brown Hotel, Louisville, Kentucky*

# 191.  Arroz Con Pollo (Chicken and Rice)

(Serves 1)

**INGREDIENTS**

**DIRECTIONS**

¼ of a 3-lb. chicken
2 ozs. olive oil

Saute for 3 minutes.

garlic to taste—
chopped
1 onion—chopped
½ green pepper—
chopped

Add to above and cook for 2 minutes.

1 fresh tomato—peeled
and cut in small
pieces

Add to mixture and cook 2 minutes.

1 bit of red pepper
½ cup rice
1 cup chicken broth
2 grains saffron

Add to mixture and place in 400 F. oven and
cook for 17 minutes.  Take out of oven and
keep hot over a low flame.

2 tablespoons fresh
cooked peas
2 or 3 slices red pepper
1 teaspoon parsley—
chopped

Decorate the top.  Put cover on casserole and
serve piping hot.

The most important part about cooking this
dish is that it must be cooked in an earthen-
ware casserole and after the rice is in, use a
wooden spoon and go all around the edges
without taking out the spoon so as not to
break up the rice.  Do not put the spoon in
the center and stir the chicken and rice but
go all around the edge and work to the center
gradually.

*El Chico, New York City, N. Y.*

*Better that grease clog the sink than your stomach.*

## 192.  Breast of Chicken

INGREDIENTS

DIRECTIONS

3 two and half pound
   chickens— (use fillets)
3 pieces larding pork
3 tablespoons butter

Remove skin and lard.  Place in buttered
sautoir and cook in 400 F. oven until a golden
brown.  Place on heart-shaped pieces of toast,
fried in butter and spread with pate de fois
gras.  Dress on a round platter.

*SAUCE*

2 tablespoons butter
2 shallots—chopped
1 julienne of
   mushrooms
1 slice truffle

Fry lightly in the sautoir.

2 tablespoons sherry
   wine
2 tablespoons white
   wine

Moisten mixture.

½ cup cream

Add to mixture and cook until sauce is thick.

salt and cayenne
pepper to taste

Add to mixture and serve with chicken.

*Hotel St. Regis, New York, N. Y.*

## 193.  Chicken a la King

(Serves 20)

INGREDIENTS

DIRECTIONS

1 quart heavy cream
1 quart milk

Mix together and heat in a double boiler.

3 cups chicken fat—
   melted

Add to the above.

½ lb. butter
2 cups flour
2½ tablespoons salt
½ teaspoon pepper

In another double boiler, melt butter and
whisk in the flour and seasoning.

Add the cream mixture, whisking contin-
ually, until smooth and well-blended.

½ lb. jar pimientos—
   diced
1 quart fresh
   mushrooms—diced

Add to mixture and let stand for 1 hour.

2½ quarts cooked chicken
   —diced

Add to sauce and heat for serving.

*Hartwell Farm, Lincoln, Massachusetts*

## 194. Chicken a la King on Swiss Fondue

(Serves 8 to 12)

INGREDIENTS

DIRECTIONS

3 tablespoons butter
5 tablespoons flour
1 cup chicken stock
1 cup cream
1 teaspoon salt
¼ teaspoon paprika

Make a cream sauce.

2 cups cooked chicken—diced
1 cup chopped mushoooms
⅓ cup ripe olives—cut
2 tablespoons pimientos —chopped
1 teaspoon lemon juice

Put into the sauce and heat for 5 minutes.

2 egg yolks—beaten
2 tablespoons milk

Beat together and add to mixture. Stir and cook slowly for 2 minutes.

### FONDUE

2 cups milk—scalded
2 cups stale soft bread crumbs
½ lb. sharp cheese cut in bits
2 tablespoons butter
1 teaspoon salt

Mix all these ingredients together.

6 egg yolks—beaten

Add to the above mixture.

6 egg whites—beaten

Cut and fold into mixture.

Pour into buttered baking dish. Bake in 350 F. oven for 20 minutes.

Cut hot fondue in 2-inch squares, partly covered with chicken a la King. Garnish with parsley and paprika.

*The Barclay House, Oregon City, Oregon*

## 195. Chicken a la Stroh (Serves 2)

| INGREDIENTS | DIRECTIONS |
| --- | --- |
| 1 chicken | Boned and diced. |
| 2 calves sweetbreads | Diced. |
| 2 tablespoons flour | Roll in flour and brown in butter. |
| 3 tablespoons butter | |
| 2 artichoke bottoms | Cut in quarters and add to the above. |
| 3 oz. sherry wine | Add to mixture and let boil until the liquid is reduced to ⅓ it's original contents. |
| ½ pint cream | Add to above and let simmer for 15 minutes. |
| 2 sausages | Fry and add to the above. |
| seasoning to taste | Put all ingredients in a casserole. |
| 6 pieces of corn-meal mush | Cut in diamond shape and top the casserole. |
| 6 ripe stuffed olives | Place in casserole as a decoration. |

*Clift Hotel, San Francisco, California*


## 196. Chicken Croquettes

| INGREDIENTS | DIRECTIONS |
| --- | --- |
| 1 chicken—5 lbs. | Simmer until tender. |
| 3 cups water | |
| 1 loaf bread | Pour the broth over the bread. |
| 1 cup chicken broth | |
| ½ lb. butter | Add to mixture and make soft panada by cooking. Let cool. |
| 4 eggs—beaten | |
| 2 eggs | Add to mixture. |
| 1 cup cream | |
| 1 teaspoon onion—minced | Grind the chicken. Add seasoning and blend into the above mixture. Mold into croquettes, dip in raw beaten egg and cracker crumbs and fry in boiling lard. |
| salt and pepper to taste | |

*Mrs. Orlando Brown, Frankfort, Kentucky*

## 197. Chicken a la Waleski

(Serves 2)

**INGREDIENTS**

**DIRECTIONS**

1 chicken—spring—
disjointed
1 can chicken broth
1 carrot—sliced
1 onion—sliced
2 tablespoons chopped
parsley
1 pinch thyme
1 bay leaf
1 whole clove
2 peppercorns

Simmer gently for 15 minutes. Drain and
save the broth. Dry the chicken on a cloth.

2 tablespoons butter

Brown the chicken.

*SAUCE*

3 tablespoons butter
2 tablespoons flour

Blend and let cook 5 minutes.

1 cup chicken broth
1 glass white wine

Gradually add to the above stirring into a
smooth sauce, bring to a boil and remove fat
and strain through a sieve. Let the sauce simmer and reduce.

1 egg yolk
2 tablespoons cream

Add to the sauce.

½ lb. mushrooms
2 tablespoons butter

Saute until light brown.

Place browned chicken in serving dish, place
mushrooms all around, cover with a little
gravy.

1 lemon—juice

Pour over all. Serve excess gravy in a gravy
boat.

*L'Omelette, Los Altos, California*


## 198. Chicken All'ucceletto

(Serves 4)

**INGREDIENTS**

**DIRECTIONS**

1 fryer chicken—2 lbs.

Cut in 4 pieces.

½ cup olive oil
¼ cup butter

Have hot before putting in the chicken.
Brown on both sides.

sage—chopped fine
garlic—chopped fine
salt and pepper
½ glass white wine

Season to taste. Let mixture simmer for 15
minutes. Then serve.

*Amelio's, San Francisco, California*

# 199. Chicken Fricassee

(Serves 6)

**INGREDIENTS**

**DIRECTIONS**

1 chicken—5 lbs.
1 quart boiling water
1 onion
4 stalks or stems of celery

Put in large kettle, cover and bring to a boil, then simmer gently for 30 minutes.

2 teaspoons salt
6 or 7 carrots

Add to above and continue simmering for about 2 hours. Remove fowl and carrots, keep hot. Strain stock, remove all fat and measure stock. There should be 2 or 3 cups.

4 to 6 tablespoons chicken fat
4 to 6 tablespoons flour

(Should be 2 tablespoons of each for each cup of broth.) Blend these ingredients over a low flame, add the stock and stir until thick and smooth. Add more seasoning, if necessary.

2 cups cooked rice

Remove skin from fowl and take meat off the bones. Arrange pieces in center of platter, place carrots around chicken and outside of that place a ring of rice. Pour a little gravy over the chicken and carrots and serve the rest in a gravy boat.

*Waldorf Astoria, New York City, N. Y.*


# 200. Chicken Lucrecio

(Serves 4)

**INGREDIENTS**

**DIRECTIONS**

4 lb. chicken

Unjoint.

8 tablespoons flour
2 tablespoons chili powder

Blend these ingredients and roll the chicken in it.

½ cup olive oil

Fry chicken in oil until a golden brown.

1 toe garlic—chopped fine

Add to chicken as it is browning.

1 teaspoon camino seeds —chopped fine

After the chicken is browned, cover with water and let simmer for 3 hours. Remove the chicken from the sauce. Strain the sauce

1 tablespoon butter

Add to the sauce while stirring and pour over the chicken.

2 tablespoons shredded almonds

Brown in butter and top the chicken.

*LaFonda, Santa Fe, New Mexico*

## 201. Chicken Macaroni (Serves 15)

INGREDIENTS | DIRECTIONS

1 chicken—5 lbs.
1 bay leaf
1 onion
1 bunch celery tops
salt and pepper to taste

Simmer slowly until the chicken is tender. Remove meat from bones and cut into 1-inch squares.

1 cup chicken fat or butter
¾ cup flour

Melt butter and add flour.

5 cups chicken broth
1 cup milk

Slowly add to the above and cook until thick.

1 cup celery—cut fine
1 can mushrooms
1 can tomato puree
1 can pimientos
2 cloves garlic—cut fine

Add to sauce and let cook.

Add the chicken to the sauce and let stand for at least 1 hour.

⅔ lb. macaroni

Blanch the macaroni and add to the above.

½ cup grated Parmesan cheese

Cover with cheese and bake in 350 F. oven for 45 minutes.

*Mrs. W. B. Taylor, Bowling Green, Kentucky*

## 202. Chicken Matt Brady

INGREDIENTS | DIRECTIONS

3 chickens
4 tablespoons flour
½ lb. butter

Joint as many chickens as you wish. Roll in flour and fry in butter until browned.

3 calf sweetbreads
2 tablespoons butter

Fry in another pan.
Add both together.

1 jigger brandy

Add to mixture and set on fire to burn alcohol.

1 pint cream

Cover with cream. Do not boil too hard.

bacon
corn fritters

Serve with a couple slices of bacon and corn fritters.

*Villa Chartier, San Mateo, California*

## 203.  Chicken Pie

INGREDIENTS

DIRECTIONS

1 large chicken
1/4 lb. salt pork

Cover with hot water and simmer until nearly tender.

salt to taste

Add to chicken and cook until tender.  Cool. Remove the skin and bones and cut meat in rather large pieces.

Simmer the broth down to about one-half to make it strong.

2 tablespoons butter— melted
2 tablespoons flour

Cook together until crumbly.

1½ cups broth

Add slowly to the above stirring constantly and cook until it thickens.

salt and pepper to taste

Add to gravy.

Roll light biscuit dough 1½ inches thick and cut to fit baking dish.  Line the dish and bake.  Fill with chicken and gravy.  Heat.

Bake the biscuit top in a separate pan and when done, place on top of chicken.  (When baked separately like this, the crust is always crisp and perfect.)

*This is an old family recipe.*

*Old Hundred, Southbury, Connecticut*


## 204.  Chicken with Rice

(Serves 4 to 6)

INGREDIENTS

DIRECTIONS

4 lb. chicken

Cut into pieces.

1 onion—minced
1 tablespoon parsley
2 whole cloves
2 tablespoons butter

Braise with chicken for a few minutes.

1 cup tomato sauce
2 cups soup stock
salt and pepper to taste

Add to mixture and let simmer until done.

Serve with cooked rice.

*Pilot Butt Inn, Bend, Oregon*

## 205.  Chicken Pie

(Serves 6 to 8)

INGREDIENTS

DIRECTIONS

1 chicken

Cook and remove meat from bones.  Put into bottom of a baking dish.  Cover with gravy.

*GRAVY*

3 tablespoons butter—melted
3 tablespoons flour

Blend.

4 cups chicken broth
1 cup milk or cream
salt and pepper to taste

Add slowly to the above and stir.  Boil until it is smooth and thick.  Pour over chicken.

*CRUST*

2¼ cups flour
2 tablespoons butter
2 teaspoons baking powder
1 teaspoon salt

Cut in with blender until like coarse sand.

1 egg—beaten
1 cup milk

Mix together and add to the above.

Cut as for biscuits and place over the chicken, or roll out as for a pie and cover the entire top of the dish.  Bake in 400 F. oven for 15 to 20 minutes.

*From a friend in Cincinnati, Ohio*


## 206.  Chicken Saute Marengo

(Serves 6)

INGREDIENTS

DIRECTIONS

3 chickens—broilers
salt and pepper to taste
1 cup olive oil

Cut chickens in halves and season.  Saute until brown.

1 onion—diced
1 clove garlic—cut fine
1½ lbs. fresh mushrooms
2 No. 2 cans tomatoes
or
6 fresh tomatoes

Add to the chicken and let simmer for 15 minutes.

*Kuglers, Philadelphia, Pennsylvania*

## 207.  Chicken Valencienne (Serves 6)

INGREDIENTS

DIRECTIONS

2 3-lb. chickens
4 tablespoons flour
  salt and pepper to
  taste
¼ lb. butter

Joint chickens, roll lightly in flour and brown.
Place in a heavy bottom pot.

1 doz. baby artichoke
  hearts (trim all leaves
  and tops)
2 lbs. shelled fresh peas
3 cups washed Italian or
  Carolina rice
½ can pimientos—
  chopped
1 pint white wine
2 cups broth or
  consomme
15 to 20 grains saffron
  salt and pepper to
  taste

Add to chicken, cover pot.

25 minutes before serving place on medium
fire and cook without stirring.

*Villa Chartier, San Mateo, California*


## 208.  Country-Fried Chicken

INGREDIENTS

DIRECTIONS

1 spring chicken

Dress and joint chicken the day before it is
to be used.  Put joints in cold salt water
for at least an hour, then put them on ice.

2 tablespoons flour

Roll each piece in flour.

⅓ butter
⅔ lard

Fry slowly until brown.

salt and pepper to
taste

Season after the pieces are in the skillet.
When the chicken is brown put in roaster and
pour a little water and melted butter over
it, cover and steam in 300 F. oven for 1
to 1½ hours.  Add a little more water to
keep the pieces from getting too dry.

Add to a lightly browned (not too thin)
cream gravy all the scrapings from the skillet
and roaster.

*Mr. John T. McCutcheon (Chicago Tribune); recipe given to him by
Mary Fletcher, a cook on George Ade's farm in Indiana*

## 209. Fried Chicken, Southern Style (Serves 3)

INGREDIENTS

1 2-lb. chicken
salt and pepper and
seasoning to taste
3 tablespoons flour

DIRECTIONS

Cut chicken in pieces, dip in milk and the seasoning and dip in flour.

¼ lb. butter
4 slices of bacon

Fry bacon in butter until a light brown. Take out the bacon and put in chicken to fry. When chicken is brown, put on cover and simmer for 30 minutes. Arrange chicken in a dish with the bacon and pour off most of the butter from the pan.

2 tablespoons flour
1 cup cream
seasoning to taste

Stir in flour, making a smooth paste. Add cream and let boil for a few minutes. Season and pour over chicken.

*The Greenbrier, White Sulphur Springs, West Virginia*

## 210. A Different Fried or Broiled Chicken
(Serves 8 to 10)

INGREDIENTS

2 hens
2 slices onion
1 celery stalk
salt and pepper to
taste

DIRECTIONS

The day before using, boil until tender. (Save stock for broth.)

¼ lb. butter
salt and pepper to
taste

Cut chicken in pieces and broil or fry slowly in butter until brown, adding salt and pepper to taste.

*Mrs. A. Scott Hines, Bowling Green, Kentucky*

*We frequently cook the chickens and take them to the country place down on Gasper River where they are fried or broiled for lunch.*

# 211.  Oven Broiled Chicken

INGREDIENTS

DIRECTIONS

3 spring chickens

Cut in quarters, removing the backs and necks.  Use these undesirable pieces with the livers and gizzards to make a cup of stock.

1½ teaspoons salt

Salt each piece separately and place in small covered roasting pan, skin side down.

½ cup butter

Dot generously with butter.

Bake until brown, turn and brown other side, putting bottom pieces on top and browning all evenly.  Keep covered to retain moisture.  Bake for 1 to 1½ hours.  When chicken is browned, remove to another pan to keep hot.

2 tablespoons flour

Add to butter in roaster and brown.  Add the stock and make gravy.

Serve at once.  Put gravy in gravy boat.

*High Hampton, Cashiers, North Carolina*


# 212.  Smothered Chicken

(Serves 4)

INGREDIENTS

DIRECTIONS

1 chicken—spring— quartered
salt and pepper to taste
2 tablespoons flour

Season and dredge with flour.  Place in a baking dish.

1 lb. butter—melted

Pour over the chicken, cover and bake in 450 F. oven for 1 hour, basting every fifteen minutes.  When brown, pour off the butter.

1 quart chicken stock
salt and pepper to taste
2 tablespoons flour

Blend and put in the pan, cover and bake in 350 F. oven for 1½ hours.  This method makes its own gravy.

*Tally-Ho Tea Room, Park Ridge, Illinois*

# 213. Cream De Volaille

(Serves 20)

### INGREDIENTS

1 chicken—spring
2 lbs. pork
1 lb. salt pork

1 lb. butter
6 eggs
1 pint milk
1 onion—chopped
1 tablespoon parsley—
  chopped
  crumbs from inside a
  loaf of bread
  salt and pepper to
  taste
  mace to taste
  nutmeg to taste

### DIRECTIONS

Put through a meat grinder.

Mix all together and add to meat mixture.

Place in individual molds and steam for 3 hours.

*Virginia Duvall Greenhow, Frankfort, Kentucky*


# 214. Roast Duckling in Casserole

(Serves 4)

### INGREDIENTS

1 duck—4 lbs.
  salt and pepper to
  taste
3 tablespoons oil or lard

1 onion—diced
1 carrot—sliced
1 stalk celery
1 bay leaf
1 pinch thyme

6 small pearl onions
3 oz. melted butter

3 slices bacon—minced

1½ lbs. shelled peas
½ heart shredded lettuce
½ teaspoon salt
1 teaspoon sugar
2 cups water

2 oz. butter

### DIRECTIONS

Season duck and place in roasting pan, in a 425 F. oven until it browns, basting every 10 or 15 minutes.

Add to the duck and let simmer in 325 F. oven for 45 minutes to 1 hour. Remove the duck and make a gravy. Quarter the duck and place on a platter with wing and drum stick bones upright. Place holders on them.

Let brown.

Add to onions and simmer for 5 minutes.

Add to mixture. Cover with oiled paper or a tight lid and cook for 30 to 35 minutes. Remove from the fire.

Fold into the mixture, and circle the duck with the peas. Pour gravy over the duck. Apple sauce may be served with this dish.

*El Prado, San Francisco, California*

# 215.  Pressed Duck

(Serves 8)

### INGREDIENTS

4 wild mallards

Note: 1 can of condensed bouillon may be used, if press is not available.

### DIRECTIONS

Roast in 400 F. oven for 12 minutes. Carve breasts in one piece. Remove skin and set aside. Place carcasses in duck press and extract the essence.

### SAUCE NO. 1

¼ lb. butter
5 tablespoons currant jelly

Cook slowly and stir until thoroughly melted.

1 teaspoon salt
3 pinches cayenne pepper

Add to the above and stir.

6 tablespoons Worcestershire sauce
5 dashes Tabasco sauce
essence extracted from ducks

Add to the mixture and set aside.

### SAUCE NO. 2

4 duck hearts
4 duck livers
salt and fresh ground black pepper to taste
2 tablespoons butter

Saute in butter and run through a meat grinder.

1 bunch celery— chopped
1 carrot—chopped
2 onions—chopped
2 tablespoons butter

Fry until brown.

4 ozs. sherry wine

All these ingredients are pureed through a sieve with the wine.

The breasts are now cooked in Sauce No. 1 to taste in a chafing dish on the table. Add Sauce No. 2 and cook for 1 minute. Add Bourbon to sauces and pour over ducks. Serve with wild rice, string beans and rolls.

4 ozs. Bourbon

*Dr. E. Vernon Mastin, St. Louis, Missouri*

# 216. Boned Squab, Martha Washington (Serves 6)

| INGREDIENTS | DIRECTIONS |
|---|---|
| 6 squabs (¾ lb. each) —boned<br>salt and pepper to taste<br>6 strips of bacon | Season squabs and wrap a piece of bacon around each one. Stuff them with dressing. |

### DRESSING

| | |
|---|---|
| 1 teaspoon parsley—chopped<br>1 celery heart—cut fine<br>1 onion—cut fine<br>⅛ lb. butter | Saute for ten minutes over a slow fire. |
| 5 ozs. chicken livers—chopped<br>⅛ lb. butter | Saute for 3 minutes and add to the above. |
| 8 ozs. bread—cut in small pieces<br>¾ lb. butter | Toast bread in butter and add to the mixture. |
| ½ lb. wild rice | Boil for 15 minutes and add to bread mixture. |
| 2 ozs. almonds—chopped<br>1 slice of truffle—minced<br>1 pinch of thyme<br>salt and pepper to taste<br>¼ cup chicken broth | Add to mixture and blend thoroughly.<br><br>Stuff the squabs, and place them in roasting pan. |
| 1 onion—diced<br>1 stalk celery—cut fine<br>4 ozs. butter | Put in pan with squab and dot with butter. Bake in 450 F. oven for 20 minutes. Sprinkle squabs with chicken broth. Then in 350 F. oven for 10 minutes. Remove squabs and make a gravy. |
| 1 tablespoon flour<br>1½ cups warm chicken broth<br>4 tablespoons white wine<br>1 tablespoon brandy | Mix into the fond of the squabs, let come to a boil and strain through a fine sieve. Serve separately. |

*Stirrup-Cup Castle, Oakdale, Long Island, New York*

# 217. Roast Mallard

(Serves 2)

INGREDIENTS

DIRECTIONS

1 wild mallard duck

Wash and dry.

1 whole onion
1 tablespoon vinegar
1 stalk celery—cut in
long pieces

Put inside the duck, set in a covered pan in
a cold place overnight. This is for the purpose of eliminating all fishy flavor and should
be removed and discarded next day.

1 apple—sliced
1 stalk of celery—cut

Stuff the duck and discard after it is roasted.
Seldom are wild ducks cooked in this manner, stuffed with dressing.

2 slices salt pork
salt and pepper to
taste

Lay diagonally across the breast of the duck
and season.

½ cup olive oil
3 tablespoons butter

Put in small roaster and be certain it is very
hot before putting in the duck. Roast in
a 500 F. oven for 15 to 20 minutes, basting
every 4 to 5 minutes.

My favorite accompaniment is wild rice and cranberry relish.

*Duncan Hines, Bowling Green, Kentucky*


# 218. Sour Cream Quail

(Serves 6)

INGREDIENTS

DIRECTIONS

6 pieces salt pork
6 quails
3 tablespoons butter

Wrap pork around quail and fasten with tooth-
pick. Fry in butter, turning from side to side
until brown.

12 juniper berries—
crushed
1 cup boiling water

Mix together in a pot and put in the quails.
Simmer for 1½ to 2 hours. Add water from
time to time if necessary.

salt and pepper to
taste

Put on the quails.

1 pint sour cream (to
be 5 or 6 days old)

Pour over quail and boil well for 30 minutes.

If the cream curdles, add a teaspoon of hot
water slowly until the cream becomes smooth.

*Huntington Hotel, Pasadena, California*

# 219. Quail

INGREDIENTS | DIRECTIONS

6 quail
1 tablespoon flour
salt and pepper to taste

Dredge the birds lightly.

½ cup butter
1 tablespoon lard

Heat as much as possible without scorching. Add the birds and brown fast to seal in the juices. Keep turning.

1 cup boiling water

Lower temperature and add to birds, cover the pan and cook until tender. Add water as needed until ready to brown the breasts.

After the water is gone, place breast side down in butter and brown over low flame on top of stove. Take the birds out and make the gravy.

1 tablespoon flour

Stir into the butter.

1 to 1¼ cups water

Add to flour mixture and scrape all the brown coating of the roaster into the gravy. Stir and cook until thick.

*Duncan Hines, Bowling Green, Kentucky*

*If the overfed were underfed and the underfed had enough we would have no wars.*

## 220.   Breast of Turkey and Ham, Mary Christine

(Serves 4)

| INGREDIENTS | DIRECTIONS |
|---|---|
| 4 slices of ham | Place in bottom of a buttered casserole. |
| 4 slices breast of turkey | Place over the ham. |
| 2 cups turkey stock<br>1 stalk celery—cut<br>1 onion—chopped<br>salt and pepper to taste | Boil down to reduce to a strong stock.  Strain through a cloth. |
| 1 tablespoon butter | Melt. |
| 1 teaspoon cornstarch<br>1 tablespoon cold water | Dissolve and add to the butter.  Stir until smooth and add to the stock. |
| ½ lb. fresh mushrooms<br>1 tablespoon butter | Cut in pieces and saute in butter.  Add to sauce. |
| 2 tablespoons sherry wine | Add to sauce and pour over the ham and turkey in the casserole.  Cook in 350 F. oven just long enough to heat all and serve. |

*Normandy Inn, Carmel, California*


## 221.   Huntington Special Steak

(Serves 10)

| INGREDIENTS | DIRECTIONS |
|---|---|
| 2 lbs. breast of turkey<br>1 lb. veal | Put through a meat grinder several times to be sure it is ground fine. |
| salt and pepper to taste<br>1 pinch of nutmeg<br>3 egg whites—beaten | Add to the above. |
| ½ cup whipped cream | Add enough whipped cream to the mixture to mold into balls.  The patties should weigh about 5 or 6 ounces each. |
| 3 tablespoons butter | Fry patties. |

Serve with creamed mushroom sauce.  Put the sauce on the plate first then the patty on top.

Supreme sauce may also be used, in which case, put a whole mushroom on top of the patty and serve under glass.

*Huntington Hotel, Pasadena, California*

# 222. Sliced Turkey, John Paffrath

| INGREDIENTS | DIRECTIONS |
|---|---|
| 1 cluster boiled broccoli | Place in oblong casserole that has been well buttered. |
| 1 tablespoon melted butter<br>1 tablespoon grated cheese | Sprinkle over broccoli. |
| ⅓ of 1 gill sherry wine | Douse broccoli. |
| 4 slices white meat of turkey | Arrange over the broccoli. |
| 1 tablespoon grated cheese<br>⅓ gill sherry wine | Sprinkle over the turkey. |
| 1 cup cream sauce<br>2 egg yolks<br>salt and pepper to taste | Beat these ingredients together. |
| 1 tablespoon whipped cream | Fold into sauce, and pour over the turkey so it is completely covered. |
| 1 tablespoon grated cheese<br>⅓ gill sherry wine | Put over the top and bake in 350 F. oven for 12 minutes until a golden brown and slightly souffled. |

*The Brown Hotel, Louisville, Kentucky*

*The temper of a host is judged by his carving.*

## 223. Boulghour Pilaff (Cracked Wheat)

INGREDIENTS

¼ lb. butter—melted
3 cups Boulghour
   (cracked wheat)

1 onion—chopped
1 tablespoon butter

6 cups clear broth
   salt and pepper to
   taste

DIRECTIONS

Braise for 5 minutes.

Fry on the side and add to the boulghour.

Add to mixture, stir well, cover the pot and bake in 350 F. oven for 30 minutes.

Take out, mix well, cover and bake for another 10 minutes.

Very good used as a turkey, duck, or chicken dressing.

*Omar Khayyam's, San Francisco, California*

## 224. Filling for a Turkey

INGREDIENTS

1 loaf bread—stale

6 white onions—sliced
½ cup parsley
1 cup celery
¼ lb. butter

2 eggs—beaten

1 teaspoon salt
1 teaspoon thyme (if
   desired)
¼ teaspoon pepper

DIRECTIONS

Break into small pieces, crust and all.

Saute until thoroughly browned. Add the bread and stir until thoroughly blended.

Stir into mixture.

Blend together and stir into mixture. Set aside to cool. Fill the fowl and roast breast side down.

*Mrs. Edmund H. Singmaster, Germantown, Pennsylvania*

## 225.   Poultry Dressing

| INGREDIENTS | DIRECTIONS |
|---|---|
| ¼ lb. butter | Cream. |
| 2 eggs<br>2 egg yolks | Stir into butter. |
| 1½ tablespoons cornstarch<br>½ pint cream | Mix together and blend into mixture. |
| 1 onion—grated<br>mace<br>thyme<br>bread crumbs | Stir into mixture, using enough breadcrumbs to make the consistency of oatmeal or mush. |

*Roy C. Neuhaus, Evanston, Illinois*


## 226.   Turkey Dressing

| INGREDIENTS | DIRECTIONS |
|---|---|
| 1¼ lbs. French bread | Bread should be stale enough to grate, crust and all. |
| 2½ teaspoons salt<br>1¼ teaspoons pepper<br>3 teaspoons sage—crushed<br>1¼ teaspoon poultry seasoning<br>1 teaspoon celery salt | Mix together and add to grated bread, blending thoroughly. |
| 1¾ to 2 cups butter | Melt in a large pan. |
| 4 onions—cut fine<br>1 cup celery hearts—cut fine<br>1 lb. chestnuts—cooked, blanched, and quartered | Add to the butter, and when onions are a little done add the bread, stirring all together. Brown the bread slightly. |
| ½ cup cream | Add to mixture. |
|  | Stuff the turkey, but do not pack, if you want a light dressing. |
|  | Rub the turkey with butter and flour and season well with the same dry seasonings that were used in the dressing. |

*Gertrude Tidd Chaffin, Los Angeles, California*

## 227.  Chicken Curry

(Serves 4)

INGREDIENTS

DIRECTIONS

1 chicken--boned and
  cut in small pieces
2 tablespoons flour
2 tablespoons olive oil
½ lb. butter

Dust chicken with flour and saute until brown.

4 onions—chopped
1 clove garlic or more
  —cut fine
1 tablespoon butter

Saute and when chicken is about half done,
add to above.

1 tablespoon curry
  powder
1 tablespoon flour
3 tablespoons cream
  salt and pepper to
  taste

Mix into a smooth paste and add to above.

1 can lima beans—juice

Add to mixture and cook slowly for 2 hours.

½ can lima beans
¼ lb. blanched almonds
  —chopped

About 15 minutes before serving, add these
to the above ingredients.

1 tablespoon chopped
  parsley

Serve with rice and relishes.  Chutney, hard
boiled egg yolks put through a sieve, chopped
almonds, etc.

*Cora Aron, Chicago, Illinois*


## 228.  Curried Chicken

INGREDIENTS

DIRECTIONS

1 chicken—cut in pieces
1 onion—sliced

Brown the onion in some of the chicken fat.
Add the chicken.

1 teaspoon salt
2 tomatoes or 1 cup of
  canned tomatoes

Add to chicken and cover with water.  Simmer
for 1 hour.  Bone chicken.

2 tablespoons curry
  powder

Add to chicken and cook until the chicken is
tender.  Keep covered with water.

Make a gravy of the stock.  Add the meat
which is taken off the bones.

Serve on hot rice.

*Quaker Bonnet, Orchard Park, New York*

# 229.   A Curry Dinner

| INGREDIENTS | DIRECTIONS |
|---|---|
| 2 lbs. rice—cooked | Put in large tureen and use as a center piece. |

2 boiled chickens— boned and diced
12 hard boiled eggs— diced
36 pickles—chopped
36 stuffed olives—sliced
3 Spanish onions—cut fine
6 bunches celery—cut fine
2 bunches radishes— sliced thin
2 cups nut meats
2 cups grated cheese
6 oranges—diced
6 apples—diced
1 loaf of bread—diced and toasted into buttered croutons

Put each of these into separate bowls and place around the tureen.   Add any other combination that will add to color and taste. They need not be hot.   Let each guest help himself, first to rice and then to any of the ingredients in the surrounding bowls.   Top all with plenty of hot curry sauce.

### CURRY SAUCE

3 onions—cut fine
½ lb. bacon—cubed

Fry together until brown.

4 tablespoons curry powder
salt and pepper and red pepper to taste
½ cup flour

Mix together and add to above, keeping free of lumps.

2 quarts of milk

Boil and add to the above mixture, stirring constantly.   Cook until the consistency of gravy.

Nothing else is needed for this meal, unless an ice for dessert is desired.

*Mrs. Otto J. Sieplein, Miami, Florida*

## 230. Indian Curry

INGREDIENTS

DIRECTIONS

1 onion—sliced
3 slices of bacon

Cook until brown.

1 quart chicken stock

Add to the above and as it comes to a boil add:—

4 teaspoons curry powder
2 tablespoons milk

Mix these together and add to above and let boil for 20 minutes. Strain, and return to the fire.

1 apple—chopped
1 cup fresh cocoanut—grated
½ cup cream

Add to the mixture and thicken to the consistency of heavy cream.

cooked chicken, cold meat, or hard boiled eggs

Add whatever base desired and serve with cooked rice and condiments.

*Casa de Manana, La Jolla, California*

## 231. A Bengal Curry                               (Serves 6)

INGREDIENTS

DIRECTIONS

2 onions—sliced
⅓ cup butter

Fry to a golden brown and take out of pan.

2 lbs. veal

Cut into small squares.

2 tablespoons flour
1½ teaspoons salt
2 tablespoons curry powder

Mix these ingredients and dredge pieces of meat. Brown in the pan the onions were cooked in. Take out of pan.

1 apple

Cut in pieces and fry slightly.

1 clove of garlic—minced
2 tablespoons brown sugar
2 tablespoons seeded raisins
1 tablespoon Worcestershire sauce
1 lemon—sliced
2 tablespoons unsweetened cocoanut
⅓ cup walnuts
2 cups of hot water

Mix all these ingredients together and add the flour and curry mixture that was left after dredging. Put all the ingredients in a sauce pan, bring to a boiling point, cover and let simmer until the meat is tender. Thicken if necessary. Serve with boiled rice.

Serve cold chopped ham, grated cocoanut, fried onions, mustard pickles, Major Grey's Chutney, minced egg yolk and whites, Bombay duck, or substitute sardines spread with anchovy paste and dried in 300 F. oven, which are taken in the fingers and crumbled on the rice.

*Pelican Cafe, Klamath Falls, Oregon*

## 232.  Curry

| INGREDIENTS | DIRECTIONS |
|---|---|
| 3 cups lean meat in ½-inch dices. | Pork, lamb, veal, or chicken leftovers—cut Shrimp, either fresh or canned may also be used. |
| 1½ cups chopped celery, including the tops<br>1 onion—chopped fine<br>2 tablespoons butter | Saute until a golden brown. |
| ¾ cups beef or chicken broth<br>2 tablespoons flour | Make into a gravy and add to celery and onion combination. |
| ¼ teaspoon curry powder<br>3 dashes Tabasco sauce<br>2 tablespoons butter | Add to mixture and taste. If more curry is desired it may be added. Blend thoroughly by stirring smoothly. Add the meat and let simmer. Salt to taste. If necessary, put |

in double boiler. If it becomes too dry by evaporation, add boiling water to bring back volume. Serve heaped in center of warmed plate surrounded by a ring of boiled rice, garnished with parsley and accompanied by Major Grey's Chutney.

*Dr. T. J. LeBlanc, Cincinnati, Ohio*


## 233.  Curry of Sea Food Rizotto
(Serves 12)

| INGREDIENTS | DIRECTIONS |
|---|---|
| 1 onion—cut fine<br>1 apple—cut fine<br>1 tablespoon butter | Saute. |
| 2 tablespoons curry powder<br>1 cup cocoanut milk<br>1 tablespoon shredded cocoanut | Blend together and add to the above. |
| ½ lb. fresh lobster<br>½ lb. crab meat—fresh<br>½ lb. scallops—fresh<br>½ lb. oysters—fresh | Parboil first and then cut in large pieces. (Save the stock.) Add to the curry sauce and bring to a boil. |
| 1 jigger white wine<br>3 tablespoons cream | Add to the above mixture. |
| 3 tablespoons butter | Serve with rizotto. |

### RISOTTO

| | |
|---|---|
| 1 tablespoon chopped onion<br>2 tablespoons butter | Saute. |
| 3 cups washed rice<br>celery salt, maggi sauce and salt—to taste | Add to the onion and place on warming shelf to dry. |
| 5 cups consomme or stock sea food was boiled in | When the mixture is very dry, add liquid and bring to a boil.<br>Bake in 350 F. oven for 15 minutes. |

*Monument Inn, Bennington, Vermont*

*There is a wide variation in the quality of meats. Prime grades are found in comparatively few markets and not in many eating places because, first, there is not a sufficient amount of prime quality to supply the demand and also the price is necessarily high.*

*At the present time (Fall, 1939) the amount of beef coming into packing plants will not grade more than 8 per cent prime. At other seasons of the year, the amount will drop to 2 per cent or lower.*

*The next best grades are known as U. S. Choice No. 1, No. 2, No. 3 and at present these three additional grades amount to about 19 or 20 per cent of the total. Beyond these four grades, the quality rapidly drops and finally there is approximately 49 per cent which consists of old cows, bulls, low grade yearlings, etc.*

*In selecting your meat purchases, I believe the first consideration should be to buy only U.S. Government inspected meats and then select the best grades your pocket book will permit.*

*It so happens that I have a number of friends at Swift & Company who have very generously gone to the trouble to supply me with descriptive matter and photographs of various cuts, which I hope will be a help to you in selecting better quality meats.*

> *"When mighty roast beef*
> *Was the Englishman's food,*
> *It ennobled our hearts,*
> *And enriched our blood.*
> *Our soldiers were brave*
> *And our courtiers were good.*
> *Oh! the roast beef of old England!"*

More than three hundred years ago, an English poet praised roast beef! And today, there is no meat more universally popular than a sizzling steak or succulent roast of beef, and beef is generally far better today than it was in the days gone by, for through the breeding of finer cattle there has been a large increase in the amount of quality beef available to consumers.

## You Can Recognize Fine Beef

Buying fine beef is principally a matter of looking for certain definite characteristics. Good cuts of beef are plump—well filled out, with a thick smooth covering of white fat. The color of top grade beef is bright red, and the lean is streaked throughout with pure white fat. This latter quality, typical of all of the finest beef, is called "marbling." To make it easier for you to be sure of excellent beef, the packers are now branding their names *right on the meat.*

These two photographs clearly demonstrate the characteristics of good beef. Illustrated above is a rib of beef from which is cut the lordly standing rib roast.

Below are pictured boneless beef sirloins, probably the most delicious of all fine steaks. The most choice steaks, served by the better class hotels and restaurants, are made from this cut. Notice the "marbling" and even covering of white fat.

# Lamb Offers Variety
# To Your Menu Year 'Round

✤     ✤     ✤

Good lamb is always in season, offering a multitude of piquant meat dishes to enliven the weekly menu. All lamb cuts are richly flavorful, and all lamb cuts are tender because lamb is young meat. Breeders have done much to improve the year 'round quality of lamb, so now you can always buy tender, delicious lamb.

## Lamb Easy to Prepare

Because of its natural tenderness, all cuts of lamb, except the neck and breast, can be prepared either by roasting or broiling. But, remember, lamb is a meat that should be served piping hot or cold! Never serve it lukewarm!

## French Leg of Lamb
## For Family Dinners

Here is a fine roast that the entire family can enjoy. Excellent flavor and tenderness, combined with the high nutritive value and easy digestibility of lamb, makes this a perfect meat dish.

## Loin and Rib Chops Always Popular

The lamb loin chop, evenly broiled to a golden brown, yet juicy and tender, is always a favorite. If you prefer a smaller and somewhat less expensive chop, the rib chop is just the answer.

## Try Blade or Arm Chops

These cuts come from a square cut shoulder of lamb. These two cuts of lamb are the most economical lamb chops. In addition, they are larger cuts and will be preferred by those who like good-sized chops. Blade or arm chops are delicious broiled.

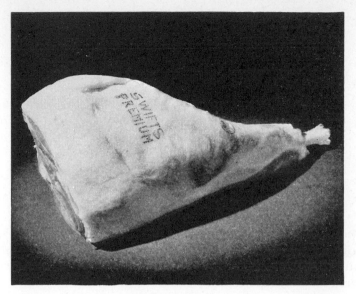

*Leg of Lamb*

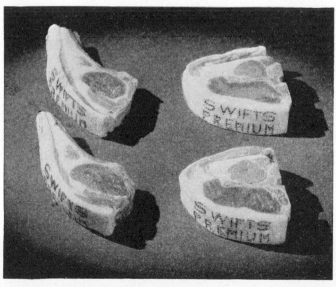

*Lamb Chops*

# Veal Has Great Possibilities

✤    ✤    ✤

Veal is a delicately flavored meat which may be served in an infinite number of ways.  There are many unusual veal dishes, often served with tasty cheese or mushroom sauces.  But equally delicious are flavorful roasts served with simple meat gravies.

## Veal Is Young Meat

Veal comes from calves from three to twelve weeks of age.  The characteristics of veal are, for this reason, different from those of mature beef.  Good veal is white, firm, and velvety in texture. There is no development of fat covering, and no "marbling."

## Veal Roll

The rolled veal shoulder is rapidly becoming a popular roast on many a housewife's weekly menu.  It is made from a boned shoulder of veal, and is covered with a layer of beef fat which adds flavor and tenderness.

## Veal Rib Chop

Veal rib chop, or cutlet as it is sometimes called, is often breaded and fried in deet fat or pan fried.  It offers an excellent, easy to prepare dish for luncheons or suppers.

## Leg of Veal

The leg not only makes a delicious roast, but in addition $\frac{1}{4}$-inch slices from the butt end provide delicious chops.

Now buying veal has been made easier.  Like beef, you can buy veal by brand name.

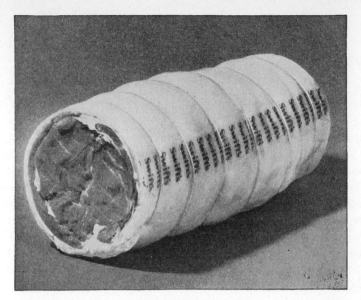

*Veal Roll*

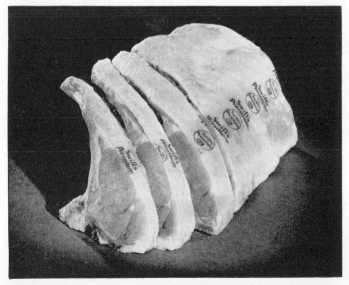

*Veal Rib Chops*

# Pork Provides Interesting
# Variety to Your Meals

✢   ✢   ✢

According to a story made famous by Francis Bacon man's first taste of roast pork was the result of a fire which destroyed the cottage of a certain Chinese farmer, many centuries ago. The farmer's shock at losing his home and livestock was quickly turned to pleasure when he accidentally tasted the extraordinary flavor of cooked meat for the first time. As the story goes, the farmers throughout the district developed the strange custom of burning their homes as fast as they could build them—in order to eat the wonderful cooked pig.

And today fresh pork provides the menu with many delightful dishes, although the quaint custom of firing one's home has been replaced by more modern methods of cookery. Along with better methods of cooking and new ways to serve pork, there has been a marked improvement in the quality of hogs through better breeding and modern scientific feeding.

## You Can Always Get Good Fresh Pork

Grades of pork do not vary greatly, and the pork you buy these days will be uniformly good in quality. To get the best flavor and true tenderness, pork should always be well done. Roasts should be cooked at a moderate temperature to keep in the juices and to prevent the hardening of the surface meat.

## Delicious Roasts and Chops

Pork loin is one of the most popular cuts of pork. It makes a rich, flavorful roast, and chops cut from the loin, pan fried or braised, have long been a favorite American dish.

## Fresh Hams

Fresh hams make excellent roasts. Steaks cut from the choice portions of these hams are deliciously tender pan fried. Individual ham steaks are just the right size for sandwiches.

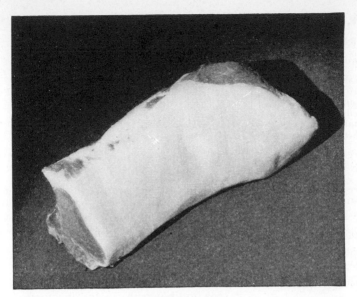

*Pork Loin Roast*

*Pork Chops*

## 234. Asparagus Souffle (Serves 12)

| INGREDIENTS | DIRECTIONS |
|---|---|
| 1 quart asparagus | Cut in ¼-inch pieces and cook. |
| 8 tablespoons butter<br>⅞ cup flour<br>1 cup milk<br>1 cup asparagus water<br>1½ tablespoon salt<br>⅓ teaspoon pepper | Make cream sauce. |
| 9 egg yolks | Beat until thick and add to sauce, and mix with asparagus. |
| 9 egg whites—beaten stiff | Fold in above mixture. Place in hot water bath and bake in 350 F. oven for 1 hour, or |

until a fork inserted in center, comes out clean. Serve with cheese sauce.

### CHEESE SAUCE

| | |
|---|---|
| 4 tablespoons butter<br>½ cup flour | Melt butter, add flour and cook 5 minutes. |
| 3 cups milk | Heat milk and gradually add to above and cook until smooth—15 to 20 minutes. |
| ½ teaspoon salt<br>speck of pepper<br>8 tablespoons snappy cheese | Add and stir until the cheese is melted. |

*Grace E. Smith Service Restaurant and Cafeteria, Toledo, Ohio*


## 235. Cheese Fondue (Serves 6)

| INGREDIENTS | DIRECTIONS |
|---|---|
| 2 tablespoons butter<br>½ lb. American cheese | Cut in small pieces and place in bowl. |
| 4 tablespoons bread crumbs | Add to butter and cheese. |
| 1 cup sweet milk | Heat to scalding and pour over mixture. |
| 3 egg yolks—beaten<br>1 pinch of salt | Add to mixture and mix well. Place over low fire and stir occasionally until dissolved. |
| 3 egg whites—beaten | Fold in egg whites and put in buttered baking dish. Bake in 350 F. oven for 20 to 30 minutes. This has to be watched. |
| | Serve the moment it is taken from the stove. |

*Miss Katharine L. Little, Chicago, Illinois*

## 236. Cheese Souffle

INGREDIENTS

DIRECTIONS

4 tablespoons butter—
  melted
4 tablespoons flour

Blend together.

1⅓ cups milk

Slowly add to the above. Cook until a creamy sauce.

1 cup cheese—cut fine
½ teaspoon salt
½ teaspoon baking
  powder
¼ teaspoon paprika
¼ teaspoon celery salt

Add to the mixture, and then remove from the stove.

4 egg yolks
1 tablespoon parsley—
  chopped
1 tablespoon pimiento—
  chopped

Add to the mixture and beat 2 minutes.

4 egg whites—beaten

Fold into mixture. Pour into buttered baking dish and bake in pan of hot water, 50 minutes.

*Mrs. Louie M. Weathers, Elkton, Kentucky*


## 237. Cheese Souffle

(Serves 6)

INGREDIENTS

DIRECTIONS

8 square soda crackers
1¾ cups milk

Put in pan 10x3 inches deep and let stand in refrigerator 3 or 4 hours. Mash crackers thoroughly.

3 egg yolks—beaten
¾ lb. grated cheese
  dash of Tabasco

Mix well with crackers and let stand until ready to heat and serve.

3 egg whites—beaten
  stiff, but not dry

Fold into mixture and bake for about 30 minutes in oven that has been preheated and turned down to 300 F. Turn up temperature and brown for 2 minutes.

*Shadow Hill Tea Room, Hernando, Mississippi*

## 238. Cheese Souffle

(Serves 6)

INGREDIENTS

DIRECTIONS

1 cup bread crumbs
1 cup grated cheese
1 cup milk
3 egg yolks
½ teaspoon salt
1 tablespoon butter

Thoroughly beat all these ingredients together. Cook over a low fire until it begins to thicken. Let cool.

3 egg whites—beaten

Fold into mixture and pour into buttered baking dish. Bake in 375 F. oven for 25 minutes.

*Miss Laura Pepper*


## 239. Cheese Souffle

(18 rings)

INGREDIENTS

DIRECTIONS

3 cups milk—hot
9 tablespoons minute tapioca

Cook until thick.

3 cups grated snappy cheese

Add to mixture and let cool.

9 egg yolks—beaten

Blend into mixture.

9 egg whites—beaten
3 teaspoons salt

Beat together and fold into mixture.

Bake in greased ring mold in 350 F. oven for 30 minutes.

Turn out and fill with creamed mushrooms.

*The Hearthstone, Winnetka, Illinois*


## 240. Egg Plant Souffle

(Serves 8 to 10)

INGREDIENTS

DIRECTIONS

1 egg plant—large

Peel and cut in small chunks. Boil in clear water until tender. Drain well by pressing lightly in colander.

4 eggs
1 cup cream
¼ cup melted butter
salt to taste

Thoroughly mix and beat in with eggplant, using a potato masher. Bake in pyrex dish in 325 F. oven for 30 minutes, or until it puffs up like a sponge cake. Serve very hot.

*William Jack Latta, Goshen, Indiana*

## 241.  Spinach Souffle                                    (Serves 14)

| INGREDIENTS | DIRECTIONS |
|---|---|
| 2½ cups spinach—cooked, and drained dry | Press through a colander. |
| ¼ teaspoon salt | Add to spinach. |
| 1 quart of milk | Heat until steaming. |
| 5 eggs—beaten | Whip until frothy and add slowly to hot milk.  Add milk and egg mixture to spinach and pour into buttered baking dish or individual cups.  Bake in 300 F. oven for 30 minutes. |
| 1 cup sliced mushrooms<br>2 tablespoons butter | Saute in butter and put some on top of each serving. |

*Fallen Leaf Lodge, Lake Tahoe, California*


## 242.  Spinach Souffle                                  (Serves 5 or 6)

| INGREDIENTS | DIRECTIONS |
|---|---|
| ¾ cup cooked spinach, chopped fine | |
| 2 tablespoons butter<br>2 tablespoons flour<br>½ cup milk | Make cream sauce. |
| ½ cup grated cheese<br>3 egg yolks—beaten<br>½ teaspoon salt<br>pepper to taste | Add to sauce and mix with spinach. |
| 3 egg whites—beaten | Fold in mixture.  Pour in buttered pan and set in hot water in 350 F. oven and bake for 30 minutes.  Let stand a few minutes after taking it out of oven. |

*Mrs. R. T. Cooksey, Madison, Wisconsin*

## 243.  Sweet Potato Souffle

(Serves 8)

| INGREDIENTS | DIRECTIONS |
|---|---|
| 6 sweet potatoes, medium size | Peel and boil in salted water, until tender. Put through a potato ricer and mash thoroughly. |
| 2 egg yolks—beaten<br>½ cup milk | Mix together. |
| ½ cup sugar<br>½ cup raisins<br>1 teaspoon nutmeg<br>3 tablespoons melted butter | Add to egg mixture and stir in mashed potatoes.<br><br>Put in buttered casserole and bake in 350 F. oven for about 30 minutes, or until light brown on top and bottom. |
| 2 egg whites—beaten<br>4 tablespoons sugar<br>1 teaspoon lemon juice or orange juice | Make a meringue and place on top and put under broiler a few minutes to brown. |

*The House by the Road, Ashburn, Georgia*


## 244.  Apple Casseroles

(Serves 6)

| INGREDIENTS | DIRECTIONS |
|---|---|
| 6 big Northern Spy or Morgan apples | Wash, pare and quarter and core. Pack quarters close together in open casserole. |
| ¼ cup sugar<br>2 tablespoons butter | Sprinkle with sugar and dot with butter.<br><br>Bake in 350 F. to 375 F. oven until tender and brown or about 30 to 40 minutes.<br><br>These are sent bubbling to the table and eaten as a vegetable. |

*High Hampton, Cashiers, North Carolina*

## 245. Apple Crunch (Serves 8)

INGREDIENTS                                    DIRECTIONS

8 apples—thinly sliced        Fill greased baking dish 2-3 full of apples.

¼ cup butter                          Crumble together and spread over apples.
½ cup flour
¾ cup sugar
1 teaspoon cinnamon

½ cup light wine              Pour over all and bake in 300 F. oven for 45
  or                         minutes, or until apples are done.
¼ cup sherry and ¼ cup
  water

                             Serve with hard sauce.

*Althea, Lewisburg, West Virginia*


## 246. Apple Sauce (Serves 8)

INGREDIENTS                                    DIRECTIONS

8 medium apples—tart          Peel and cut in large pieces.  Cook and drain
¼ cup water                   and put in bowl.

½ cup sugar                   Add to apples.
1 teaspoon butter
1 teaspoon nutmeg

1 dozen marshallows           Put apples in baking dish and cover with
                              marshmallows, stick in oven until brown.

*The House by the Road, Ashburn, Georgia*


## 247. Fried Apples (Serves 8)

INGREDIENTS                                    DIRECTIONS

6 to 8 winesap apples         Core (peel or not as desired), slice in ½-inch
                              slices, like the sections of an orange.

½ cup water                   Add to apples and cook in covered frying pan
                              until almost tender.  Remove the cover and
                              let the water evaporate.

4 tablespoons bacon           Add to apples and fry until a deep golden
  drippings                   brown and candied.  Turn frequently while
⅔ cup sugar                   browning.

*Duncan Hines, Bowling Green, Kentucky*

## 248.  Virginia Apples

(Serves 6)

INGREDIENTS

DIRECTIONS

6 apples (York
Imperial)
1¼ cups boiling water

Peel and core and place in baking dish.  Add
water and let boil five minutes in covered
dish.

1½ cups sugar
3 lemon slices

Add sugar and lemon and bake in 400 F. oven
for 45 minutes, basting often.

*Elmhurst Farm, Caldwell, West Virginia*


## 249.  Baked Tomatoes

(Serves 4)

INGREDIENTS

DIRECTIONS

1 can tomatoes (quart
size)

Drain off juice.

1 cup toasted bread
½ cup sugar
1 teaspoon salt
3 tablespoons butter

Mix into tomato pulp.

¼ cup bread crumbs

Pour into buttered baking pan and cover
with bread crumbs.  Bake in 300 F. oven for
about 30 minutes.

*Valley View Inn, Hot Springs, Virginia*


## 250.  Fried Tomatoes

(Serves 6 to 8)

INGREDIENTS

DIRECTIONS

2 tablespoons butter

Place in pan and let melt.

6 to 8 tomatoes

Slice in thick slices.

½ cup flour
salt and pepper to
taste

Dust tomato slices and fry in the butter.

1 cup milk

Just before taking tomatoes out of pan, pour
milk over them and let them boil up.

*Mr. Fred Waring, New York City, N. Y.*

## 251. Blushing Cauliflower                    (Serves 6)

INGREDIENTS                DIRECTIONS

1 large cauliflower        Place cauliflower upside down in cold water.
1 tablespoon salt          Sprinkle with salt and let stand 30 minutes.
                           Place in boiling water and cook until just
                           tender. Time will vary from 10 to 20 min-
                           utes. Drain and place on platter and cover
                           with tomato sauce.

                                *TOMATO SAUCE*

2 tablespoons butter       Melt butter and cook onion.
1 tablespoon minced
  onion

1 tablespoon curry         Blend and add to butter and onion.
  powder
1 tablespoon cold water
¼ teaspoon salt

1 cup tomato soup          Add to above mixture and let simmer slow-
  (condensed)              ly for 10 minutes.
  few drops condiment
  sauce

*Valley View Inn, Hot Springs, Virginia*


## 252. Carrot Loaf                             (Serves 10)

INGREDIENTS                DIRECTIONS

3 bunches carrots          Cover carrots with water and cook until
                           tender. Cool slightly and put through a food
                           chopper or sieve.

8 eggs—beaten until        Add to carrot mixture.
  light

1 tablespoon sugar         Add to mixture.
1 teaspoon salt
2 tablespoons melted
  butter

1 tablespoon cornstarch    Make a paste and add to mixture.
  little cold water

1 quart cream              Stir in cream and mix well. Place in buttered
                           dish and set in pan of hot water to bake.
                           Bake in 350 F. oven for 45 minutes.

*Williamsburg Inn, Williamsburg, Virginia*

## 253. Carrot Mold
(Serves 6 to 8)

INGREDIENTS

DIRECTIONS

3 bunches carrots

Cook and mash.

½ cup cream
½ cup cracker crumbs
3 tablespoons butter
5 egg yolks—beaten
salt to taste

Add to carrots.

5 egg whites—beaten

Fold into mixture. Place in buttered ring mold form pan, setting pan in hot water for 30 minutes in 350 F. oven.

Turn mold out on flat plate and fill center with peas, arranging a row of mushrooms around the outside of the ring. (Fresh lima beans, green beans, spinach, or any other vegetable may be used in the center.) Cover center vegetable with cream sauce.

*Mrs. H. G. Beebe, Chicago, Illinois*

## 254. Eggplant Supreme
(Serves 6)

INGREDIENTS

DIRECTIONS

1 large egg plant

Peel and slice thin. Boil until tender in salted water. Drain well and mash.

2 tablespoons butter

Mix in with mashed eggplant.

1 large can clams

Mince the clams. Save juice.

1 cup cracker crumbs
3 tablespoons butter

Butter individual ramakins or a casserole. Put in a layer of eggplant, a layer of clams, a layer of cracker crumbs and dots of butter.

½ cup milk
clam juice
salt to taste

Blend together and pour over mixture and bake in 350 F. oven for 30 minutes.

*Kit Carson Guest House, Kingman, Arizona*

## 255. Kentucky Fried Corn

INGREDIENTS

DIRECTIONS

8 ears tender corn

Cut close to outer edge, cutting twice around ear. Scrape the ear to remove all the milk.

8 strips of bacon

Render to make ½ cup fresh bacon drippings. Have skillet very hot, add drippings and corn. Let the corn crust, but not burn. Stir constantly for five minutes, until thick.

1 cup of milk, cream or water
salt and pepper to taste

Add to corn, cover and let simmer for 15 minutes or until thick.

*Charlot C. Moore, Owensboro, Kentucky*

## 256. Scalloped Cucumbers and Onions (Serves 6)

INGREDIENTS

DIRECTIONS

2 cucumbers—8 inch
4 Spanish onions

Pare cucumbers and cut in thin slices. Cut onions in thin slices.

4 tablespoons flour
salt and pepper to taste

Alternate cucumbers and onions in baking dish. Sprinkle each layer with flour and salt and pepper.

2 cups ketchup or chili sauce

Pour over all.

2 tablespoons butter

Add. Bake in 350 F. oven 20 to 30 minutes, or until tender.

*Phelps and Phelps Colonial Restaurant, Chicago, Illinois*

## 257. Escalloped Eggplant (Serves 6)

**INGREDIENTS**

1 pint cooked eggplant

¼ cup white sauce
¼ cup grated cheese
1 teaspoon chopped onion
½ cup tomatoes

**DIRECTIONS**

Peel eggplant, cube and boil in salted water until tender. Drain.

Place layer of eggplant in bottom of baking dish, then alternate layers with sauce, cheese, onion and tomatoes. Have the top layer of eggplant. Cover with buttered bread crumbs and bake in 350 F. oven for 20 to 30 minutes.

*The Anna Maude, Oklahoma City, Oklahoma*

## 258. Garden Peas Francaise (Serves 10)

**INGREDIENTS**

1 head of lettuce
1 bunch green onions— chopped fine, using green and all
½ lb. butter
salt and pepper to taste
¼ cup sugar
1 cup consomme or broth
10 lbs. shelled peas

**DIRECTIONS**

Place in a heavy pot, cover and cook for about 20 minutes at 380 to 400 F. temperature.

*Villa Chartier, San Mateo, California*

## 259. Green Peas in Cream (Serves 4)

**INGREDIENTS**

2 lbs. fresh peas
1¼ cups boiling water

½ teaspoon salt, or to taste
1 teaspoon butter
6 tablespoons milk
6 tablespoons cream

**DIRECTIONS**

Peas must be fresh and crisp. Boil briskly until water has boiled away and peas are tender—about 10 minutes. Careful watching is necessary to prevent burning.

Add to peas and heat thoroughly, but do *not* allow to boil.

Success of this recipe is dependent on quality of peas and watchfulness in cooking.

*Ward G. Foster, Battle Creek, Michigan*

# 260.   Guinea Squash Pie

(Serves 6)

INGREDIENTS

DIRECTIONS

1 eggplant—medium
  size

Peel and boil eggplant in salted water.  When
done drain and mash.

3 slices toasted bread
  little milk

Soak bread until soft.  Mix with mashed
eggplant.

2 eggs—beaten slightly

Add to above mixture.

1 onion—chopped
3 tablespoons of melted
  butter
1 teaspoon salt
  pepper to taste

Blend in with mixture and put in buttered
casserole.

2 tablespoons cream

Put over top and bake in 350 F. oven for
25 minutes until a golden brown.

*The House by the Road, Ashburn, Georgia*


# 261.   Maryland Corn Pie

(Serves 6)

INGREDIENTS

DIRECTIONS

3 strips of bacon

Lay bacon in bottom and sides of baking dish

1 cup bread crumbs
1 cup tomatoes—sliced
½ cup green peppers—
  sliced
1 teaspoon salt
1 teaspoon sugar
2 tablespoons butter
2 cups uncooked corn

Fill up dish with these ingredients, alternating layers.  See that a lot of uncooked corn is
in the center.  The top layer to be of corn.
Top with bread crumbs, and dot with butter.
Bake in 350 F. oven until done.

Grated cheese may also be used on top if
desired.

*Mrs. W. B. Taylor, Bowling Green, Kentucky*

## 262. Mushrooms Chantilly

(Serves 5 or 6)

**INGREDIENTS**

**DIRECTIONS**

1 lb. fresh mushrooms

Wash carefully, but do not allow to soak in water. Cut in 1-inch chunks. Stems may also be used, if they are tender and not dry.

3 tablespoons butter
1 teaspoon salt

Saute slowly for 15 minutes, or until done. Stir occasionally to prevent sticking. Add salt about middle of cooking. Mushrooms vary in moisture so if there is too much juice when they are done, remove cover and cook until moisture has evaporated.

*SAUCE*

1 tablespoon butter
1½ tablespoons flour

Melt butter and add flour and cook until smooth.

1 cup milk
1 cup cream 25%

Bring to boiling point and add to base, stirring quickly to keep from lumping. Bring to boil once and remove from fire in 1 or 2 minutes.

Combine mushrooms and sauce and let come to boiling point. Set aside for 1 or 2 hours before serving.

6 tablespoons sherry wine

When ready to serve, re-heat and add sherry. Do not cook after the sherry is added.

May be served on sauteed or broiled egg-plant, broiled tomatoes, toasted English muffins, or as a sauce for steaks or chops.

*From One of America's Finest Restaurants.*


## 263. Mushroom Dish

(Serves 5 or 6)

**INGREDIENTS**

**DIRECTIONS**

6 green peppers

Cook in just enough water.

3 Bermuda onions

Cook in just enough water.

1 lb. fresh mushrooms

Saute in butter.

Put all in white sauce and cook long enough to get the flavor.

*Mrs. R. T. Cooksey, Madison, Wisconsin*

## 264. Stuffed Mushrooms

INGREDIENTS

DIRECTIONS

1 lb. large fresh
mushrooms

Remove stems, wash and dry on a towel.

1 cup cooked spinach—
drained
1 clove of garlic
1 hard boiled egg
4 tablespoons chopped
parsley
2 small cans anchovies
flat fillets
mushroom stems

Put all through a meat grinder.

salt and pepper to
taste

Add to mixture. Use sufficient amount of oil from anchovies to hold mixture together, using a few soft bread crumbs if mixture is too moist.

Stuff mushroom heads with this mixture, and place in buttered casserole, stuffed side up. Pour a heavy white sauce over them and sprinkle with grated cheese and bake in 450 F. oven for about 45 minutes.

*Mrs. R. T. Cooksey, Madison, Wisconsin*


## 265. Rice and Carrot Casserole Dish

INGREDIENTS

DIRECTIONS

1 cup ground raw
carrots
1 tablespoon grated
onion

Bring to a boil and drain.

1 cup grated cheese
1 egg—beaten
1 cup cooked rice
salt and pepper to
taste

Combine with carrot and onion. Place in buttered casserole and dot with butter. Place in pan of hot water and bake in 400 F. oven for 40 minutes.

Serve with sauce of creamed dried beef, peas or mushrooms, or any rich cream sauce.

*H. M. Carruth, Cleveland, Ohio*

## 266. Rice Ring (Serves 6)

INGREDIENTS

1 cup cooked rice
½ cup chopped parsley
4 egg yolks—beaten
4 egg whites—beaten
2 tablespoons melted butter
salt and pepper to taste

DIRECTIONS

Combine all and place in mold. Steam 30 minutes in 350 F. oven.

*Mrs. W. B. Taylor, Bowling Green, Kentucky*


## 267. Spinach au gratin (Serves 16)

INGREDIENTS

4 bunches of spinach

DIRECTIONS

Cook spinach for 5 minutes in hard boiling water to which a pinch of soda has been added. Drain.

2 tablespoons flour
a little cold water

Make a paste. Put spinach in pot on stove and add the paste.

salt and pepper to taste

Add to mixture.

1 cup grated cheese
2 tablespoons melted butter
4 hard boiled eggs—chopped fine

Add to mixture and stir well. Place in casserole.

½ cup grated cheese

Cover with cheese and bake in 350 F. oven for 25 minutes.

*Inn by the Sea, Pass Christian, Mississippi*


## 268. Spinach Ring (Serves 6)

INGREDIENTS

½ peck spinach

DIRECTIONS

Cook, drain, and chop fine.

2 eggs

Beat up together.

1 tablespoon cornstarch
1 tablespoon butter
1 tablespoon sugar
salt and pepper to taste

Mix in with eggs, and add to spinach.

1 cup whipped cream

Add to mixture and put in mold. Steam for 1 hour or more.

*Mrs. W. B. Taylor, Bowling Green, Kentucky*

## 269.  French Fried Potatoes

INGREDIENTS

DIRECTIONS

Use fancy Idaho potatoes.  Peel and soak in water overnight.  Cut in French fry shape.

Fry in pure leaf lard, moving them up from lower temperature lard to higher temperature lard for browning.

Salt the potatoes immediately after taking them from the last fry kettle.

*Phil Johnson, Northbrook, Illinois*


## 270.  Scalloped Potatoes                    (Serves 6)

INGREDIENTS

DIRECTIONS

1 can mushroom soup
1 cup of milk
   salt and pepper to
   taste

Mix soup and milk, heat and pour over scalloped potatoes.

*Mrs. A. Scott Hines, Bowling Green, Kentucky*


## 271.  Sweet Potato Surprise               (Makes 12)

INGREDIENTS

DIRECTIONS

2 cups sweet potatoes—
   mashed
3 tablespoons milk

Mix together so as to have a creamy mixture.

12 marshmallows

Roll potato around the marshmallow to make balls.

crushed corn flakes

Roll in crushed cornflakes and let stand for 30 minutes before cooking, so they can set.

Fry in hot deep fat.  Serve hot.

*Santa Fe Inn, Santa Fe, New Mexico*

## 272. American Rice

INGREDIENTS

2 cups dry rice

DIRECTIONS

Wash rice in colander until it is absolutely clear. (This may take 10 times.) Then wash 5 times more.

Have a large kettle filled with boiling water and add rice slowly so that the water never stops rolling. After all the rice is in, let boil 10 minutes. Then take out a kernel and bite. If the rice bites smooth, take off fire and put into a sieve. Set the pot back on the fire and put in the sieve with the rice in it and let dry in the hot air coming up from the pot.

Now, it is ready to serve.

*Dr. T. J. LeBlanc, Cincinnati, Ohio*


## 273. Cheese Loaf and Spaghetti

INGREDIENTS

3 eggs
1 cup milk

1 lb. cheese
1 can pimientos

1 cup bread crumbs
2 lemons—juice

salt and cayenne pepper to taste

1 pkg. spaghetti

DIRECTIONS

Beat eggs in milk.

Grind cheese and pimiento together.

Add to cheese and pimiento mixture. Add to milk and egg mixture.

Blend into mixture. Pour in greased baking dish and bake in 350 F. oven for 30 minutes.

Cook in salted water until done. Drain. Cover cheese loaf with spaghetti and pour over all a heavy cream sauce. Serve hot.

*Mrs. W. B. Taylor, Bowling Green, Kentucky*

## 274.  Chicken Liver and Rice Mold    (Serves 4)

INGREDIENTS | DIRECTIONS
---|---

1 lb. rice—cooked

Keep rice warm.

¾ lb. chicken livers
2 tablespoons butter

Saute slowly and when done cut in small pieces.

1 lb. fresh mushrooms—
cut in small pieces
2 tablespoons butter
1 onion—grated

Saute slowly.   Add to chicken livers and mix into rice.

2 tablespoons chopped
parsley

Add to mixture.

Put into buttered mold and place in pan of water.  Bake in 350 F. oven for 30 minutes, or until rice sets.  Center of mold can be filled with any vegetable.

*Mrs. Cora S. Aron, Chicago, Illinois*


## 275.  Macaroni Loaf

INGREDIENTS | DIRECTIONS
---|---

1 cup macaroni—broken

Blanch macaroni.

1 cup cream
½ cup butter

Heat.

3 eggs—beaten

Add to cream mixture.

1 cup soft bread crumbs
2 tablespoons chopped
parsley
1 teaspoon chopped
onion

Add to above mixture, and then stir in macaroni.

½ cup grated cheese
1 can (small) pimientos
1 teaspoon salt

Turn into a buttered mold and bake in 350 F. oven for 1 hour.

*SAUCE*

1 lb. fresh mushrooms
2 tablespoons butter

Saute mushrooms.

2 tablespoons butter
3 tablespoons flour
2 cups cream
salt to taste

Make a cream sauce.

Add mushrooms and pour over macaroni loaf

*Mrs. W. B. Taylor, Bowling Green, Kentucky*

## 276.  Rice Pilaff

INGREDIENTS

DIRECTIONS

¼ lb. butter—melted
2 cups dry rice

Braise well, until butter begins to bubble.

4 cups broth (chicken, lamb, or beef)
salt and pepper to taste

Add to the above.  Mix well and bake in 400 F. oven for 30 minutes.

Take out of the oven, mix well, and bake for another 10 minutes.

*Omar Khayyam's, San Francisco, California*


## 277.  Cheese Sauce

INGREDIENTS

DIRECTIONS

½ cup butter
3 tablespoons flour
½ tablespoon prepared mustard

Blend together in a sauce pan.

1½ cups milk

Add to the above and place on an asbestos mat, or slow electric current, stirring constantly.

½ lb. grated cheese
½ teaspoon salt
1 dash red pepper
1 dash paprika
1 tablespoon onion juice
1 tablespoon Worcestershire sauce

Add these ingredients, when the mixture is rather warm.  It will thicken gradually.  When thick, remove from the heat.

This is a perfect sauce for cauliflower.

1 tablespoon chopped pimiento

Added for au gratin potatoes.

½ cup tomatoes

Added for shrimp creole.

½ cup chopped mushrooms

Added for crab meat au gratin.

*Charlot C. Moore, Owensboro, Kentucky*

## 278. Cocktail Sauce for Shrimp (Serves 6)

INGREDIENTS

1 cup tomato catsup
2 tablespoons vinegar
a few drops Tabasco sauce
1 tablespoon horseradish
½ cup mayonnaise
1 teaspoon lemon juice
1 teaspoon Lea & Perrins

DIRECTIONS

Mix all these ingredients together and chill.

*Tarpon Inn, Port Aransas, Texas*

## 279. Cooked Dressing for Sandwich Spread

INGREDIENTS

1 cup sour—very thick—cream
⅓ cup milk
⅓ cup vinegar
3 egg yolks

DIRECTIONS

Put into a double boiler and mix together.

1 tablespoon flour
2½ tablespoons sugar
1 teaspoon salt
1 teaspoon dry mustard
½ teaspoon celery seed

Blend together and add to the above mixture. Let cook until it gets thick.

grated onion to taste

This may be added if desired.

This is a delicious dressing; can be used with odds and ends of baked ham leftovers, as a sandwich spread.

*Note: When the ground ham is placed in the refrigerator, it should be put in an uncovered container as it will quickly mold if covered. To be mixed with the dressing as needed.*

*Duncan Hines, Bowling Green, Kentucky*

## 280. Dressing for Avocado Cocktail

**INGREDIENTS**

3 tablespoons cream
2 tablespoons catsup
1 tablespoon lemon
   juice
6 drops Tabasco sauce
¼ teaspoon salt

½ cup mayonanise

**DIRECTIONS**

Blend together.

Mix well with above.

*This dressing may also be used on sea food cocktails.*

*Mrs. W. B. Taylor, Bowling Green, Kentucky*


## 281. Guacamole (Mexican Sandwich Spread)

**INGREDIENTS**

3 ripe tomatoes—peeled
1 onion
1 avocado pear
   salt and fresh ground
   pepper—to taste

**DIRECTIONS**

Grind and mix ingredients together to form a paste consistency.

These same ingredients may be used as a salad or for hor d'oeuvres, in which case, ingredients to be cut in pieces. Serve with melba or a thin toast.

*Mrs. Douglas Broadhurst, Bloomfield, New Jersey*


## 282. Hollandaise Sauce                    (Serves 6)

**INGREDIENTS**

3 tablespoons butter
½ teaspoon cornstarch
¼ teaspoon salt

2 egg yolks

2 tablespoons lemon
   juice
½ cup boiling water

**DIRECTIONS**

Cream together. Place in double boiler over warm (not boiling) water.

Add to mixture, one at a time.

Blend together and stir into mixture. Keep stirring. When the water in the bottom of double boiler starts to boil, cook 5 to 8 minutes. Let cook until consistency of boiled custard. This recipe will not curdle if directions are closely followed.

*Shadow Hill Tea Room, Hernando, Mississippi*

## 283.  Sauce for London Style Steak

(Serves 4)

INGREDIENTS

⅛ lb. butter
⅛ teaspoon black pepper
2 tablespoons mild
  prepared mustard

4 tablespoons Escoffier
  provencale sauce

¼ lemon—juice

DIRECTIONS

Melt butter, stir in pepper and mustard making a smooth paste.

Add to the above and stir.

Cut the steak in pieces to serve.  Add the juice from the steak to the sauce and let it come just to a boiling point.

Add to sauce and serve piping hot on plate, alongside the steak.

*Boston Oyster House, Chicago, Illinois*

## 284.  Tomato Sauce

(Serves 20)

INGREDIENTS

15 onions—sliced
½ cup butter
3 bottles chili sauce
3 chili sauce bottles of
  water

2 cups chicken soup

DIRECTIONS

Put in a heavy stew pan and simmer slowly for 1 hour, or longer if you want it thicker.

When nearly done add to mixture.

*Hartwell Farm, Lincoln, Massachusetts*

## 285.  White Sauce

INGREDIENTS

2 slices of onion
2 tablespoons butter

2 tablespoons flour

1 cup chicken broth or
  1 can may be used

1 small piece of celery—
  chopped
1 teaspoon parsley—
  chopped
  salt and pepper to
  taste

⅓ cup cream

DIRECTIONS

Saute onion in butter.

Blend with butter.

Stir in butter and flour mixture slowly and cook until thick.

Add to above mixture and let simmer 5 minutes.

Add to mixture and let boil up twice.  Strain and serve.

*Mrs. W. B. Taylor, Bowling Green, Kentucky*

# 286. White Sauce

INGREDIENTS

DIRECTIONS

1 cup milk
½ cup cream

Heat in double boiler.

2 tablespoons flour
2 tablespoons butter

Brown in pan and add a little milk or water to thicken into paste. Add to hot milk and cream in double boiler and cook until it thickens.

salt and pepper to taste

Add to sauce.

1 lb. fresh mushrooms—cut—or 1 large can may be used

If fresh mushrooms are used, saute them in butter before adding to sauce.

*Mrs. W. B. Taylor, Bowling Green, Kentucky*

# 287. Omelette                    (Serves 2)

INGREDIENTS

DIRECTIONS

2 tablespoons flour—mixed with a little water
2 tablespoons butter
salt and pepper to taste
1 cup milk

Blend and cook until quite thick. Allow to cool.

4 egg yolks—beaten

Add to the above and stir thoroughly.

4 egg whites—beaten

Fold into mixture.

Pour into hot well-buttered large frying pan and set over flame until the mixture sets. Place in 400 F. to 450 F. oven until straw tests done. Remove from oven and run spatula around the entire pan loosening omelette, then make an incision on opposite sides of the omelette and slide the spatula beneath one side and slide it over on other half at the same time sliding omelette out on dish.

Garnish with crisp bacon or parsley or Spanish sauce.

To make a larger omelette use 6 eggs and make a little more sauce.

*Mrs. Edmund H. Singmaster, Germantown, Pennsylvania*

## 288. Bogberry Omelet (Serves 1)

INGREDIENTS

DIRECTIONS

1 egg
3 egg yolks

Beat together for 1 minute.

½ teaspoon salt
2 tablespoons butter

Add salt and make thin unfolded omelet.

3 egg whites—beaten
2 tablespoons butter

Place in center of omelet and gently fold half over. Place in 200 F. oven and bake 8 minutes. (Too hot an oven will ruin the omelet.)

2 slices ham—broiled or fried
2 tablespoons Bogberry jelly

Garnish with ham and jelly and serve with sweet potatoes.

2 candied sweet potatoes

*Stirrup-Cup Castle, Oakdale, Long Island, New York*

## 289. Baked Eggs au gratin (Serves 1)

INGREDIENTS

DIRECTIONS

2 hard boiled eggs

Cut lengthwise and remove yolks. Mash the yolks.

2 fresh mushrooms—chopped
1 onion—chopped
2 tablespoons butter
salt and pepper to taste

Saute and let cool. Add to egg yolks. Fill the whites with this mixture. Place in casserole side by side and cover with a rich cream sauce. Some of the grated cheese to be added to the sauce.

½ lb. grated cheese

Sprinkle top with grated cheese and bake in 350 F. oven for 30 minutes.

*From a friend in Cincinnati, Ohio*

## 290.  Oeufs a la Russe (Eggs Russian Style) (Serves 4)

| INGREDIENTS | DIRECTIONS |
|---|---|
| 4 teaspoons caviar<br>4 artichoke hearts—<br>  cooked | Place caviar on artichoke hearts and heat in oven. |
| 4 poached eggs<br>Hollandaise sauce | Place poached egg on each artichoke heart and cover with Hollandaise sauce. |
| 4 slices of truffles | Tip with slice of truffle and sauce. |

*Antoines Restaurant, New Orleans, Louisiana*


## 291.  Scrambled Eggs and Mushrooms (Serves 1)

| INGREDIENTS | DIRECTIONS |
|---|---|
| 3 eggs—for each person<br>3 teaspoons hard butter | Whip eggs and put in small pieces of butter. |
| 3 strips of bacon | Cut in small pieces and fry crisp. Remove bacon and leave drippings in pan. |
| ½ small can mushrooms | Cook mushrooms in bacon drippings with cover on pan for 15 minutes. Remove cover and brown. |
| 2 teaspoons chopped onion<br>salt and pepper to taste | Mix with eggs and bacon and add to pan containing mushrooms. Stir while cooking. Do not cook too long, and eat at once. |

*Al Carder's Restaurant, Chicago, Illinois*


## 292.  Scrambled Eggs (Serves 3)

| INGREDIENTS | DIRECTIONS |
|---|---|
| 2 tablespoons butter<br>6 tablespoons cream | Melt butter in double boiler and add cream. |
| 6 eggs | Break in the eggs and when they become hot, start breaking them up. |
| salt and pepper to taste | Add seasoning and let cook until they are the consistency you like—either soft or hard scrambled. |

*McDonald Tea Room, Gallatin, Missouri*

## 293.   Sauce for Stuffed Eggs                    (12 eggs)

**INGREDIENTS**

1 can cream of tomato soup
1/4 lb. butter
1 can mushrooms and juice
1 can grated cheese
Worcestershire sauce to taste
Tabasco sauce to taste
salt and pepper to taste

12 stuffed eggs

**DIRECTIONS**

Heat in double boiler.   If too thick, add cream.

Pour over stuffed eggs.

*Inn by the Sea, Pass Christian, Mississippi*


## 294.   Baked Beans

**INGREDIENTS**

1 lb. dry small beans
10 dry white onions— sliced thin

1 1/4 cups brown sugar
4 tablespoons dry mustard
1/4 lb. bacon, cut in 2 inch pieces
1/2 bottle catsup

**DIRECTIONS**

Soak beans and sliced onion in cold water overnight.   Pour off water and add fresh water to cover and boil slowly until the beans are done.

Place alternate layers of beans, onions, sugar, mustard, bacon, and catsup spread over all until the casserole is filled.   Top generously with sugar and bake in 350 F. oven until a crusty brown.

Reheating almost improves the flavor.

*Mrs. Edmund H. Singmaster, Philadelphia, Pennsylvania*


## 295.   Quick Baked Beans                    (Serves 3)

**INGREDIENTS**

1 can baked beans
2 onions—chopped
2 tablespoons syrup
1 teaspoon dry mustard

1/2 lb. salt pork

**DIRECTIONS**

Thoroughly mix all ingredients and place in casserole.

Decorate top of casserole with salt pork and bake in 375 F. oven for about 20 minutes.

*Mrs. Cora S. Aron, Chicago, Illinois*

## 296. Frijoles Con Queso (Fried Beans with Cheese)

(Serves 5)

| INGREDIENTS | DIRECTIONS |
|---|---|
| ½ lb. pink beans<br>salt to taste | Wash and thoroughly clean the beans and boil until soft. |
| 3 tablespoons of lard | Fry beans in skillet, just as you would a piece of meat. The beans should be added to the |

hot lard spoonful by spoonful and add some of the water they were boiled in. Let simmer for 5 or 10 minutes. Then mash like potatoes until creamy and let simmer 5 or 6 minutes more. Put out the fire.

| | |
|---|---|
| 2 tablespoons of grated mild cheese | Add to mixture and serve. |

*If any frijoles are left, refry in a little lard and water.*
*This dish is to Mexicans what potatoes are to Americans.*

*El Cholo Spanish Cafe, Long Beach, California*


## 297. Spanish Beanpot

(Serves 4 to 6)

| INGREDIENTS | DIRECTIONS |
|---|---|
| 2 large cans red kidney beans | Put in beanpot. |
| 2 lbs. bacon fat<br>1 clove garlic—minced<br>1 pinch English thyme<br>1 pinch Rosemary<br>1 small bay leaf<br>2 whole cloves<br>1 teaspoon salt<br>2 teaspoons dry mustard<br>¼ teaspoon pepper<br>2 tablespoons cider vinegar<br>½ cup juice from pickled peaches, pears, or any fruit that is not too sweet | Mix all these ingredients and pour over the beans. Stir and bake in 275 F. oven for 1 hour. |
| 1 onion—sliced thin<br>4 slices of bacon | Put onion on top of beans and bacon on top of onion. Turn up oven to 400 F. and bake for 15 minutes longer. |
| ¼ cup strong black coffee | Pour over bacon and bake until the bacon is crisp. |
| 1 jigger brandy | Add the brandy and leave in hot oven until the brandy is thoroughly heated. Serve hot. |

*Madeleine H. Normand, Berkeley, California*

## 298.  Armenian Fritters

INGREDIENTS

2 eggs—beaten
1 pint milk
½ cup sugar
⅓ teaspoon salt

3 cups flour
2 tablespoons baking powder
1 tablespoon olive oil
1 teaspoon vanilla

bananas, apples, pineapple, pears, peaches, oranges, or any fresh fruit

DIRECTIONS

Mix well.

Add to mixture and beat until smooth.

Dip fruit in batter and fry in hot fat or oil until brown.

*Omar Khayyam's, San Francisco, California*


## 299.  Apple Dumplings                    (Serves 6)

INGREDIENTS

2 cups cake flour
2 teaspoons baking powder
½ teaspoon salt

⅔ cup shortening

⅓ cup of milk, or perhaps ½ cup

6 to 8 apples

½ teaspoon cinnamon
¼ teaspoon nutmeg
¾ cup brown sugar

6 tablespoons butter

½ cup brown sugar
½ cup granulated sugar
2 cups water
½ cup butter

DIRECTIONS

Mix and sift dry ingredients.

Work shortening in lightly with the tips of fingers.

Make hole in flour and add milk gradually while mixing lightly.  Knead lightly into a ball and roll into a rectangular-shaped piece of dough about ¼ inch thick and cut into six pieces.

Peel and slice apples and divide between six squares of dough.

Mix these ingredients and add to the apples.

Dot each square with a tablespoon of butter and bring up the corners of the dough and pinch together to make dumpling.

Make a syrup of these ingredients and while hot, set in dumplings and bake in 350 F. to 375 F. oven for 1 hour, or until apples are done.  Dumplings are best when made of quick cooking apples, though winter apples may be used if slowly cooked.

*Richards Treat Cafeteria, Minneapolis, Minnesota*

## 300. Potato Dumpling (Makes 6 dumplings 1½ inch)

**INGREDIENTS**

1 cup dry mashed potatoes
½ cup bread crumbs
1 teaspoon chopped onion
1 teaspoon chopped parsley
1 egg
salt and pepper to taste

**DIRECTIONS**

Mix and shape in small balls. Drop in boiling salted water and cook 7 to 10 minutes.

### LIVER DUMPLINGS

½ cup finely chopped calf or chicken livers

Add to above mixture for a nice luncheon entree.

*Phelps & Phelps Colonial Restaurant, Chicago, Illinois*

## 301. Spiced Iced Coffee (Serves 6)

**INGREDIENTS**

Make coffee as usual. only a little stronger

1 stick cinnamon
2 whole cloves
6 teaspoons sugar
cream to taste
½ cup whipping cream

**DIRECTIONS**

Strain and cool.

Add cinnamon, cloves, sugar, and cream. Strain while filling glasses. Serve with a lot of cracked ice and top with dab of whipped cream.

*Crestmont Hotel, Eagles Mere, Pennsylvania*

## 302. Cafe Diablo (Serves 6)

**INGREDIENTS**

6 demi-tasses of coffee

6 whole cloves
½ stick cinnamon
2 bay leaves
1 orange peel
¼ cup whole roasted coffee beans
6 lumps of sugar
2 oz. Jamaica rum
4 oz. brandy

**DIRECTIONS**

Make in Silex or drip.

Mix in deep chafing dish and set liquor afire. Keep stirring with a ladle and very slowly add the coffee, stirring all the time to keep the flame burning.

Serve in demi-tasse cups, using ladle and a spoon to remove coffee beans.

*Boston Oyster House, Chicago, Illinois*

## 303. Apricot Rickey (1 drink)

INGREDIENTS

DIRECTIONS

½ lime
2 oz. apricot syrup

Add ice and seltzer water.

*Stevens Hotel, Chicago, Illinois*


## 304. Fruit Punch (1 gallon)

INGREDIENTS

DIRECTIONS

1 quart lemon juice
⅔ quart orange juice
1 pint pineapple juice
1 pint white grape juice
grenadine to taste
fruits in season

Mix all together and add a little seltzer water.

*Stevens Hotel, Chicago, Illinois*


## 305. Grenadine Rickey (1 drink)

INGREDIENTS

DIRECTIONS

½ lime
2 oz. grenadine syrup

Add ice and seltzer water.

*Stevens Hotel, Chicago, Illinois*


## 306. Loganberry Punch (1 gallon)

INGREDIENTS

DIRECTIONS

1 quart lemon juice
1 quart loganberry juice
⅔ quart orange juice
loganberry syrup to
taste
fruit in season

Mix all together and add a little seltzer water.

*Stevens Hotel, Chicago, Illinois*


## 307. Loganberry Rickey (1 drink)

INGREDIENTS

DIRECTIONS

½ lime
2 oz. loganberry syrup

Add ice and seltzer water.

*Stevens Hotel, Chicago, Illinois*

# 308. Duncan Hines Mint Julep (Serves 1)

INGREDIENTS

DIRECTIONS

2 jiggers Bourbon
whiskey
1 tablespoon whole
mint leaves

Let stand for about 2 hours, then remove the
mint leaves.

1½ teaspoons simple
syrup (more if you
like it sweeter)

Simple syrup is made by slowly cooking cane
sugar and water until it becomes syrupy. If
you prefer, honey may be used instead to
sweeten liquor.

Rim the julep cups with a piece of lime or
lemon, dip in powered sugar and set in refrigerator to frost.

6 or 8 mint leaves
cracked ice (not
shaved)

Crush mint in bottom of julep cups and fill
half full with cracked ice. Pour in the sweetened liquor and fill the cup with ice.

3 sprigs of mint leaves
½ teaspoon powdered
sugar

Sprinkle mint sprigs with powdered sugar for
decoration and serve.

*Duncan Hines, Bowling Green, Kentucky*

# 309. Hot Brick (1 drink)

INGREDIENTS

DIRECTIONS

1 teaspoon butter
1 teaspoon sugar
1½ jiggers boiling water

Put in glass and stir until butter is melted
and sugar dissolved.

1½ jiggers Bourbon
whiskey

Add and stir. Drink while hot.

*Mr. A. Scott Hines, Bowling Green, Kentucky*

# 310. Omar's Delight (Makes 1 drink)

INGREDIENTS

DIRECTIONS

1 jigger Southern
Comfort
½ lime—juice
⅓ oz. lemon juice
1 dash curacoa
½ teaspoon sugar

Frappe thoroughly.

*Omar Khayyam's, San Francisco, California*

## 311.   Fireman's Shirt          (Serves 2)

INGREDIENTS                    DIRECTIONS

½ canned peach                 Blend until you are satisfied.
 1 jigger lemon juice
¼ jigger peach juice

 2 or more jiggers gin         Mix with above and put in electric mixer.
   lots of cracked ice         Fun in making this drink is to vary contents
   some charged water          until you get what you want.

*Warren R. Gibbs, Berkeley, California*


## 312.   Gibbs' Favorite

INGREDIENTS                    DIRECTIONS

½ large canned peach           Frappe thoroughly.
 1 lime juice
 1 jigger Southern
   Comfort
½ teaspoon sugar
 2 glasses cracked ice

*W. R. Gibbs, Berkeley, California*


## 313.   A Favorite "Old Fashioned" Cocktail

INGREDIENTS                    DIRECTIONS

 1 lump sugar                  Muddle in a glass until dissolved.
 1 teaspoon cold water
 1 dash Angostura
   Bitters

 1 cube of ice                 Put into the glass.

1½ jiggers Southern            Pour over the ice and stir.
   Comfort

½ slice orange                 Put over side of glass, add cherry and serve.
 1 maraschino cherry

*Duncan Hines, Bowling Green, Kentucky*

# 314.  Wild Moose Milk—A Different Eggnog

(Makes about 6 quarts)

INGREDIENTS

DIRECTIONS

1 quart milk
1 quart cream
6 cups sugar

While liquid is slowly heating, add the sugar and stir until dissolved.

9 nutmegs whole— cracked
2 or 3 sticks cinnamon

Put in bag and add to mixture.

3 dozen strictly fresh eggs

Break 6 eggs at a time and remove egg germ. (The germ is apt to make the mixture stringy, if not removed.)   Beat eggs until thoroughly mixed, but do not beat until foamy.   Do not try to beat all the eggs at one time.   Put beaten eggs in a pitcher and add drop by drop to hot milk mixture, stirring all the while.   The addition of the eggs is very important and cannot be hurried or the mixture will become lumpy.   This process will take about three or four hours and when done the mixture will be a smooth custard.   Remove from fire and allow to cool.

1 bottle rum (1/5 size)
2 bottles brandy (1/5 size)

Stir into mixture and put in bottles.   Cork tightly and keep in cool place.   Keeps indefinitely.

When serving, the eggnog can be thinned with milk, cream, or water.   Can be served either hot or cold.

*John F. Heck, New Freedom, Pennsylvania*


# 315.  Aunt Delia's Piccallili

INGREDIENTS

DIRECTIONS

1 peck green tomatoes
1 cup salt

Chop tomatoes, sprinkle with salt and let stand overnight.   In the morning, drain.

3 quarts vinegar
5 cups sugar

Let come to a boil.

1 tablespoon mustard seed
2 tablespoons cassia
1 tablespoon ground cloves
½ tablespoon allspice
2 large sticks horseradish

Add to hot vinegar and boil for 5 minutes.

3 peppers
3 onions

Chop and add to tomatoes.   Mix in with vinegar and boil slowly for 1 hour.

*Pecketts on Sugar Hill, Franconia, New Hampshire*

## 316. Beet Relish

INGREDIENTS | DIRECTIONS

1 teaspoon salt
¼ teaspoon pepper
¾ cup sugar
½ tablespoon flour

Mix thoroughly.

½ cup vinegar

Add to dry ingredients and cook in double boiler until thick.

4 cups cooked beets—diced small
2 cups celery—chopped
½ cup onion—chopped

Mix thoroughly with above and cool.

*The Old House, Lexington, Massachusetts*


## 317. Brandied Peaches

INGREDIENTS | DIRECTIONS

4 lbs. sugar
2 cups water

Make syrup of sugar and water.

8 lbs. peaches

Peel peaches and put in cold water to prevent discoloring. Add a few at a time to the syrup and let simmer until tender. Do not let get too soft, or they will break. Place on plate to cool.

1 pint or more brandy

Take syrup from fire and add 1 pint of brandy to every quart of syrup and stir until cool. Put cooled peaches in jars (sterilized) and pour syrup over them. Seal jars tight.

*Mrs. Thomas A. Hannon, Chicago, Illinois*


## 318. Cranberry Relish          (About 16 servings)

INGREDIENTS | DIRECTIONS

1 quart raw cranberries

Grind through meat chopper.

2 oranges—pulp and juice
1 orange rind—chopped
1 lemon—juice
1⅔ cups sugar

Mix with cranberries and let stand 24 hours before using. Will keep in jar in ice box for weeks.

*Althea, Lewisburg, West Virginia*

# 319. Dill Pickles

INGREDIENTS

DIRECTIONS

18 cups water
2 cups salt—do not use iodized salt

Make a brine and boil for 5 minutes. Cool.

6 cups vinegar

To every 3 cups of brine, add 1 cup of vinegar.

cucumbers
dill to taste

Pack cucumbers and dill into jars, pour on the brine and seal.

If cucumbers are not absolutely fresh, soak in ice water for 2 hours.

*Mrs. Voijt F. Mashek, Chicago, Illinois*


# 320. Gooseberry Jam          (Makes 13 pints)

INGREDIENTS

DIRECTIONS

8 lbs. gooseberries
7 lbs. sugar

Snip blossom end from the gooseberries and mix with the sugar. Let stand for 12 hours.

Boil in an open kettle for 20 minutes after it comes to a good rolling boil. Stir constantly. Skim if necessary.

Pour into sterilized jars and seal tightly.

*Hartwell Farm, Lincoln, Massachusetts*


# 321. Orange Marmalade

INGREDIENTS

DIRECTIONS

12 oranges—not too ripe, but firm
6 lemons

Remove ends and slice. Take out seeds. Measure fruit and add half as much water. Let stand overnight. Then boil fruit in same water until tender. Remove from fire and weigh.

sugar

To each pound of fruit and liquid, add 1 lb. sugar.

Boil until it jellies, which should be about 20 minutes.

*Mission Inn, Riverside, California*

# 322.   End of the Garden Pickles   (About seven quarts)

INGREDIENTS

DIRECTIONS

(These vegetables to be fresh)

1 quart green tomatoes 1 inch cubes
1 pint sweet pepper mangoes—red—cut 1 inch cubes
1 pint sweet pepper mangoes—green—cut in 1 inch cubes
1 quart cucumbers 1 inch long—whole

Wash and clean.  Place in separate vessels, cover with water and salt to taste and let stand overnight.  Then drain.  Pour boiling water over them again and drain.

1 quart green beans— break in ½ inch pieces
1 quart lima beans
1 quart small white onions—whole
1 quart white onions— chopped
1 quart cabbage— chopped coarse
1 quart carrots—½ inch cubes

Cook separately in salted water.  *Do not cook until too tender.*  Thoroughly drain.

1 quart celery—½ inch cubes
1 quart muskmelon—½ inch cubes

Place in colander and pour boiling water over them.

Put all ingredients in kettle and stir with wooden spoon.

6 cups sugar
2 teaspoons celery seed
1 quart cider vinegar
2 tablespoons white mustard seed

Add to vegetables.

1 cup flour
1 teaspoon tumeric
1 pint vinegar

Make a thickening, and add when mixture is heated.  Cook until the mixture thickens.

*Roy C. Neuhaus, Evanston, Illinois*

## 323.  Peach Conserve

**INGREDIENTS**

12 peaches—peeled and sliced
1 lb. seedless grapes—cut in half
1 lb. red plums, stoned and cut fine
2 oranges, unpeeled—cut fine
3½ lbs. sugar
12 kernels of peach pits—chopped

**DIRECTIONS**

Mix all ingredients and cook slowly over low heat until thick.  Seal in jelly glasses.

*Marjorie Mills, Boston, Massachusetts*


## 324.  Pottsfield Pickle          (Makes 4 quarts)

**INGREDIENTS**

3 pints green tomatoes
3 pints ripe tomatoes
1 quart onions
3 red peppers
3 green peppers
1 bunch celery
1 cabbage
½ cup salt

3 pints vinegar
3 pints sugar
½ cup white mustard seed
½ teaspoon cinnamon
1 teaspoon ground cloves
¼ cup mixed spices (tied in bag)

**DIRECTIONS**

Chop coarsely or put through a meat grinder. Add salt and let stand overnight.  Drain well.

Add these ingredients to drained vegetables and cook slowly for 1 hour.

Bottle in jars and seal tightly.

*Sawyer Tavern, Keene, New Hampshire*

## 325. Sawyer Tavern Relish

INGREDIENTS

DIRECTIONS

1 tablespoon flour
1 tablespoon sugar

Combine.

1 egg—beaten

Add to above and mix well.

½ cup milk

Stir in milk gradually and cook in double boiler 7 to 10 minutes, or until thick.

2 tablespoons vinegar
1 tablespoon butter—melted

Remove from fire and stir in vinegar and butter.

1 pkg. cream cheese

Pour hot dressing over cheese.

2 hard cooked eggs—chopped
1 tablespoon onion—chopped
1 green pepper—chopped
1 pimiento—chopped
speck red pepper
salt and pepper to taste

Add these ingredients to mixture.

This relish can be used to stuff tomatoes for a salad, as a sandwich filling, or served as a relish.

*Sawyer Tavern, Keene, New Hampshire*

## 326. Rhubarb Conserve          (Makes 5 or 6 pints)

INGREDIENTS

DIRECTIONS

6 cups diced rhubarb
1 cup raisins—chopped
1 cup crushed canned pineapple
1 cup orange juice
½ cup grated orange rind
1 lemon—juice and grated rind
4 cups sugar
1 teaspoon salt

Mix all together and let come to a boil. Cook slowly for 4 to 5 hours until it becomes very thick.

1 cup broken nut meats

Add to mixture about 30 minutes before it is done.

Seal in hot jars.

*Old Hundred, Southbury, Vermont*

## 327. Sliced Cucumber Pickles

INGREDIENTS

2 quarts boiling water
1 cup salt
1 peck cucumbers—
 sliced

DIRECTIONS

Pour mixture of boiling water and salt over the cucumbers and let stand 3 days. Pour off the brine and let come to boiling point. Pour over cucumbers again and let stand 3 days. Pour off brine again and let come to boiling point and pour over cucumbers and let stand 3 days. This makes a total of 9 days in brine.

1 gallon boiling water
1 tablespoon alum

Pour this mixture over cucumbers and let stand 6 hours. Drain and place cucumbers in stone jar.

4 quarts vinegar
6 lbs. brown sugar
4 sticks cinnamon
2 tablespoons allspice
2 tablespoons whole cloves
4 tablespoons white mustard seed
4 tablespoons celery seed
4 tablespoons mixed spices
6 pieces horseradish
6 cloves of garlic

Heat all ingredients and pour over cucumbers, repeat for 9 consecutive days.

*Virginia Duvall Greenhow, Frankfort, Kentucky*

## 328. Spiced Blackberries

INGREDIENTS

4 cups brown sugar
2 cups vinegar

DIRECTIONS

Boil together for 5 minutes.

5 lbs. blackberries

Add to the syrup.

2 sticks cinnamon
1 tablespoon whole cloves
½ tablespoon whole allspice

Tie spices in a bag and let mixture simmer for 20 to 25 minutes, until it has cooked down thick.

Remove spice bag and pour berries into clean sterilized jars. Seal at once.

*Pauline Johnson, Berkeley, California*

# 329. Strawberry Jam

| INGREDIENTS | DIRECTIONS |
|---|---|
| 1 quart strawberries | Pour boiling water over berries to cover and let stand 3 minutes. Drain. |
| 1 cup sugar | Add to berries and boil 5 minutes. Remove from fire. |
| 2 cups sugar | Add to berries and boil 20 minutes. Remove and pour the berries in earthenware crock |

and let stand 24 hours stirring occasionally. Pour into glasses and paraffin.

*Headley Inn, Zanesville, Ohio*


# 330. Strawberry Preserves

| INGREDIENTS | DIRECTIONS |
|---|---|
| 1 pint water<br>9 cups sugar | Boil until sugar is well melted. |
| 2 quarts strawberries | Add to syrup and boil for 17 to 20 minutes. Do not stir, just shake the kettle and skim. |

When done remove from fire and shake constantly until cold. The shaking is the secret of success, as it causes the berries to absorb the syrup and to remain plump and whole. When cold, seal in jars.

Never make more than 2 quarts of berries at one time.

*Mrs. Voijt Frank Mashek, Chicago, Illinois*


# 331. Tomato Relish

| INGREDIENTS | DIRECTIONS |
|---|---|
| 1 peck tomatoes (not too ripe—do not peel)<br>6 onions<br>6 red peppers (remove seeds) | Grind through meat chopper. Squeeze and remove what juice you can from the tomatoes. |
| 1 quart vinegar<br>3 lbs. brown sugar<br>2 tablespoons white mustard seed<br>1 tablespoon cinnamon<br>⅞ cup salt | Boil and let cool. Mix with above ingredients and put in jars and seal. |

*Mrs. Voijt Frank Mashek, Chicago, Illinois*

# 332.   Tutti-Frutti

INGREDIENTS

DIRECTIONS

1 quart brandy

Place brandy in large stone crook with a cover to it.

1 quart strawberries
1 quart pineapple
  (peeled and sliced)
1 quart cherries
1 quart currants
1 quart raspberries
1 quart gooseberries
1 quart apricots (peeled
  and sliced)
1 quart peaches (peeled
  and sliced)
32 cups of sugar

Add fruit as they come in season with an equal amount of sugar to the brandy. Stir mixture every day until the last of the fruit has been added.

Cover well and store in a cool place. Will keep indefinitely.

To be served as sauce for ice cream, puddings, or with meat course.

*Mrs. Thomas A. Hannon, Chicago, Illinois*


# 333.   De Luxe Salted Peanuts

INGREDIENTS

DIRECTIONS

1 lb. raw peanuts in
shell

Shell and scald with boiling water. Remove red skin and let dry thoroughly. (May take overnight.) Put in 350 F. hot oven and keep shaking until browned.

1 teaspoon butter

Glaze nuts with butter. Do not use too much butter in glazing, but just enough so

1 teaspoon salt

that the salt will stick. Sift on the salt.

*Mrs. Edmund H. Singmaster, Philadelphia, Pennsylvania*

*At least 25% of good cooking is visual.*

# 334.  Apricot and Peach Turn-Overs

(Makes 8)

INGREDIENTS

DIRECTIONS

½ lb. dried apricots
½ lb. dried peaches
1½ cups water

Cook until the consistency of mush.

1 cup sugar
⅓ cup butter
½ grated nutmeg
1 tablespoon flour

Add to the above.

Cut pastry into saucer-shaped rounds and put in ample filling.  Fold over and seal the edges.  With a fork, prick the top so the steam can escape.

Place on a baking sheet and bake in 350 F. oven for 15 minutes, then lower to 300 F. and bake until a golden brown and the crust seems crisp on both sides.

*Duncan Hines, Bowling Green, Kentucky*

# 335.  Aunt Susan's Clabber Cake

(Serves 16)

INGREDIENTS

DIRECTIONS

½ lb. butter
2 cups sugar

Cream together.

2 eggs—beaten

Add to the above.

2 cups clabber
3½ cups flour—cake
⅔ tablespoon soda
3⅓ tablespoons cocoa

Add to the mixture.  Stir well.

Bake in a 350 F. oven for 45 minutes.

*The Anna Maude, Oklahoma City, Oklahoma*

# 336. Blackberry Jam Cake

(Serves 15 to 20)

INGREDIENTS

DIRECTIONS

1 cup butter
2 cups sugar

Cream butter and gradually add the sugar.

1 cup buttermilk
1 teaspoon soda
4 egg yolks—beaten

Dissolve soda in buttermilk and add eggs, then alternate this mixture with blended mixture of:

3 cups flour
2 teaspoons cinnamon
1 teaspoon nutmeg
1 teaspoon cloves
1 teaspoon allspice

Blend mixture, sifted together, and alternately add to creamed butter and sugar.

1 teaspoon vanilla
1 cup blackberry jam

Add to mixture.

4 egg whites—beaten

Fold into mixture. Bake in large pan with tube in center at 300 F. for 15 minutes, then at 350 F. for 15 minutes and then 360 F. for 30 minutes. Test with wire tester before removing from oven.

*Headley Inn, Zanesville, Ohio*


# 337. Bohemian Cake

INGREDIENTS

DIRECTIONS

¾ cup milk—scalded
1 cup poppy seed

Pour over poppy seed and let stand overnight.

2 cups sifted flour
3 teaspoons baking powder
½ teaspoon salt

Sift together three times.

½ cup shortening
1½ cups sugar

Cream together and add the poppy seed mixture.

¾ cup milk

Add to creamed mixture, alternately with the dry ingredients.

4 egg whites—beaten

Fold into mixture and pour into well-greased layer pans, or a spring form pan and bake in 350 F. oven for 45 minutes.

Cover with your favorite chocolate frosting and serve with whipped cream.

*Suk's Tavern, King City, California*

## 338. Burnt Sugar Cake

| INGREDIENTS | DIRECTIONS |
|---|---|
| 1 cup butter<br>3 cups sugar | Cream together. |
| 2 cups milk<br>4 tablespoons brown sugar syrup | Mix these ingredients together. |
| 6 cups flour | Add to butter alternately with the milk mixture. |
| 4 eggs | Add to mixture, 1 at a time, stirring well each time. |
| 11/12 tablespoon baking powder<br>2 teaspoons vanilla | Add to mixture. Bake in 350 F. oven for 45 minutes. |

*The Anna Maude, Oklahoma City, Oklahoma*

## 339. Cherry Sponge                    (Serves 4)

| INGREDIENTS | DIRECTIONS |
|---|---|
| 3 egg yolks—beaten<br>3 tablespoons sugar | Beat into yolks until smooth and lemon colored. |
| 3 egg whites—beaten | Put on top of yolks. |
| 3 teaspoons flour | Sift over the egg whites. Fold in lightly. |
| | Put mixture in an 8-inch square or round cake pan 1½ inches deep. |
| 1½ cups sweet black cherries | Wash and dry. Drop into the egg batter so they are distributed evenly over the surface. |
| | Bake in 320 F. oven for 10 to 15 minutes until lightly browned. Let cool, slice, and then dust with powdered sugar and serve. |

*Mrs. A. E. R. Peterka, Cleveland, Ohio*

# 340. Chocolate Cake

(Makes one pan, 8x13 inches)

## INGREDIENTS

## DIRECTIONS

4 tablespoons butter
2 cups sugar
2 egg yolks

Cream together.

1½ cups flour
2 teaspoons baking powder
1 pinch of salt

Sift these ingredients together three times. Add to the above mixture.

4 squares bitter chocolate

Melt and add to mixture.

1½ cups milk
2 teaspoons vanilla
1 cup nuts—chopped

Gradually add to mixture.

2 egg whites—beaten

Fold into mixture and pour into greased and floured baking pan. Bake in 300 F. for 60 to 70 minutes. (The dough will seem thin, but it is all right.) Leave the cake in the pan and put icing on it.

### ICING

3 cups powdered sugar —sifted
1 tablespoon cocoa
5 tablespoons melted butter
½ cup cream

Mix these ingredients and beat until it is thoroughly creamed, then spread on the cake.

*H. M. Carruth, Cleveland, Ohio*

*Your hostess may say "It is perfectly all right" when you are thirty minutes late for dinner but it comes not from the heart.*

# 341.  Chocolate Fudge Upside Down Cake

INGREDIENTS

DIRECTIONS

¾ cup sugar
1 tablespoon butter

Cream together.

½ cup milk

Add to the above and stir.

1 cup flour
¼ teaspoon salt
1 teaspoon baking
powder
1½ tablespoons  cocoa

Sift together and add to mixture.  Stir well
and put in 9-inch buttered pan.

½ cup walnuts—chopped

Sprinkle with nuts.

½ cup sugar
½ cup brown sugar
¼ cup cocoa

Mix well together and spread over top.

1¼ cups boiling water

Pour over the top of all.  Bake in 350 F.
oven for 30 minutes.

*Cathryn's Portland, Oregon*


# 342.  Date and Nut Confection

INGREDIENTS

DIRECTIONS

1 cup pitted dates—
diced
½ cup black walnuts—
broken
1 cup granulated sugar
1 teaspoon baking
powder
pinch of salt

Thoroughly mix together.

4 egg whites—beaten

Fold into above mixture and bake in buttered tin in 300 F. oven for 20 minutes.

When cool, serve with whipped cream.

*Gurney's Inn, Montauk, Long Island, New York*

# 343. Dark Fruit Cake

(Makes about 12 lbs.)

INGREDIENTS

DIRECTIONS

¾ lb. butter
2 cups sugar

Cream together.

8 egg yolks

Add to above.

4 cups flour
1 tablespoon cinnamon
½ teaspoon cloves
1 teaspoon nutmeg

Hold out a little flour to mix later with fruits. Sift dry ingredients together and add to mixture.

3 teaspoons soda
½ cup cold water

Mix together and stir into mixture.

8 egg whites—beaten

Fold into mixture.

2 lbs. moist raisins
2 lbs. currants
¼ lb. candied orange peel—cut
¼ lb. candied lemon peel—cut
½ lb. citron—cut
¼ lb. candied cherries—cut
¼ lb. candied pineapple —cut
¼ lb. candied fruit mix
¾ lb. walnuts—broken
½ lb. pecans—broken

Mix fruits and nuts with the flour held out. Stir into mixture.

1 cup sherry wine

Stir in the wine.

Bake in 350 F. oven for about 75 minutes. then turn oven down to 300 F. and bake another 75 minutes, or about 3 hours. Be careful and not bake too fast, or it will burn.

*Mrs. M. E. Houser, Des Plaines, Illinois*

*When a dish is "cute" I have my suspicions.*

# 344.  Devils Food Cake

INGREDIENTS

DIRECTIONS

2 cups sugar
2 tablespoons
  shortening
3 eggs
1/4 teaspoon salt
2 teaspoons vanilla

Cream together.

1 cup milk

Add to the above.

3 cups cake flour
2 teaspoons of soda

Sift together and add to mixture.

4 squares chocolate
1 cup milk

Cook until dissolved then add to the batter.

Bake in 325 F. to 350 F. oven for 1 hour.

*Buckley Tea Room, Walworth, Wisconsin*


# 345.  Allenwood Fudge Cake

INGREDIENTS

DIRECTIONS

2 squares bitter
  chocolate
1/2 cup milk

Melt chocolate in the milk, stirring constantly, until like a custard.

1 tablespoon butter
1 egg yolk

Add to the above mixture.   Let cool.

1 cup sugar
1/2 cup milk
1 teaspoon vanilla

Add to mixture.

1 3/4 cups flour
1 teaspoon soda

Blend these together and add to mixture.

Pour into greased and floured tins and bake in 375 F. oven for about 10 minutes, then lower the temperature to about 350 F. and bake for another 25 or 30 minutes.

*Allenwood, Burlington, Vermont*

## 346.   8-Yoke Fudge Cake

(Serves 16)

INGREDIENTS

DIRECTIONS

2 cups sugar—sifted
¾ cup butter

Cream until light and fine grained.

8 egg yolks—beaten

Add to above.

2 squares bitter
chocolate

Melt and add to mixture.

2½ cups flour
¾ teaspoon soda
2 teaspoons baking
powder
¼ teaspoon salt

Sift dry ingredients four times.   Alternately
add to above mixture with:

1¼ cups buttermilk

To be added alternately with dry ingredients.

1 teaspoon vanilla

Add to mixture.

8 egg whites—beaten

Fold into mixture and pour in three layer
pans.   Bake in 350 F. oven for 30 minutes.

*Violet Bray Berry, Berkeley, California*


## 347.   Fudge Squares

(Serves 6)

INGREDIENTS

DIRECTIONS

½ cup butter
2 ozs. bitter chocolate
or
⅓ cup cocoa plus
1 tablespoon butter

Melt butter and chocolate.

½ cup cake flour
1¼ cups sugar
⅛ teaspoon salt

Sift twice and add to above.

3 eggs—beaten
1 teaspoon vanilla
¾ cup chopped nuts
(walnuts or pecans)

Mix into mixture and bake in 350 F. to 375
F. oven for 25 minutes.

*Phelps and Phelps Colonial Restaurant, Chicago, Illinois*

# 348. Gateau St. Honore'

INGREDIENTS

DIRECTIONS

1 pie shell

Make a pie crust shell about 18 inches in diameter with a rim about 1½ inches high.

### PASTRY PUFFS

¼ lb. butter
½ pint milk
2 tablespoons sugar
1 pinch of salt

Bring to a boil, stirring constantly. Remove from the fire.

1 cup flour

Add to mixture.

4 eggs

Stir into the mixture and put into a pastry bag. Make small mounds on a baking sheet and bake in 350 oven for about 20 minutes. Then place them around the edge on the rim of pie shell and in the center in the form of a flower.

¾ cup sugar
½ cup pistachio nuts

Melt sugar and glaze the puffs. Sprinkle nuts over the melted sugar.

### PASTRY CREAM

1 cup sugar
1 cup flour
½ teaspoon salt
1 pint milk—hot

Mix all together and heat.

6 eggs

Add to mixture and stir constantly until it thickens. Cool.

½ pint whipping cream
—whipped
vanilla and curacoa—
to taste

Add to mixture and fill pastry shell.

*Monument Inn, Bennington, Vermont*

*The hardest dish to sidestep is something "I made especially for you."*

## 349. Grandmothers Chocolate Cake (Serves 8 to 12)

INGREDIENTS

2 tablespoons butter
2 cups sugar
2 eggs—beaten
1½ cups milk
½ cup cream
2½ cups cake flour (sift and measure between sifts)
2 teaspoons soda
4 oz. bitter chocolate
½ teaspoon salt
2 teaspoons vanilla

DIRECTIONS

Put in bowl in order given and beat with wire whip, or put into machine at low speed. Do not over-mix, especially in warm weather. Milk and cream should be room temperature.

Pour into two cake tins that have been greased and dusted with flour. Level the mix by tapping the bottom of the pan on a level table.

Bake in 348 F. oven for 20 to 25 minutes, or until cake springs to the touch.

### CHOCOLATE FUDGE FROSTING

½ cup melted butter
½ cup cream
3 lbs. powdered sugar
2 oz. bitter chocolate
1 egg (this fluffs up the frosting and gives better volume)

Whip up in order given and spread between layers, on top and sides of cake, after it has cooled.

*Phelps and Phelps Colonial Restaurant, Chicago, Illinois*

## 350. Oat Cakes

INGREDIENTS

3 cups Quaker Oats

½ cup corn meal
½ cup butter or shortening
1 cup flour
3 teaspoons sugar
1 teaspoon salt
½ teaspoon soda
1 teaspoon baking powder

⅔ cup hot water

DIRECTIONS

Put through a meat chopper.

Add to the above and mix thoroughly.

Add to mixture.

Roll thin, cut and bake in 350 F. oven for 30 to 40 minutes.

*Mrs. David Donald, Pittsfield, Massachusetts*

# 351. Ice Box Cake

| INGREDIENTS | DIRECTIONS |
|---|---|
| 3 tablespoons butter<br>¾ cup powdered sugar | Cream together. |
| 3 egg yolks—beaten | Add to above. |
| ½ cup strong cold coffee | Add to mixture, drop by drop, constantly stirring. |
| 2 tablespoons brandy | Add to mixture, droy by drop, constantly stirring. |
| 3 egg whites—beaten | Fold into mixture. |
| 24 lady fingers—dipped in sherry wine | Line the bottom and sides of a mold. Cover with half the mixture. |
| 1 pint whipping cream —whipped | Cover the mixture and on top of the cream, put the rest of the mixture. Top that with nuts and fruit. |
| candied orange peel<br>candied lemon peel<br>candied cherries<br>pistachio nuts | Cover mold and pack in ice and salt for 3 hours. Serve with chocolate sauce. |

## CHOCOLATE SAUCE

| | |
|---|---|
| 1½ cups sugar<br>½ cup water | Boil together for five minutes. |
| 4 squares bitter chocolate | Melt over hot water and when the syrup is partially cooled add to above. |
| ½ teaspoon vanilla | Add to mixture, and put in double boiler to keep warm until ready to serve. |
| ¼ cup cream | Add to sauce just before serving. |

*Mrs. C. H. Welch, Mitchell Field, Long Island, New York*

*Whipped cream has its place. Ripe olives have theirs. Pickles are nice. But let's be reasonable.*

## 352. Macaroon Charlotte Russe with Butterscotch Sauce

(Serves 15)

| INGREDIENTS | DIRECTIONS |
|---|---|
| 1 pint whipping cream —40% whipped<br>½ tablespoon almond extract<br>½ tablespoon vanilla | Blend into whipped cream. |
| ½ lb. macaroons— crumbled | Fold into the above. |
| 5 ozs. egg whites— beaten<br>1/16 teaspoon salt | Beat together and fold into mixture. |
| sponge cake may be used in place of lady fingers if cut the same shape. | Arrange lady fingers as desired in glasses in which the Charlotte Russe is to be served and fill with creamy mixture. Place in refrigerator until ready to serve. Serve with butterscotch sauce. |

### BUTTERSCOTCH SAUCE

| | |
|---|---|
| 1 lb. brown sugar<br>1 can evaporated milk (14½ oz. size)<br>4 tablespoons butter | Put all ingredients in a double boiler and cook until it coats the spoon. |

This sauce is very necessary as its richness complements the Charlotte Russe.

*Jane Davis Restaurant, New York City, N. Y.*

*Every good cook should have an oven and stove thermometer and test the stove front and back, top and bottom, to see that the oven heats evenly.*

# 353.  Lane Cake

| INGREDIENTS | DIRECTIONS |
|---|---|
| 1 cup butter<br>2 cups sugar | Cream together until very light. |
| 3¼ cups flour<br>3 teaspoons baking powder | Sift together 4 times. |
| 1 cup milk | Add to creamed mixture, alternately with the flour. |
| 8 egg whites—beaten<br>1 tablespoon vanilla | Add vanilla to egg whites and fold into mixture.  Bake in two layers or one tube pan in 350 F. oven for 40 to 50 minutes, or until cake springs to touch.  Test with straw. |

*LANE CAKE FILLING*

| | |
|---|---|
| ½ cup butter<br>1 cup sugar | Cream together. |
| 7 egg yolks—beaten | Add egg yolks and cook in double boiler, stirring constantly until smooth and thick.  Remove from fire. |
| 1 cup raisins—chopped<br>1 cup nut meats—chopped<br>1 teaspoon vanilla | Add to mixture while it is still hot. |
| 1 wineglass brandy | Add to mixture and spread over the cake. |

*This is a rich but distinguished cake.*

Dr. T. J. LeBlanc, Cincinnati, Ohio

# 354. Orange Cake

INGREDIENTS | DIRECTIONS

1 tablespoon grated orange rind
¼ cup orange juice—strained

Put rind in juice and let stand while making the cake. Save the pulp for filling.

¾ cup butter
1½ cups sugar

Cream butter, add sugar gradually and cream thoroughly.

3 egg yolks—beaten

Add to mixture.

2¼ cups cake flour
3½ teaspoons baking powder
½ teaspoon salt

Sift together and add to mixture, alternately with:

¾ cup water

Add water to the orange juice and add alternately with the sifted ingredients.

3 egg whites—beaten

Fold into mixture. Pour into well greased layer pans and bake in 350 F. oven for 30 to 35 minutes.

### CLEAR ORANGE FILLING

2 tablespoons butter
4 tablespoons cornstarch
2 tablespoons grated orange rind
1 cup sugar
½ teaspoon salt
1½ teaspoons lemon juice
1 cup orange juice and pulp

Mix all together and spread between layers and on top and sides of cake.

*Francis Fowler, St. Louis, Missouri*

# 355. Orange Tea Cakes

INGREDIENTS | DIRECTIONS

1¼ cups almonds—chopped about the size of rice kernals
½ lb. orange peel—chopped
2 cups cake flour
2½ cups powdered sugar

Place in a mixing bowl. Blend all ingredients.

1 pint heavy cream
a few drops orange coloring

Mix into ingredients and put into pastry bag with a No. 5 or No. 6 tube.

Lay out in little mounds on a heavily greased pan. Bake in 340 F. oven. Do not allow to get brown, as they should retain their orange color. Ice the bottoms with temperate sweet chocolate.

*Chalet Suzanne, Lake Wales, Florida*

## 356. Poppy Seed Cake

| INGREDIENTS | DIRECTIONS |
|---|---|
| 1 cup poppy seed<br>¾ cup scalding milk | Soak overnight. |
| 1½ cups sugar<br>¾ cup butter | Cream together. |
| ¾ cup cold milk<br>3 teaspoons baking<br>powder<br>3 cups flour | Sift together three times and blend all ingredients together. |
| 4 egg whites—beaten | Fold into mixture. |
|  | Bake in three layers 9-inch cake tins in 350 F oven for 25 to 30 minutes. |

### FILLING

| | |
|---|---|
| 2 egg yolks<br>1 lemon—juice<br>1 cup sugar<br>2 tablespoons cornstarch<br>1 cup scalding water<br>1 pinch salt | Cook until thick and fill each layer with lemon filling. |
| ½ cup chopped nuts | Sprinkle with nuts and top with icing. |

### ICING

| | |
|---|---|
| 2 egg whites<br>1 cup sugar<br>4 tablespoons cold water | Mix together and cook in double boiler until thick. Beat constantly with an egg beater while cooking. Put on cake while hot. |

*Angus McDonald's Lake Breeze Resort, Three Lakes, Wisconsin*

## 357.   Prune Layer Cake

INGREDIENTS

DIRECTIONS

⅓ cup butter
1⅛ cups sugar

Cream together.

2 egg yolks—beaten
1 egg—beaten
5 tablespoons milk

Add to above mixture, and stir well.

1⅛ cups stewed prunes—
   chopped
1 teaspoon lemon juice

Add to mixture and stir.

1½ cups flour
½ teaspoon baking
   soda

Sift together and add to mixture and stir
lightly.

1½ teaspoons baking
   powder
¼ teaspoon salt
1 teaspoon cinnamon
1 teaspoon cloves
1 teaspoon nutmeg

Put in two cake tins and bake in 375 F. oven
for 25 to 30 minutes, lowering temperature
gradually until it is properly baked.

Cover with boiled white icing.  This delicious
cake remains fresh for some time.

*Mrs. Alonzo Newton Benn, Chicago, Illinois*


## 358.   Sour Cream Chocolate Cake

INGREDIENTS

DIRECTIONS

2 eggs—beaten
1 cup sugar

Mix together.

½ cup sour cream
½ cup sour milk
1 teaspoon soda
1 teaspoon vanilla

Mix together and add to the above.

1½ cups flour
¼ teaspoon salt

Sift together and add a little at a time to the
mixture, stirring well.

1 square chocolate

Melt and add to mixture.  Beat well, and pour
into two 9-inch layer cake pans.  Bake in a
350 F. oven until a straw comes out clean or
it is springy to the touch.

*The Rice Ranch, Hammett, Idaho*

## 359.  Spice Layer Cake with Seafoam Frosting

(Makes 2 layers, 8-inch or 9-inch pans)

| INGREDIENTS | DIRECTIONS |
|---|---|
| 1/3 cup butter | Cream thoroughly. |
| 1 cup sugar | Add to butter gradually and cream until light and fluffy. |
| 1 egg<br>1 egg yolk | Add to butter mixture and beat well. |
| 2 tablespoons molasses | Add and mix thoroughly. |
| 3/4 cup milk | Add to cream mixture alternately with dry ingredients a little at a time, beating after each addition until smooth. |
| 2 cups flour—sift once and measure<br>2 teaspoons baking powder<br>1/4 teaspoon salt<br>1/4 teaspoon ginger<br>1/4 teaspoon mace<br>1/4 teaspoon allspice<br>1/4 teaspoon nutmeg<br>3/4 teaspoon cloves<br>3/4 teaspoon cinnamon | Sift together three times.  Add alternately with milk.<br><br>Bake in greased layer pans in 375 F. oven for about 25 minutes, or until done. |

*SEAFOAM FROSTING*

| | |
|---|---|
| 1½ cups brown sugar<br>½ cup water<br>1/4 teaspoon cream of tartar | Boil until it spins a thread. |
| 4 egg whites—beaten | Slowly add the above syrup to eggs, beating all the time. |

*Williamsburg Inn, Williamsburg, Virginia*

# 360. Sponge Cake

| INGREDIENTS | DIRECTIONS |
|---|---|
| 12 egg yolks—beaten<br>½ cup sugar | Beat in sugar with egg yolks, a teaspoon at a time. |
| 1 lemon—juice<br>1 cup flour—sift 4 times | Alternately add juice and flour to above until it becomes a smooth dough. |
| 12 egg whites—beaten<br>1 pinch of salt<br>½ cup sugar | Slowly beat sugar and salt into the egg whites. Cut into the batter. |
| 1 teaspoon vanilla | Add to mixture. |

Cut a paper the size of the pan to be used and place on the bottom. Bake in an ungreased pan in 325 F. oven for 1 hour and 15 minutes, using an angel food cake pan for baking.

(This delicious sponge cake we use to make our famous "Ice-Cream Sandwiches." One slice of cake, coffee ice cream with butterscotch sauce. It's "Yummy.")

*The Smith's Rainbows End, Valatie, New York*


# 361. Sponge Cup Cakes     (Makes 24 cakes)

| INGREDIENTS | DIRECTIONS |
|---|---|
| 1 cup sugar<br>2 eggs | Beat together. |
| 1 cup flour<br>1 teaspoon baking powder | Sift together and add to above. Beat well. |
| 1 teaspoon lemon extract | Add to above. |
| ½ cup boiling milk | Pour into greased cups or greased Gem pans and bake in 375 F. oven for 20 to 30 minutes. Cover with icing. |

### CHOCOLATE ICING

| | |
|---|---|
| 2 tablespoons hot coffee<br>1 cup powdered sugar<br>2 tablespoons butter<br>2 teaspoons cocoa | Mix thoroughly and spread on cakes before removing them from the containers. |

*Mrs. Otto J. Sieplein, Miami, Florida*

## 362. Sultana Cake (Makes 3 loaves)

| INGREDIENTS | DIRECTIONS |
|---|---|
| 1 lb. butter<br>1 lb. sugar | Cream together. |
| 8 eggs | Mix into the above. |
| 1½ cups milk | Slowly add to the mixture. |
| 8 cups cake flour<br>3 teaspoons baking powder | Sift and add to mixture. |
| 1 lb. sultana raisins<br>½ lb. orange peel<br>orange and lemon to flavor | Add to mixture.<br><br>Bake in 350 F. oven for 1 hour, or more. |

*Mrs. David Donald, Pittsfield, Massachusetts*

## 363. Sunshine Cake

| INGREDIENTS | DIRECTIONS |
|---|---|
| 1 cup flour<br>1 teaspoon baking powder<br>1½ teaspoons cornstarch<br>½ teaspoon salt | Sift three times. |
| 4 egg yolks—beaten<br>½ cup sugar | Beat together. |
| 2 tablespoons flour<br>3 tablespoons cold water<br>1 teaspoon vanilla | Add to egg mixture and stir into dry ingredients. |
| 4 egg whites—beaten<br>½ cup sugar | Fold into mixture and pour into angel food pan. Bake in 300 F. oven for 45 minutes, then in 350 F. oven for 15 minutes. Invert pan until the cake is cold. |

*Sawyer Tavern, Keene, New Hampshire*

# 364. Torte

INGREDIENTS

DIRECTIONS

6 egg whites—beaten
  stiff
1½ cups sugar

Beat into the egg whites adding sugar gradually.

1½ teaspoons vinegar
1 teaspoon vanilla
¼ teaspoon almond
  extract

Add to the above. Drop on brown paper placed on cookie sheet, using a spoon that holds about 2 tablespoonsful. After they are placed on the sheet, make an indentation with the back of the spoon. Bake in 300 F. oven for 45 minutes, then raise the temperature to 325 F. for 15 minutes. Remove from paper, using a spatula. If they stick, re-heat the sheet and try again.

1 quart strawberries
½ cup sugar—superfine

Do not crush the berries. Add sugar and fill each indentation with berries.

1 cup whipping cream—
  whipped

Top each meringue with whipped cream.

If berries are not used peaches may be upturned and filled with a soft custard.

*CUSTARD*

3 cups milk and ½ cup
  sugar, or
2 cups milk and 1 cup
  peach juice and ⅓
  cup sugar

Scald.

6 egg yolks—beaten
⅓ cup sugar
1 teaspoon salt
⅛ teaspoon almond
  flavoring

Put in double boiler and pour hot milk over. Cook slowly until mixture coats a spoon. Stir while cooking. Cool.

*Valley Green Lodge, Orick, California*

## 365.  Whipped Sour Cream Cake    (Makes 3 layers)

INGREDIENTS | DIRECTIONS
---|---

2 egg yolks
½ cup cold water — Whip together.

1 cup sour cream—whipped — Add to the above.

2 cups cake flour—sifted once
1¼ cups sugar
1 teaspoon soda
3 teaspoons baking powder
½ teaspoon salt — Sift together three times.  Add to the mixture.

1 teaspoon vanilla — Add to mixture.

2 egg whites—beaten — Fold into mixture.

Pour into 3 well greased and floured cake pans.  Bake in 350 F to 375 F. oven for 20 to 25 minutes.  Cool and frost.

### FROSTING

Make a 7-minute frosting, spreading it on real thick and use a whole fresh grated cocoanut between layers and on top.

*Ruggles' Manor, Ridgeway, Wisconsin*


## 366.  White Cake

INGREDIENTS | DIRECTIONS
---|---

1 cup butter
2½ cups sugar — Cream together.

1 cup milk
3 cups flour — Add alternately with the flour, a little at the time and keep batter very smooth.

1 cup flour
4 teaspoons baking powder — Sift together and add to the mixture.

1 teaspoon bitter almond — Add to mixture.

10 egg whites—beaten — Fold into mixture.

Bake in 4 layers in 350 F. to 400 F. oven for 20 to 35 minutes.

*The Chaya, Petersburg, Virginia*

# 367. White Cake

INGREDIENTS

½ cup butter
1¾ cups sugar—sifted

4 egg yolks

3 cups flour

1 cup milk

½ teaspoon salt
3 teaspoons baking
powder

2 egg whites—beaten

2 teaspoons lemon
extract

DIRECTIONS

Cream together.

Add to above.

Sift three times. Add just a little to mixture.

Add alternately with flour. Hold out 1 cup of flour.

Add to final cup of flour and stir into mixture.

Fold into mixture.

Add to mixture.

Pour into two 9-inch cake tins and bake in 350 F. oven for 35 minutes.

Fill and frost when cold.

*Marshlands Inn, Sackville, N. B., Canada*


# 368. Boiled Icing

INGREDIENTS

4 cups sugar
1⅓ cups water

4 egg whites—beaten
¼ teaspoon cream of
tartar
1 teaspoon vanilla

DIRECTIONS

Cook with a cover on the pan until the sugar is thoroughly dissolved and begins to boil. Remove the cover and boil up to 238 F.

Pour the syrup in slow stream over the egg whites, beating continuously until thick and creamy.

*The Chaya, Petersburg, Virginia*

## 369.  Betty Cass' Brown Sugar Cookies

**INGREDIENTS**

2 cups brown sugar
½ cup shortening
½ cup butter
2 eggs
2 cups flour
1 teaspoon baking
   powder
2 teaspoons vanilla
1 cup chopped pecans

**DIRECTIONS**

Mix in the order given and drop by a teaspoon on buttered baking sheet. Press half pecan in each one. Bake in 350 F. oven for 15 minutes.

*Mrs. R. T. Cooksey, Madison, Wisconsin*

## 370.  Jackson Cookies

**INGREDIENTS**

1 cup butter
1½ cups sugar

**DIRECTIONS**

Cream together.

3 eggs—beaten

Add to above.

¼ cup milk
½ teaspoon soda
1 pinch of salt

Stir into mixture.

2 cups flour
1 teaspoon nutmeg
1 teaspoon cinnamon

Blend and add to mixture

1½ cups raisins
½ cup chopped pecans
   or walnuts

Mix well and stir into mixture.

Spread on shallow well-greased pans and bake in 375 F. oven for 10 to 12 minutes. Remove from oven and cut into squares.

*Mrs. Mathew Jackson, Chicago, Illinois*

## 371. Brownies

(Makes 1 pan 12x12 inches)

INGREDIENTS | DIRECTIONS

2 squares bitter chocolate
½ cup butter

Melt together over hot water.

1 cup sugar
2 eggs

Add to above and beat thoroughly.

1 teaspoon vanilla
1 cup nuts—broken

Add to mixture.

¾ cup flour
½ teaspoon baking powder
½ teaspoon salt

Sift together and add to mixture. Stir in thoroughly.

Pour into a greased and floured baking pan and bake in 350 F. oven for 25 to 30 minutes. When cool, cut into squares. These may be iced before serving.

*The Old House, Lexington, Massachusetts*


## 372. Brownies

INGREDIENTS | DIRECTIONS

1 cup sugar
½ cup melted butter
2 squares chocolate
2 eggs
1 teaspoon salt

Blend together.

½ cup flour
1 cup walnuts—chopped

Stir into mixture.

1 teaspoon vanilla

Add to mixture. Pour into a shallow tin and bake in 350 F. oven for 20 minutes.

*The Krebs, Skaneateles, New York*


## 373. Butter Cookies

INGREDIENTS | DIRECTIONS

6 cups flour
1 cup sugar
1 pinch of salt

Sift together.

1 lb. butter

Cream and add to the above.

Roll out thin, cut and bake in 375 F. oven 10 to 12 minutes.

*Mr. Francis E. Fowler, Jr., St. Louis, Missouri*

## 374.  Cherry Nut Cookies

(60 cookies)

INGREDIENTS

DIRECTIONS

1⅓ cups butter
  2 cups brown sugar

Cream together.

  4 cups flour
  1 teaspoon soda
  1 teaspoon salt

Sift these ingredients and mix and add a portion to the above.

  3 eggs

Add the eggs and continue mixing. (If a power mixer is used, the bowl and beater should be scraped down thoroughly.) Add nearly all the remaining flour.

1⅓ cups chopped nuts
    (pecans or walnuts)
1⅓ cups candied cherries
1⅓ cups dates

Dredge with the remaining flour and add to the mixture.

Drop cookies on a greased and floured sheet pan and bake about 15 minutes in 375-400 F. oven until brown.

This dough can be kept in refrigerator and baked as needed.

To facilitate dishing and keep the cookies uniform, a No. 40 ice-cream scoop may be used.

*Richards Treat Cafeteria, Minneapolis, Minnesota*


## 375.  Date and Nut Cakes

(Makes 20 cakes)

INGREDIENTS

DIRECTIONS

  1 package of dates, cut
    fine
  2 cups boiling water

Pour water over dates.

  2 tablespoons butter
  1 teaspoon soda

Add to dates.

  2 eggs—beaten
  2 cups sugar
  3 cups flour

Blend these ingredients and add to above mixture.  Stir well.

  1 cup walnuts—broken
  1 teaspoon vanilla

Fold into mixture and pour into greased muffin tins.  Bake in 350 F. oven for 30 minutes.

*Irelands Rustic Lodge, Gold Beach, Oregon*

## 376.   Chocolate Drop Cookies with Icing

(Makes 36 cookies)

INGREDIENTS | DIRECTIONS
--- | ---
½ cup butter<br>1 cup brown sugar | Cream together.
1 egg—beaten | Add to the above.
2 cups flour—sifted before measuring<br>½ teaspoon salt<br>½ teaspoon soda | Sift dry ingredients and alternately add to the mixture, with
¾ cup milk | Add to mixture, alternately with flour.
2 squares melted chocolate<br>½ cup nuts—chopped<br>1 teaspoon vanilla | Blend together and add to the mixture. Drop on greased pans and bake in 400 F. oven for 15 minutes.

### ICING

INGREDIENTS | DIRECTIONS
--- | ---
2 tablespoons melted butter<br>2 squares chocolate—melted<br>4 tablespoons cream<br>2 cups powdered sugar | Melt together.
1 pinch salt | Blend all these ingredients.
1 egg—beaten | Fold into mixture and spread on cakes.

*Grace Peterson Adams, Chicago, Illinois*


## 377.   French Cookies (Tulles)

(Makes 40)

INGREDIENTS | DIRECTIONS
--- | ---
4 egg whites—beaten<br>1 cup sugar<br>1 teaspoon vanilla | Beat together.
1 cup almonds | Blanch and grind fine. Add to the above.
¼ lb. butter—melted | Add to mixture.
1 cup flour | Stir in slowly. Drop by teaspoonful on a buttered pan. Bake in 350 F. oven for 15 minutes. Let cool on rack before putting them away.

*Villa LaFayette, Mountain View, California*

## 378.  Ginger Crisps

INGREDIENTS | DIRECTIONS

1 cup shortening

Cream until soft and waxy.

1 cup granulated sugar

Add gradually to above and cream until fluffy.

2 eggs—beaten

Stir in eggs.

½ cup molasses

Add molasses and beat until well blended.

4½ cups flour
3 teaspoons ginger
1 teaspoon soda
1 teaspoon salt

Sift together and add to the mixture.  Bake in 325 F. oven until the cookies are brown.

*Miss Katharine L. Little, Chicago, Illinois*


## 379.  Little Apple Cakes

INGREDIENTS | DIRECTIONS

½ cup lard
1 cup sugar

Cream together.

1 egg—beaten

Add to above.

2 cups flour
½ teaspoon soda
1 teaspoon salt
2 teaspoons baking
  powder
½ teaspoon cinnamon
½ teaspoon cloves
½ teaspoon nutmeg
½ cup nuts—broken
1 cup chopped apples
1 teaspoon vanilla
½ cup cold coffee

Stir all these ingredients into mixture, in their order, and bake in Gem tins in 350 F. oven for about 40 minutes.

*Mrs. Mathew Jackson, Chicago, Illinois*

## 380.   Maple Ice Box Cookies          (Makes 48 cookies)

INGREDIENTS                    DIRECTIONS

½ cup butter                   Cream together.
1 cup maple sugar

2 eggs                         Stir into above.

1 cup cake flour               Sift dry ingredients and add to mixture. This
2 teaspoons cream of           should make a stiff dough. Form into roll and
   tartar                      place in ice box overnight.  Slice thin and
1 teaspoon soda                bake in 350 F. oven for 10 to 12 minutes.
½ teaspoon salt

*Maple Cabin, Johnsbury, Vermont*


## 381.   Nut Macaroons          (Makes 6 or 7 dozen)

INGREDIENTS                    DIRECTIONS

2 cups powdered sugar          Blend these ingredients.
   —sifted
½ cup flour—sifted
1 teaspoon baking
   powder

5 egg whites                   Do not beat.  Stir into the dry ingredients.

1 lb. chopped nuts             Add the nuts.  Drop from a teaspoon onto a
                               greased cookie sheet.  Bake in 300 F. oven
                               until set.  Do not bake too hard, or they won't
                               be good.

*McDonald Tea Room, Gallatin, Missouri*


## 382.   Orange Cookies          (Makes 36)

INGREDIENTS                    DIRECTIONS

½ cup butter                   Mix in the order given.  More flour may be
1 cup sugar                    required.
1 orange rind—grated
1 egg—beaten                   Roll into a sheet, cut in mounds, dredge with
½ cup orange juice             sugar and bake in 350 F. oven for about
3 cups flour                   20 minutes, or until brown.
4 teaspoons baking
   powder                      This recipe makes soft cookies, if crisp ones
                               are desired, use ¼ cup of orange juice.

*Villa LaFayette, Mountain View, California*

## 383. Pecan Drop Cakes

(Makes about 30)

INGREDIENTS

DIRECTIONS

1 egg white—beaten
1 cup brown sugar

Beat sugar into egg whites.

1 cup pecans (whole or broken)

Add nuts and drop from a spoon onto a buttered cookie sheet.

Bake in 300 F. oven for 40 minutes. Should be a light brown when done.

*Mrs. George P. Meier, Indianapolis, Indiana*


## 384. Pecan Puffs

INGREDIENTS

DIRECTIONS

½ cup butter

Beat until soft.

2 tablespoons sugar
1 teaspoon vanilla

Blend until creamy.

1 cup pecans—put through a meat grinder
1 cup cake flour—sifted

Mix these together and stir into the butter mixture.

Roll into small balls and place on greased baking sheet. Bake in 300 F. oven for 45 minutes. While hot, roll in powdered sugar and when cooled, roll again in powdered sugar.

*Mrs. Louie M. Weathers, Elkton, Kentucky*


## 385. Quick Brown Sugar Drop Cookies

INGREDIENTS

DIRECTIONS

1 lb. butter
2 cups brown sugar
2 egg yolks
3½ cups flour
2 teaspoons vanilla

Mix all together.

1 cup chopped nuts

Drop mixture from the end of a teaspoon into the nuts.

Place on baking sheet and bake in 400 F. to 450 F. oven.

*The Hearthstone, Winnetka, Illinois*

## 386.  Vanilla Cookies

| INGREDIENTS | DIRECTIONS |
|---|---|
| 8 teaspoons butter<br>8 teaspoons lard | Cream together. |
| 1 cup sugar<br>1 egg, well beaten<br>¼ cup milk<br>2 cups flour<br>2 teaspoons baking<br>   powder<br>½ teaspoon salt | Add to cream mixture.<br><br>Sift dry ingredients and add to mixture. |
| 2 teaspoons vanilla | Add to mixture.  Roll thin and cut with cutter.<br><br>Bake in 375 F. oven for 6 minutes. |

*Pecketts on Sugar Hill, Franconia, New Hampshire*


## 387.  Angel Food Pie

| INGREDIENTS | DIRECTIONS |
|---|---|
| 4 egg whites—beaten<br>¾ cup sugar | Gradually fold in sugar with beaten egg whites. |
| ½ teaspoon baking<br>   powder<br>1 teaspoon vanilla | Add to egg whites and pile into *uncooked* pie shell and bake in 300 F. oven for 45 minutes, until a light brown. Allow to cool. |
| 1 cup whipping cream—<br>   whipped<br>¼ cup chopped nuts | Spread with whipped cream and top with nuts. Strawberries may be used instead of nuts. |

*Garden Grill, Daytona Beach, Florida*

## 388. Apple Pie

**INGREDIENTS**

1 cup of sugar
2 tablespoons flour
½ grated nutmeg
½ cup orange juice
⅓ cup melted butter

    winesap apples cut
    into fine blocks
    (enough to fill a pie
    pan)

**DIRECTIONS**

Mix all together.

Add to the above and thoroughly mix together.

Butter a pie pan heavily before putting in the pastry, then fill with the apple mixture and make strips for the top.

Bake in 400 F. oven for 15 minutes, then reduce oven to 250 F. and bake for 35 to 40 minutes.

*Duncan Hines, Bowling Green, Kentucky*


## 389. Apple Pie

(9-inch pie)

**INGREDIENTS**

**DIRECTIONS**

### CRUST

1½ cups flour
1 teaspoon salt

Sift 2 times.

¾ cup shortening

Cut in shortening.

½ cup cold water

Add water and roll on floured board.

### FILLING

10 to 12 apples—sliced
1 cup sugar
1 tablespoon butter
1 teaspoon ground cinnamon
1 teaspoon nutmeg

Line pie plate with pastry and fill with these ingredients.

Put on top crust and place a wet cloth around the edges (about 1-inch wide) to prevent pie from cooking over. Bake in 425 F. oven for 15 minutes, then turn oven down to 325 F. and bake 30 minutes.

*Verti Musgrove, Chicago, Illinois*

## 390. Blueberry Pie

INGREDIENTS

1 quart blueberries
1¼ cups sugar
4 tablespoons melted butter

DIRECTIONS

Bake in a double crust. Do not add thickening agents. Serve runny in a fairly deep dish.

*Lowell Inn, Stillwater, Minnesota*

## 391. Blueberry Pie

INGREDIENTS

1 quart blueberries

DIRECTIONS

Fill baked pie shell with blueberries and cook the ones that are left with:

1 cup water
1 cup sugar
1 tablespoon cornstarch
pinch of salt

Cook with berries and strain over raw berries in the pie shell. Put in refrigerator until it sets.

Spread with whipped cream and serve.

*Parker Homestead, Santuit, Massachusetts*

## 392. Banana Butterscotch Pie

INGREDIENTS

1 cup brown sugar
4 tablespoons flour

DIRECTIONS

Mix and put in top of double boiler.

1 cup milk

Add slowly to the above. Stir constantly until it thickens.

2 egg yolks—beaten

Add to mixture and cook 3 minutes longer. Remove from the fire.

4 tablespoons butter

Add to mixture. Cool.

½ teaspoon vanilla

Add to mixture.

1 pie shell baked
2 large bananas

Line pie shell with bananas and pour over the mixture.

2 egg whites—beaten
2 tablespoons sugar

Make a meringue and cover pie

or

1 cup whipped cream

Cover pie with whipped cream.

*Dorothy Brehmer Klassen, Fond du Lac, Wisconsin*

## 393.  Chess Pie

INGREDIENTS | DIRECTIONS
--- | ---
1 cup butter | Cream butter.
2 cups sugar<br>1 tablespoon cornstarch | Blend together and add to butter and cream again.
4 eggs | Add eggs, one at a time, and beat well after each one is added.  Put mixture in pie crust and bake in 350 F. oven until it sets or about 35 minutes.

*Inn by the Sea, Pass Christian, Mississippi*


## 394.  Chess Pie                                 (Serves 8)

INGREDIENTS | DIRECTIONS
--- | ---
½ cup butter | Cream.
1 cup sugar | Add to butter and cream again.
2 eggs—beaten lightly | Blend into mixture.
1 pinch of nutmeg<br>1 pinch of salt<br>a little vanilla | Add to mixture and bake in pastry-lined muffin molds in a 350 F. oven for 15 minutes.

*The Meiringen, Roanoke, Virginia*


## 395.  Cocoanut Cream Pie              (Three 10-inch pies)

INGREDIENTS | DIRECTIONS
--- | ---
3 cups milk<br>2 cups sugar<br>1 pinch salt | Boil.
6 egg yolks—beaten<br>2 tablespoons cornstarch<br>3 tablspoons milk | Mix blended cornstarch and milk with eggs and add to hot milk.  Cook.
2½ tablespoons gelatin<br>6 tablespoons milk | Dissolve gelatin in milk and pour hot mixture over it.  Let set until firm.  Put in electric beater and beat well.
1½ cups cocoanut<br>3 cups whipped cream<br>1 tablespoon vanilla | Add to mixture and place in refrigerator for 10 minutes.
6 egg whites—beaten | Fold in stiff egg whites and pour in pastry shells and cover with whipped cream and sprinkle with cocoanut.

*El Encanto Tea Shop, Los Angeles, California*

## 396.  Continental Cream Pie

INGREDIENTS

DIRECTIONS

14 ginger cookies or graham crackers

Roll fine.

5 tablespoons butter—melted

Mix well with above.  Pat evenly in a 9-inch pan.  Bake in 300 F. oven for 1 minute.

### FILLING

4 egg yolks—beaten
2 cups milk—scalded

Slowly add milk to eggs.

1½ tablespoons cornstarch
½ cup sugar

Combine and stir into the above. Cook over simmering water for 20 minutes, or until custard generously coats spoon.  Remove from the fire.

1 tablespoon gelatin
4 tablespoons cold water

Soak.  Add to the custard while it is still hot. Let cool.

4 egg whites—beaten
½ cup cugar

Beat together and add to custard while it is still soft and smooth.

Fill the pie crust and set in the refrigerator. Sprinkle with candied fruit.

2 tablespoons brandy

Added to the custard makes a "special" Continental Cream Pie.

*Hilton Hotel, El Paso, Texas*


## 397.  Custard Pie

INGREDIENTS

DIRECTIONS

3 eggs—beaten lightly
2½ cups milk
1 cup sugar
1 pinch salt
2 tablespoons melted butter

Mix together and put in *uncooked* pie shell.

Sprinkle top with grapenuts or graham cracker crumbs.  Do not stir.

Bake in 400 F. oven for 12 to 15 minutes. Then reduce heat to 300 F. and cook until custard is set in the center of the pie.

*Stone's Restaurant, Marshalltown, Iowa*

## 398.  Eggnog Chiffon Pie

| INGREDIENTS | DIRECTIONS |
|---|---|
| 1 tablespoon gelatin<br>¼ cup cold water | Soak for 5 minutes. |
| 1 cup milk<br>½ cup sugar | Heat to boiling point.  Add gelatin. |
| 4 egg yolks—beaten slightly<br>¼ teaspoon salt | Beat into mixture and let cool until it starts to congeal. |
| 4 egg whites—beaten<br>½ cup sugar | Add sugar to egg whites and fold into mixture. |
| ¼ cup rum | Add to mixture and pile in baked pie shell. |
| 1 cup whipping cream—whipped<br>1 teaspoon nutmeg | Spread with whipped cream and sprinkle with nutmeg. |

*Garden Grill, Daytona Beach, Florida*


## 399.  Eggnog Pie

| INGREDIENTS | DIRECTIONS |
|---|---|
| 3 teaspoons gelatin<br>2 tablespoons cold water<br>2 cups boiling hot water | Dissolve in cold water, then add rest of hot water. |
| 8 egg whites—beaten<br>2½ cups sugar<br>4 ozs. rum | Add to egg whites the sugar and rum and then mix with gelatin. |
| 1 pint whipped cream | Fold in whipped cream and pour into previously baked pie shells.<br><br>Place in a cool place and allow to set.  Top with whipped cream. |

*Santa Maria Inn, Santa Maria, California*

## 400.  Eggnog Pie

INGREDIENTS

1 tablespoon Knox gelatin
¼ cup cold water

4 egg yolks—beaten
½ cup sugar
½ teaspoon salt
½ cup hot water

4 egg whites—beaten
¼ cup sugar
3 teaspoons rum

DIRECTIONS

Soak for five minutes.

Put ingredients in double boiler and cook until custard consistency.  Add gelatin and cool.

Fold in egg whites, sugar and rum and fill baked pie shell.  Place in refrigerator to set.  Serve with thin layer of whipped cream over top and grated nutmeg.

*The Carr House, Wolfboro, New Hampshire*


## 401.  Filling for Small Pastries, Tarts, etc.

INGREDIENTS

¼ lb. butter
¾ lb. lump sugar

2 lemons—grated rind
2 lemons—juice

6 egg yolks—beaten
4 egg whites—beaten

DIRECTIONS

Melt together.

Add to above.

Add to mixture and stir until it thickens.

*Columbia Gorge Hotel, Hood River, Oregon*


## 402.  Frozen Lemon Pie

INGREDIENTS

3 egg yolks—beaten
7 tablespoons sugar

4 tablespoons lemon juice
¼ lemon rind—whole piece

1 egg white—beaten
1 tablespoon sugar

1 cup whipping cream—whipped

DIRECTIONS

Beat together and place in double boiler.

Add to above mixture while it is heating, and cook until thick.  Remove from fire and take out rind.  Chill.

Beat sugar into egg whites.

Fold into egg whites and stir into mixture.  Pour into buttered freezing tray, sprinkle with crumbled vanilla wafers and freeze several hours.

*Althea, Lewisburg, W. Virginia*

## 403.  French Cream Cocoanut Pie    (Serves 6 to 8)

INGREDIENTS | DIRECTIONS

1 pint milk
1 cup sugar

Scald.

4½ tablespoons cornstarch
5 egg yolks
⅔ cups milk

Mix together and add slowly to above, stirring constantly until mixture thickens. Remove from fire.

4⅔ tablespoons butter
1 pinch of salt

Add to above mixture and stir until butter is dissolved.

1 tablespoon vanilla

Stir into mixture, and pour immediately into baked pie shell.

½ can cocoanut or
½ fresh cocoanut—grated

Put on top of filling.

½ pint whipping cream
—whipped

Put on top of cocoanut.

To vary this pie, stir into finished cream filling 3½ squares melted chocolate, or top with fresh fruit such as red raspberries, before topping with whipped cream. Place in ice box before serving.

*Phelps and Phelps Colonial Restaurant, Chicago, Illinois*

## 404.  Graham Cracker Pie    (Makes 2 pies)

INGREDIENTS | DIRECTIONS

30 graham crackers—
   crushed
 2 tablespoons flour
 2 tablespoons cinnamon
½ cup sugar
 1 cup melted butter
½ cup lard

Mix ingredients and press in pie pan. Add the filling.

Bake in 300 F. oven for 1 minute.

### FILLING

1 quart milk

Heat and add.

8 egg yolks—beaten
4 tablespoons cornstarch
2 teaspoons vanilla
1 pinch of salt
2 tablespoons melted
  butter
½ cup sugar

Cook filling until thick and fill pie shells.

8 egg whites—beaten
½ cup sugar
1 pinch of salt
1 teaspoon vanilla

Make a meringue of these ingredients and cover pies. Brown in 350 F. oven.

*Sanders Court and Cafe, Corbin, Kentucky*

## 405. Heavenly Pie

INGREDIENTS

DIRECTIONS

3 egg whites—beaten
½ cup sugar

Beat together.

⅓ cup confectioners sugar

Fold into mixture.

Bake in ungreased glass pie plate in 275 F. to 325 F. oven for 1 hour.

About 2 hours before serving, crush the top slightly.

1 cup whipping cream

Whip and spread over the pie. Place in the refrigerator until ready to serve.

Shred bitter chocolate over the top.

*The Weathervane, Middlebury, Vermont*


## 406. Jefferson Davis Pie          (Makes 2 pies)

INGREDIENTS

DIRECTIONS

3 cups sugar
1 cup butter

Cream together.

4 eggs—beaten lightly

Add to the above.

1 cup milk

Stir into mixture.

1 tablespoon flour
¼ teaspoon salt
1 teaspoon vanilla

Blend into mixture. Then beat all the above like the devil.

Line 2 pie pans that have first been well-buttered, with pie crust. Pour in the filling and bake in 450 F. oven for 10 minutes, then reduce heat to 350 F. for another 30 to 35 minutes.

*Mrs. McKenzie Moss, Bowling Green, Kentucky*

## 407. Lemon Chiffon Pie

**INGREDIENTS**

4 egg yolks—beaten
½ cup sugar
1 lemon—juice
1 lemon rind—grated
1 pinch salt

1 tablespoon gelatin
¼ cup cold water

4 egg whites—beaten
½ cup sugar

**DIRECTIONS**

Cook in double boiler, stirring constantly until consistency of custard.

Soak until gelatin is dissolved. Then add to hot custard.

Beat sugar into egg whites. Fold hot custard in egg whites carefully. Put in baked pie shell and chill 3 hours.

*Stones Restaurant, Marshalltown, Iowa*

## 408. Lemon Fluff Pie

**INGREDIENTS**

4 egg yolks—beaten
2 lemons—juice
1 lemon rind—grated
¾ cup sugar

2 egg whites—beaten
1 teaspoon sugar

2 egg whites—beaten
¼ cup sugar

**DIRECTIONS**

Cook in double boiler for about 12 minutes, stirring constantly. If it gets lumpy beat with egg beater after removing from fire. It is better not to let it get lumpy.

Beat sugar into egg whites and fold into mixture. Pour into baked pie shell.

Beat sugar into egg whites and cover pie with the meringue. Place in oven a few minutes to brown.

*Stoddards, Atop Butler Hall, New York City, N. Y.*

## 409. Lemon Pie

**INGREDIENTS**

1 cup sugar
⅓ cup flour
1 pinch of salt
1 cup boiling water

3 egg yolks—beaten
1 lemon—juice
1 lemon rind—grated
1 teaspoon butter

3 egg whites—beaten
½ cup sugar

**DIRECTIONS**

Mix and cook in double boiler 20 minutes.

Add to above mixture and cook for 1 minute. Put into baked pie shell and cover with meringue.

Beat sugar into whites and put on top of filling. Place in oven to brown.

*Althea, Lewisburg, West Virginia*

# 410.  Lemon Pie

INGREDIENTS                          DIRECTIONS

1 tablespoon gelatin          Soak.
¾ cup cold water

½ cup sugar                   Mix together and cook in double boiler until
½ cup lemon juice             the consistency of custard.  Remove from fire
¼ teaspoon salt               and fold into gelatin.
4 egg yolks—beaten

1 teaspoon grated             Add to mixture.
lemon rind

4 egg whites—beaten           Beat sugar into egg whites and fold into mix-
½ cup sugar                   ture.

1 cup whipping cream—         Stir in whipped cream and put mixture into
whipped                       baked pie shell.  Set in ice box for 2 hours
                              before serving.

*Mrs. H. G. Beebe, Chicago, Illinois*


# 411.  Lemon Pie

INGREDIENTS                          DIRECTIONS

                                   *CRUST*

1 cup flour                   Mix thoroughly.
½ cup lard

1 pinch of salt               Add to mixture.

¼ cup water                   Add to mixture and roll out thin.  Cover bot-
                              tom of pie tin and bake in 375 F. oven for
                              15 minutes.

                                   *FILLING*

1 lemon—juice                 Place in double boiler.
1 cup sugar
1 cup boiling water

2 tablespoons cornstarch      Add to above mixture and let boil until thick,
                              stirring to prevent lumps.  Remove from fire.

2 egg yolks—beaten            Stir into the above mixture.  Fill pie shell.
1 lemon rind—grated
1 tablespoon butter
1 egg white—beaten

1 egg white—beaten            Make a meringue and cover top.  Place in
                              oven to brown.

*Miss Katharine L. Little, Chicago, Illinois*

## 412. Lemon Tarts

(Makes 6 to 8)

INGREDIENTS | DIRECTIONS
--- | ---
½ cup sugar<br>4 tablespoons flour | Mix thoroughly.
1 cup boiling water | Add to above ingredients and cook until thick.
1 egg | Add to mixture and beat well.
1 lemon—juice<br>1 lemon rind—grated | Mix into mixture and let cool.
1 cup whipped cream | Add to cooled mixture and mix well.
 | Fill individual baked tart shells with lemon cream. Top with whipped cream and serve at once.

*The Old House, Lexington, Massachusetts*

## 413. New Orleans Pecan Pie

INGREDIENTS | DIRECTIONS
--- | ---
1 cup brown sugar<br>3 eggs<br>1 tablespoon butter | Cream together.
1 cup syrup<br>1 teaspoon vanilla<br>½ cup broken pecans | Add to above mixture and pour in to *uncooked* pie shell. Bake in 300 F. oven for 35 minutes.

*Althea, Lewisburg, West Virginia*

## 414. New Orleans Pecan Pie

INGREDIENTS | DIRECTIONS
--- | ---
1 tablespoon butter<br>1 cup brown sugar | Cream together.
1 cup syrup | Add to above.
3 eggs—well beaten<br>1 pinch of salt<br>1 cup pecans—chopped | Add to mixture.
 | Put in pan lined with a rich crust and bake in 350 F. oven for 45 minutes.

*Governor's Corner, Tucson, Arizona*

# 415.  Open Fresh Strawberry Pie

INGREDIENTS

DIRECTIONS

### PIE SHELL

2 cups flour
1 cup shortening

Blend completely.

1 teaspoon salt
2 tablespoons cold
water

Mix together and add to above mixture.

Roll out and bake in 425 F. oven for 15 minutes.

### FILLING

1 cup crushed fresh
strawberries
1 cup sugar
1 tablespoon cornstarch

Boil until transparent.

fresh strawberries—
enough to fill the pie

Put strawberries in pie shell and pour over hot berry syrup and chill.

*Lowell Inn, Stillwater, Minnesota*


# 416.  Orange Pie

INGREDIENTS

DIRECTIONS

2 cups orange juice
1½ cups sugar

Boil together until sugar is dissolved.

3 tablespoons cornstarch
½ cup water

Dissolve cornstarch in water and add to above.

3 egg yolks—beaten
slightly
½ teaspoon salt
1 tablespoon butter

Add to mixture and cook until thick.

3 orange rinds—grated

Add to mixture just before removing from fire.

3 egg whites—beaten
1 cup sugar
⅓ cup water

Whip up together until stiff.

Put filling in flaky baked pie shell which is the same temperature as the filling.  Then put egg whites on top and sprinkle with powdered sugar.  Bake in 350 F. oven for 20 minutes.

*Green Shutters, Whitewater, Wisconsin*

## 417.   Pecan Pie

INGREDIENTS

4 tablespoons butter
1 cup sugar
3 eggs
¾ cup honey
1 cup pecans

DIRECTIONS

Beat well and bake in pie crust in 375 F. oven for 45 minutes.

*Old Spinning Wheel Tea Room, Hinsdale, Illinois*


## 418.   Pecan Pie

(Serves 7)

INGREDIENTS

¼ cup butter
1 cup sugar

DIRECTIONS

Cream together.

3 eggs—beaten slightly

Add to above.

1 can syrup
1 teaspoon vanilla
1 pinch of salt

Add to mixture and stir thoroughly. Pour into 9-inch pie pan which has been lined with pastry.*

4 ozs. pecans

Sprinkle pecans on top and bake in 350 F. oven for 1 hour.

May be topped with whipped cream at time of serving.

* Pie crust should be rolled a little thicker than usual.

*H. J. Seiler Company, Boston, Massachusetts*


## 419.   Pecan Tart

(Makes 18)

INGREDIENTS

4 eggs—beaten lightly
1 cup sugar
1¼ cups syrup
1¼ cup pecans—chopped
1½ tablespoons vanilla
1½ tablespoons butter

DIRECTIONS

Stir together lightly and put into patty shell. Bake in 250 F. oven for 30 minutes.

1 cup whipping cream—whipped

Before serving top each tart with whipped cream.

*Stoddards Atop Butler Hall, New York City, N. Y.*

## 420.  Pie Crust

(Makes 2 double crusted pies)

INGREDIENTS | DIRECTIONS
--- | ---
5 cups flour<br>1 teaspoon salt | Sift together into a bowl.
1½ cups shortening | Work into the above with pastry blender.
10 tablespoons cold water | Cut into the mixture with a knife.
| Turn the mixture into a pastry cloth, fold the cloth over first on one side, then on the other and press the mixture together well. Cut off what is needed and roll the remainder in a wax paper for future use.

*Hartwell Farm, Lincoln, Massachusetts*


## 421.  Pumpkin Chiffon Pie

(10 inch pie)

INGREDIENTS | DIRECTIONS
--- | ---
1 cup brown sugar<br>3 egg yolks<br>1¼ cups pumpkin<br>2 teaspoons cinnamon<br>½ teaspoon ginger<br>¼ teaspoon allspice<br>½ teaspoon salt | Put in double boiler and cook until it begins to thicken.
1 tablespoon gelatin<br>¼ cup cold water | Soak gelatin in water for 5 minutes. Add to hot mixture and stir until thoroughly dissolved. Cool.
3 egg whites—beaten<br>2 tablespoons sugar | Beat sugar into whites and fold into mixture.
| Pour into baked pie shell and chill.
| Serve garnished with whipped cream.

*The Dinner Bell, Oakland, California*

*Things that do not mix—Alcohol and gasoline. Cigarettes and lace table cloths.*

# 422. Sunny Silver Pie

INGREDIENTS

4 egg yolks
2 or 3 tablespoons
   lemon juice
1 lemon rind—grated
⅛ teaspoon salt
½ cup sugar

1½ teaspoons gelatin
⅓ cup cold water

4 egg whites—beaten
½ cup sugar

1 baked pie shell

1 cup whipping cream

DIRECTIONS

Cook in double boiler until thick, stirring constantly. Remove from fire.

Soak and add to the above.

Beat together well. Fold into the above mixture.

Place in baked pie shell and set in refrigerator for 2 or 3 hours.

Whip and spread on top of pie.

*High Hampton, Cashiers, North Carolina*

# 423. Treasure Chest Pie

INGREDIENTS

½ cup butter
1 cup sugar

3 egg yolks—beaten
1 egg white—beaten

½ cup cooked raisins
½ cup mincemeat
½ cup walnuts—broken
½ cup pecans—broken
2 tablespoons orange
   juice
1 teaspoon vanilla
½ teaspoon salt
2 tablespoons Apple
   Jack brandy

DIRECTIONS

Cream together.

Stir into mixture until it foams.

Add to mixture and pour into pie shell *uncooked*. (Make a rich flaky crust, but do not bake it first.) Put a criss-cross crust on top and bake in 400 oven for 12 to 15 minutes until the filling sets and then cover the pie with an inverted pie pan, lower the temperature to 350 F. and bake until the top crust becomes brown and the filling is well set.

May be served with whipped cream, but that is not necessary.

*Lee Hoffman Hotel, Cresson, Pennsylvania*

# 424.   Sauce for Mince Pie

(Serves 6)

INGREDIENTS

DIRECTIONS

3 tablespoons butter
2 teaspoons sugar

Melt and mix well.

¼ lemon—juice
2 oz. hot water
2 oz. rum
2 oz. brandy
1 pinch nutmeg

Add to above and when hot, pour over slices of pie.

*Boston Oyster House, Chicago, Illinois*


# 425.   Baked Indian Pudding

(Serves 8)

INGREDIENTS

DIRECTIONS

3 cups milk

Scald the milk.

3 teaspoons Indian meal
⅓ cup molasses

Mix together and stir into hot milk and cook until it thickens.  Stir constantly to prevent scorching.  Remove from fire.

½ cup sugar
1 egg—beaten
1 tablespoon butter
½ teaspoon ginger
½ teaspoon cinnamon
¼ teaspoon salt

Add to mixture and mix thoroughly.
Pour into a buttered baking dish and put in 300 F. oven.

1 cup milk

In ½ hour pour over it the milk and continue baking for 2 hours.

*The Toll House, Whitman, Massachusetts*


# 426.   Boiled Custard Supreme

(Serves 8)

INGREDIENTS

DIRECTIONS

1 quart milk

Scald in double boiler.

¾ cup sugar
1 tablespoon flour
½ teaspoon salt
4 eggs—beaten lightly

Add to milk and cook until custard adheres to spoon, stirring constantly.  Remove from fire and cool.

¼ teaspoon vanilla
¼ cup sherry

When custard is chilled, add flavoring.  Serve in sherbert glasses, topped with sprinkle of nutmeg.  Serve cookies or cake with custard.

*The Meiringen, Roanoke, Virginia*

## 427.   Old Fashioned Indian Pudding   (Serves 8)

| INGREDIENTS | DIRECTIONS |
|---|---|
| 4 cups of milk | Scald in double boiler. |
| 5 tablespoons Indian meal | Gradually add meal and cook 15 minutes. stirring constantly. |
| 2 tablespoons butter<br>1 teaspoon salt<br>½ teaspoon ginger<br>½ teaspoon cinnamon<br>1 teaspoon salt<br>1 cup molasses<br>2 eggs—well beaten | Add these ingredients to the mixture. |
| 1 cup sweet apples—sliced very thin | Stir into mixture and turn into buttered baking dish. |
| 1 cup cold milk | Pour over all and bake in 325 F. oven for 1 hour. |
| | Serve with vanilla ice-cream. |

*The Carr House, Wolfboro, New Hampshire*


## 428.   Caramel Date Pudding   (Serves 14)

| INGREDIENTS | DIRECTIONS |
|---|---|
| 2 cups brown sugar<br>3 cups milk | Mix together and scald in double boiler until the sugar is dissolved. |
| 4 egg yolks—beaten<br>½ cup flour<br>1 cup milk<br>1 cup dates—cut up | Blend together and add to the hot mixture, stirring constantly until thick.   Cool. |
| 4 egg whites—beaten | Fold into mixture. |
| | Pour into sherbert glasses.   Chill and serve with or without cream. |

*The Weathervane, Middlebury, Vermont*

## 429. Chocolate Bread Pudding

| INGREDIENTS | DIRECTIONS |
|---|---|
| ½ cup cocoa<br>⅔ cup sugar<br>2 cups bread—cubed<br>⅛ teaspoon salt<br>3 cups milk | Heat in double boiler until the mixture is smoking. |
| 1 teaspoon vanilla<br>4 egg yolks | Add to mixture. |
| | Pour into buttered baking dish and bake in pan of water in 300 F. oven for 30 minutes. |
| 4 egg whites—beaten<br>3 tablespoons sugar | Spread with meringue and brown in oven for about 10 minutes. |

*Mrs. Belle A. Marquis, Mansfield, Ohio*


## 430. Chocolate Bread Pudding          (Serves 8)

| INGREDIENTS | DIRECTIONS |
|---|---|
| 2 tablespoons butter<br>4 squares chocolate | Melt in double boiler. |
| ½ cup sugar<br>¼ teaspoon salt | Add to the above. |
| 4 egg yolks—beaten<br>½ cup milk | Add to mixture and cook until slightly thickened. |
| 2 cups fresh bread crumbs<br>1 teaspoon vanilla<br>½ cup nut meats | Add to the above and mix thoroughly. |
| 4 egg whites—beaten | Fold into mixture. |
| | Steam for 25 minutes. |
| | Serve with butter sauce or whipped cream, either hot or cold. |

*Robert G. Brehmer, Jr., Fond du Lac, Wisconsin*

# 431. Chocolate Pudding

(Serves 6)

| INGREDIENTS | DIRECTIONS |
|---|---|
| 3 eggs—beaten<br>½ cup sugar | Beat together. |
| 1½ tablespoons<br>chocolate<br>1 tablespoon butter | Add to the above and beat well. |
| 1 pink milk | Heat in double boiler and pour the above mixture over the hot milk, beat until well mixed and smooth. |
| | Pour into custard cups and bake over water in 315 F. oven for about 15 minutes. |
| | Serve warm in cup with whipped cream on top. Also is good cold. |

*Fallen Leaf Lodge, Lake Tahoe, California*


# 432. Chocolate Pudding

| INGREDIENTS | DIRECTIONS |
|---|---|
| 1 pint milk | Cook in double boiler. |
| 4 tablespoons cornstarch<br>3 tablespoons cold milk | Stir together into smooth paste and add to milk. Cook until smooth. |
| 4 oz. of chocolate<br>or<br>4 tablespoons cocoa<br>½ cup sugar | Add to mixture. Take from the fire. |
| 4 egg whites—beaten | Fold into mixture and set away to harden. |

### CUSTARD SAUCE

| | |
|---|---|
| 4 egg yolks—beaten<br>4 tablespoons sugar | Beat together. |
| 1 pint scalding milk | Add to egg mixture and cook as you would a soft custard. |
| 1 teaspoon of vanilla | Add to mixture and pour over the pudding. |

*Mrs. Belle A. Marquis, Mansfield, Ohio*

## 433.  Chocolate Souffle

INGREDIENTS | DIRECTIONS
--- | ---
2 tablespoons butter<br>2 tablespoons flour | Blend together.
¾ cup milk | Gradually add to the above.  Cook until it reaches the boiling point.
1½ squares chocolate—melted<br>⅓ cup sugar<br>2 tablespoons hot water | Mix together and add to the mixture and stir until smooth.
3 egg yolks—beaten | Add to mixture.  Let cool.
3 egg whites—beaten<br>½ teaspoon vanilla | Fold into mixture.

Turn into baking dish and bake in 350 F. oven for 25 minutes, or until done.  Serve hot with hard sauce.

*Mrs. W. B. Taylor, Bowling Green, Kentucky*


## 434.  Chocolate Steam Pudding

INGREDIENTS | DIRECTIONS
--- | ---
3 tablespoons butter<br>⅔ cup sugar<br>1 egg—beaten | Cream and blend together.
2¼ cups flour<br>4½ teaspoons baking powder<br>½ teaspoon salt | Sift together and mix into the above.
1 cup milk | Add to mixture.
2½ squares chocolate | Melt and add to mixture.

Steam 2 hours and serve with sauce.   Do not fill molds more than half full.

*SAUCE*

| |
--- | ---
¼ cup butter | Work until very soft.
1 cup powdered sugar | Gradually add to the butter.
½ teaspoon vanilla<br>1 pinch of salt | Add to mixture.
¼ cup whipping cream | Whip and fold into the sauce.

*The Hearthstone, Winnetka, Illinois*

# 435. Cottage Pudding with Strawberry Sauce

(Serves 6 or 7)

INGREDIENTS | DIRECTIONS

2 cups of flour
2½ teaspoons baking powder
½ teaspoon salt

Mix all together.

1 egg—beaten
¾ cup sugar
3 tablespoons melted butter
1 cup milk

Mix together, and stir in the flour.

Bake in a shallow pan in 375 F. oven for 30 to 40 minutes.

## SAUCE

1 tablespoon butter
1½ cups powdered sugar

Cream together.

1 egg white—beaten

Mix into the above.

1 pint strawberries—mashed, or any other fruit

Add the fruit just before serving. It is well to have a generous serving of the sauce, and if so, double the quantities.

*Mr. H. M. Carruth, Cleveland, Ohio*

# 436. Date Souffle

(Serves 8)

INGREDIENTS | DIRECTIONS

2 tablespoons butter
3 tablespoons sugar
3 egg yolks

Cream together.

2 tablespoons flour
¾ cup milk

Add to the above, alternately with milk.

3 egg whites—beaten
1 teaspoon salt

Beat together and fold into mixture.

1 package dates—chopped (14 oz.)

Fold into mixture.

Set in pan of hot water and bake in 350 F. oven for 35 minutes. Serve with orange sauce.

## ORANGE SAUCE

1 cup sugar
1 cup orange juice
1 orange rind—grated
1 lemon—juice
1 teaspoon cornstarch
1 tablespoon butter
1 egg yolk

Mix together and cook in a double boiler, until it coats a spoon.

*The Hearthstone, Winnetka, Illinois*

## 437.  Gooseberry Mousse or Pudding  (Serves 6)

| INGREDIENTS | DIRECTIONS |
|---|---|
| 1 quart gooseberries<br>½ lb. sugar<br>½ pint water | Cook slowly until tender enough to put through a sieve. |
| 1 tablespoon brandy<br>a little green coloring | Add brandy and coloring.  Let cool. |
| 1 pint whipping cream<br>—whipped | Fold into mixture.  If made into a mousse put in refrigerator trays and freeze.<br>Any fresh fruit, minus the coloring may also be used. |

*Emelie Tolman, Chicago, Illinois*

## 438.  Lemon Pudding

| INGREDIENTS | DIRECTIONS |
|---|---|
| 1 cup sugar<br>2 tablespoons butter | Cream. |
| 2 egg yolks<br>2 tablespoons flour<br>1 lemon—juice and rind grated | Add to above and stir well. |
| 1 cup milk | Add to mixture. |
| 2 egg whites—beaten | Fold into mixture. |
| | Bake slowly in water, but do not let it bake stiff on the bottom. |
| | Preferably served hot—but it may be served cold with whipped cream. |

*Mrs. W. B. Taylor, Bowling Green, Kentucky*

## 439. Macaroon Pudding
(Serves 6 to 8)

INGREDIENTS

DIRECTIONS

4 egg yolks—beaten
½ cup sugar

Mix together.

1 tablespoon gelatin
1 cup milk

Dissolve gelatin in milk and add to the above. Let come to a boil—just to the boiling point.

4 egg whites—beaten
vanilla to taste

Stir into mixture and put in a large or individual molds.

12 almond macaroons

Break into small pieces and fill the molds.

1 cup whipped cream

Put in refrigerator until it sets. Serve with whipped cream. Sprinkle with glazed cherries and chopped nuts. If a circle mold is used, fill the center with whipped cream.

*Miss Katharine L. Little, Chicago, Illinois*


## 440. Orange Souffle

INGREDIENTS

DIRECTIONS

6 egg whites—beaten
6 tablespoons sugar

Beat together.

4 tablespoons orange marmalade
1 teaspoon orange extract

Mix into the above.

Put in a double boiler that holds 3 quarts. Cook slowly for 1 hour.

Turn out on a round platter. (It should stand up like a man's silk hat.) Pour sauce around it and serve.

### SAUCE

6 egg yolks—beaten
1 cup sugar
1 pinch of salt

Beat together until smooth.

1 pint whipped cream
2 tablespoons curacoa

Add to the sauce just before serving.

candied kumquots—sliced

Decorate each portion.

*Chalet Suzanne, Lake Wales, Florida*

# 441.  Persimmon Pudding

(Serves 6)

INGREDIENTS

DIRECTIONS

1 cup sugar
1 cup flour
2 teaspoons soda
1 teaspoon cinnamon
½ teaspoon salt

Sift together.

⅓ cup melted butter
1 egg
1 cup ripe persimmon
½ teaspoon vanilla
½ cup milk

Add to dry ingredients and steam for 1½ hours.  Serve with sauce.

### SAUCE

1 egg—beaten
2 tablespoons melted butter
⅛ teaspoon salt
2 cups powdered sugar —sifted
1 cup cream—whipped
3 or 4 tablespoons brandy or sherry wine

Mix all ingredients and pour over pudding when it is served.

*David Donald, Los Gatos, California*


# 442.  Persimmon Pudding

INGREDIENTS

DIRECTIONS

1 cup persimmon pulp
1 tablespoon butter
1 cup sugar
2 teaspoons soda
½ cup milk
1 cup flour
1 teaspoon vanilla
1½ teaspoons baking powder
1 pinch of salt

Mix together and steam for 3 hours.

Serve with sauce.

### SAUCE

2 egg yolks—beaten
1 cup sugar

Beat together.

½ cup sherry wine or Virginia Dare

Add to eggs.

½ pint whipping cream —whipped

Add to mixture just before serving.

*Mrs. Voijt Frank Mashek, Chicago, Illinois*

# 443. Plum Pudding

INGREDIENTS

½ lb. citron
¼ lb. lemon and orange peel—candied
1 lb. raisins
1 lb. currants
1 lb. suet—put through a food chopper
¼ teaspoon cloves
⅓ teaspoon cinnamon
¼ teaspoon allspice

6 eggs—beaten
2 cups sugar

1 cup sherry wine
2 cups of flour
2 teaspoons baking powder

DIRECTIONS

Mix all these ingredients together.

Mix together and stir into mixture.

Thicken the wine with flour and baking powder and pour over the fruit mixture.

Dip a cloth in hot water and line with flour. Pour in the pudding and tie. Have the water boiling and keep boiling for 6 hours. Keep the pudding covered with water during this process.

*The Viking Norwegian Restaurant, Santa Barbara, California*

# 444. Pudding Saxon   (Serves 8)

INGREDIENTS

2 cups sugar
4 eggs—beaten
3 oz. citron peel—chopped
6 oz. raisins
1 pint milk
8 slices bread—diced
1 orange rind—grated
3 oz. melted butter

DIRECTIONS

Mix and blend.

Pour into a greased form and set in hot water. Bake in 375 F. oven for 30 minutes. Serve hot.

This is a man's dessert.

*The Viking Norwegian Restaurant, Santa Barbara, California*

# 445. Rice Pudding

| INGREDIENTS | DIRECTIONS |
|---|---|
| 6 eggs—beaten<br>½ cup sugar | Beat together. |
| 1 quart milk<br>2 cups cooked rice<br>1 tablespoon butter—melted | Add to the eggs. |
| 1 cup raisins<br>nutmeg to taste | Add to mixture. Put the pudding in a dish and set in large pan so that it is surrounded by water, keeping it from the bottom of the pan with a couple pieces of wood. Bake in 250 F. oven, until a straw comes out clean. |

*Mrs. W. G. "Pete" Gibbs, Berkeley, California*

# 446. Stephanie Pudding

| INGREDIENTS | DIRECTIONS |
|---|---|
| 1 tablespoon gelatin<br>¼ cup cold water | Soak. |
| 1 cup grape or loganberry juice—hot | Dissolve gelatin with hot juice. |
| ½ cup sugar<br>¼ cup lemon juice | Add to dissolved gelatin and strain. Set in a cool place. Stir mixture occasionally and when thick whisk until frothy. |
| 3 egg whites—beaten | Add to above mixture and beat until stiff enough to hold its own shape. |
|  | Serve cold with boiled custard sauce. |

*Marjorie Mills, Boston, Massachusetts*

## 447. Cherries Jubilee

(Serves 6)

INGREDIENTS

DIRECTIONS

1 pint fresh black cherries
1 pint water
¾ cup sugar

Put into covered pot and cook slowly for 10 minutes.

Canned black cherries may be used, providing they are whole, sweet, and have the pits in them.

Drain the cherries from the syrup. Put cherries in a chafing dish.

4 teaspoons sugar
1 lemon peel—whole
½ cup cherry syrup

Let this come to a boil.

6 oz. brandy
2 oz. Grand Marnier liqueur

Pour over cherries and set aflame.

6 scoops of ice cream
6 slices of plain cake

Put cake in individual dishes, cover with ice-cream and pour blazing cherries over all.

Serve immediately.

*This dish was created for Queen Victoria of England Jubilee.*

*Boston Oyster House, Chicago, Illinois*

## 448. Angel Food Mold

(Serves 6 to 8)

INGREDIENTS

DIRECTIONS

1 envelope gelatin
½ cup cold milk

Soak.

2 cups milk
2 egg yolks
1 cup sugar

Cook in double boiler, and cool.

1 teaspoon vanilla
2 egg whites—beaten
1 pint of whipping cream—whipped

Add to cooled mixture.

Bits of angel food cake

Put bits of angel food in mold and pour mixture over them.

Serve with whipped cream into which cut and sugared strawberries have been added.

*Mrs. Voijt Frank Mashek, Chicago, Illinois*

# 449. Chocolate Cream (Serves 12)

INGREDIENTS | DIRECTIONS

3 squares of chocolate
1 cup milk

Heat, then stir until cool and thick.

1 package of gelatin
½ cup water

Dissolve.

4 egg yolks—beaten
⅔ cup sugar

Strain gelatin into yolks. Add the sugar and beat.

4 egg whites—beaten
⅓ cup sugar
1 teaspoon vanilla

Beat sugar into egg whites. Add flavoring and fold into the combined mixtures above. Put into a mold to set and serve with sauce.

*SAUCE*

3 egg yolks
1 cup milk
1 teaspoon cornstarch
⅓ cup sugar

Combine and cook until thick. Cool.

¼ teaspoon almond flavoring
½ pint whipping cream —whipped

Fold into mixture and pour over pudding.

You may increase quantity of sauce by adding another pint of whipping cream—whipped.

*Mrs. Voijt Frank Mashek, Chicago, Illinois*

# 450. Fresh Fruit Trifle (Serves 8)

INGREDIENTS | DIRECTIONS

42 macaroons
¾ cup sherry wine

Dip macaroons in wine and place in a flat serving dish.

6 egg yolks—beaten
1 cup sugar
⅛ teaspoon salt

Beat eggs 5 minutes in electric beater or with rotary beater for 15 minutes, adding sugar and beating a little longer. Add the balance of sherry and salt. Place in double boiler and cook until it thickens, stirring constantly.

Pour this mixture over the macaroons and allow to cool.

Any fresh fruit, or whipped cream and almonds

Just before serving cover with fresh sliced peaches, figs, or strawberries. Or with whipped cream and blanched almonds.

*Peter Pan Lodge, Carmel, California*

## 451.  Fried Peaches          (Serves 6 to 8)

INGREDIENTS                     DIRECTIONS

1 tablespoon butter             Place in frying pan and let melt.

6 to 8 peaches—peeled           Place whole peaches in pan.

1 cup brown sugar               Put over peaches and let simmer for 30 minutes.  Keep turning the peaches.

½ cup cream                     Just before serving, pour over peaches and let it boil up.  Serve hot.

*Fred Waring, New York City, N. Y.*


## 452.  Peaches Flambees Royale          (Serves 4)

INGREDIENTS                     DIRECTIONS

4 peaches
1 pint cold water
½ cup sugar
¼ stick cinnamon
1 lemon peel—whole

Cook peaches in this mixture with skins on. Let water come to boiling point and boil for 15 minutes, keeping the pot covered all the time.  Take out the peaches, skin, cut them in half and remove pits.  Place them in a chafing dish.

½ cup strawberries or raspberries—crushed
½ cup syrup (that the peaches were cooked in)

Put in chafing dish with the peaches and let get hot.

4 ozs. brandy
2 ozs. of curacao
3 or 4 small pieces of orange peel

Add to the above, and set aflame.

4 scoops of vanilla ice cream

Put in individual dishes and pour the flaming ingredients over all.

*The Boston Oyster House, Chicago, Illinois*

# 453.  Peaches Supreme

(Serves 8 to 10)

| INGREDIENTS | DIRECTIONS |
|---|---|
| 8 or 10 peaches—halved<br>1 vanilla bean<br>½ cup sugar<br>½ cup water | Cook just enough to tenderize peaches. Set aside to chill. |
| 1 quart raspberries—fresh | Mash into a puree. Chill. |

*Make a black currant mousse*

| | |
|---|---|
| 1 cup black currant jam or fresh currants—strained<br>½ cup powdered sugar | Combine together. |
| 2 cups whipping cream —whipped<br>1 teaspoon vanilla | Fold into mixture and freeze. If a freezer is used, it will take 3 hours. If in refrigerator trays, 2 hours. |
| 2 tablespoons Cassis Liqueur<br>1 pint whiping cream—whipped<br>3 tablespoons currant jam | Just before serving, blend this mixture.<br><br>Put the mousse on a platter, cover with brandy mixture. Put peaches on top and all around and pour puree over all. |
| ½ lb. almonds—chopped | Top with nuts. Serve at once and have all mixtures ice cold. |

*Mrs. A. Scott Hines, Bowling Green, Kentucky*


# 454.  Soubayon

(Serves 2)

| INGREDIENTS | DIRECTIONS |
|---|---|
| 2 egg yolks<br>2 tablespoons sugar<br>1 cup sherry wine | Place in double boiler (not aluminum) and beat briskly with a beater until foamy. Be careful not to cook too much as it will spoil the flavor. Remove from fire. |
| ½ cup sponge cake or macaroon crumbs (macaroons preferred) | Pour into the mixture.<br><br>Place in serving glasses and top with a cherry.<br><br>This makes a striking light dessert. |

*Dr. T. J. LeBlanc, Cincinnati, Ohio*

# 455. Strawberries Biltmore (Makes 1 quart)

INGREDIENTS

DIRECTIONS

1 quart strawberries

Stem and clean and mash thoroughly. Drain on napkin.

rum—enough to
cover berries
1/4 lb. powdered sugar

Add to berries and let stand for 2 hours before serving. Not too long however, as the berries will become soggy.

Drain and serve very cold.

### SAUCE

1 pint vanilla ice cream
2 oz. Kirschwasser

Mix and stir well.

1 cup whipping cream—
whipped
1/2 cup sugar

Fold into the above mixture and chill.

Serve over the strawberries in glass nappie.

*Biltmore Hotel, Los Angeles, California*


# 456. The Wonder Dessert (Serves 5)

INGREDIENTS

DIRECTIONS

1 cup oranges

Cut in small pieces and squeeze out some of the juice. This is important or the dessert will be soft and run.

1 cup walnuts

Break in pieces not too small.

1 cup fresh
marshallows
1/4 cup sugar

Cut with scissors and add sugar to prevent them from sticking together.

1 pint whipping cream
—whipped
1/4 teaspoon vanilla

If possible whip with an electric whipper to make stiff. Add vanilla and mix in other ingredients.

Serve in fruit cup, piled high. Will keep for a few hours in refrigerator, but is better if served at once.

*O. B. Wright, Long Beach, California*

## 457.  Butterscotch Ice-Cream Sauce

INGREDIENTS | DIRECTIONS
---|---

1¾ cups syrup (white)
2 cups sugar
1 cup butter
1 cup cream

Cook together until it reaches the soft ball stage.

1 cup cream

Add to above and cook until the candy thermometer says 218 F.

1 teaspoon vanilla

Add to mixture. Delicious either hot or cold. Serve with roasted buttered and salted pecans.

*The Farm Kitchen, Baraboo, Wisconsin*


## 458.  Chocolate Ice Cream                 (Serves 30)

INGREDIENTS | DIRECTIONS
---|---

2 eggs—beaten
1 cup sugar
1 tablespoon flour

Cream together.

1 quart milk
3 squares chocolate—
  melted over hot water

Scald and mix a little with the chocolate, making a smooth paste. Add the balance of the milk, and pour over the egg mixture. Cook in double boiler, stirring until a custard.

1½ cups sugar

Add to custard and cool.

1 teaspoon vanilla
1 pinch of salt
1 quart cream

Add to mixture. Put in freezer and freeze.

*The Santa Fe Inn, Santa Fe, New Mexico*


## 459.  Frozen Eggnog                 (Makes 2 quarts)

INGREDIENTS | DIRECTIONS
---|---

5 egg yolks—beaten
1¾ cups sugar

Beat together until light and creamy.

¾ cup Bourbon
  nutmeg to taste

Add to mixture.

5 egg whites—beaten

Fold into mixture.

1 pint whipping cream
  —whipped

Add to mixture. Put in freezer and freeze. Pack until ready to serve.
This can also be made in refrigerator trays.

*Shadow Hill, Hernando, Mississippi*

## 460.  Fresh Peach Ice Cream

(Makes 15 quarts)

INGREDIENTS | DIRECTIONS
--- | ---
5 quarts peaches—peeled and crushed | Stew the stones and skins slowly in a little water for 10 minutes.
6 cups sugar | Strain the above mixture into the sugar. Mix carefully, and add to the crushed peaches.
5 quarts heavy cream | Mix with the peaches and freeze in electric freezer using 4 measures of ice to 1 of salt.
Crushed ice<br>Rock salt | When frozen, remove to an ice-cream cabinet.

*Hartwell Farm, Lincoln, Massachusetts*


## 461.  Lemon Ice Cream

INGREDIENTS | DIRECTIONS
--- | ---
1 cup sugar<br>1 lemon—juice<br>1 cup thin cream | Combine these ingredients.
1 cup whipping cream | Whip and fold into mixture.
 | Put in trays and freeze in refrigerator, stirring two or three times.

*The Weathervane, Middlebury, Vermont*


## 462.  Lemon Ice Cream

(Makes 3 gallons)

INGREDIENTS | DIRECTIONS
--- | ---
5 teaspoons lemon extract<br>10 lemon—juice<br>10 cups sugar | Combine and let stand for 1 huor.
2 quarts whipping cream—whipped<br>5 quarts milk | Add to the above mixture and pour into freezer and freeze.

*Headley Inn, Zanesville, Ohio*

## 463. Macaroon Ice Cream (Makes 3 pints)

INGREDIENTS | DIRECTIONS

24 stale macaroons

Roll to a crumb.

1 quart whipping
cream

Scald and whip.

½ pint sherry wine
1 cup sugar

Dissolve the sugar in wine. Combine the two liquids.

1 cup shredded almonds

Add to combined liquids. Fold in crumbs and put in freezer. Freeze and pack for at least 4 hours.

*Villa Marghreti, Charleston, South Carolina*

## 464. Sherry Almond Cream (Serves 8)

INGREDIENTS | DIRECTIONS

1 tablespoon gelatin
¼ cup cold water

Soak gelatin.

1 cup boiling water
1¼ cup sugar

Add to gelatin and stir well until dissolved. Cool. When it begins to set, beat with an egg beater until frothy.

6 egg whites—beaten

Fold into mixture.

⅓ cup sherry
½ teaspoon almond
extract

Add to mixture.

1 cup almonds, chopped

Fill mold with alternate layers of mixture and nuts. Put in refrigerator and let set for 2 hours.

### SAUCE

6 egg yolks—beaten
1 pint milk

Cook in double boiler until it coats a spoon.

¼ cup sugar
⅛ teaspoon salt
½ teaspoon vanilla

Add to mixture and let cool.

3 tablespoons sherry

Add to cooled mixture.

½ pint whipping cream
—whipped

Just before serving, fold into mixture, and fill the center of the mold.

*La Chaumiere, Palm Beach, Florida*

## 465. Cranberry and Apple Ice (Serves 8 to 10)

INGREDIENTS

DIRECTIONS

2 cups cranberries
1 cup water

Cook cranberries in water rapidly until skin bursts, about 5 minutes. Strain through a medium mesh sieve. Add enough water to make 2 cups of pulp and juice.

1 cup sugar

Cook 2 minutes, adding sugar until it is dissolved. Cool.

2 cups tart apples, grated

Add equal amount of grated apples and pour in tray of refrigerator and freeze rapidly to mush. Stir once during freezing.

*Mrs. Edwin P. Morrow, Frankfort, Kentucky*


## 466. Chocolate Fudge Sauce (Serves 25 to 30)

INGREDIENTS

DIRECTIONS

1¾ cups cocoa
2 cups sugar
1 cup milk

Mix together and put on stove. When warm add:

¾ cup syrup
2 cups whipping cream
¼ teaspoon salt
¼ oz. vanilla

Add to above and place in double boiler and cook until thick.

Serve either hot or cold.

*Headley Inn, Zanesville, Ohio*

# DUNCAN HINES
## Kentucky Hickory-Smoked Hams

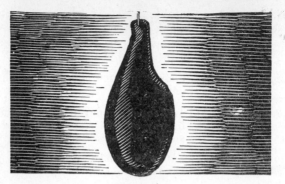

**M**Y grandfather came to Kentucky from Virginia in 1824. It was not long before his hams gained a reputation for their superior flavor and today, I adhere to his original recipe. My hams are prepared in December, January, and February, but are shipped throughout the year, *as long as the supply lasts.*

Hickory smoking requires about forty days. The long process of curing results in a shrinkage of about 24% to 33% from its original weight. This shrinkage in weight, plus the long, laborious process of curing, accounts for the necessity of pricing these hams a little above the cost of the usual meat market type.

Mold on this type of ham is like mold on some cheeses, an evidence of correct curing and aging, with this difference—it is easily washed off the ham.

Occasionally in carving one of these hams, you may notice small white specks scattered throughout the lean meat. These specks are nothing more than salt and indicate not only that the salt has thoroughly penetrated through the hams in seasoning, but it also implies that it is not too new.

While these white specks are not requisite in this type of ham, they are regarded by connoisseurs as a welcome sign.

When baked, these hams are nearly always served cold and sliced thin. In the South, we usually place a ham at one end of the table and a turkey or other hot meat at the other end. For buffet lunches or suppers, the ham may be accompanied with scalloped oysters, etc.

The best way to keep a baked ham fresh and moist, after the first day's serving, is to wrap it in a damp (not wet) napkin and place it in a crock and during hot weather, place in a refrigerator.

You need not cook the ham as soon as received. It will keep for a long period, if hung in a cool place (not refrigerator) and kept free from flies and other insects.

My Kentucky Hickory-Smoked hams are widely known for their enticing flavor and are delicious whether fried, broiled, or baked.

My supply of hams is limited. Weight runs from 13 to 22 pounds (average 15 pounds, which is the weight most people prefer). The price is 50 cents per pound uncooked.

**All shipments by Railway Express collect. Send check to**

## DUNCAN HINES
Box 538, Bowling Green, Ky.

# THE ART OF CARVING IN THE HOME

CORRECT carving is an art, which, when mastered, is an accomplishment that adds greatly to the charm and grace of dining. It brings both genuine pleasure to the carver, and an abundance of praise from the assembled guests.

In carving, as in everything else, there is a right and a wrong way to do it, and invariably, the right way is the best and easiest.

Do not take your carving duties as another one of those unnecessary evils—a task that must be performed regardless of results. Carving technique is not difficult, but requires a knowledge of how and where to cut.

The best flavor of meats and fowl is emphasized when it is carved and served in an appetizing manner.

How distressing it is, when guests see a host hack and slash across one bone after another and bespatter the table with odds and ends. Such performance always dampens the appetite of those present. But what a pleasing contrast it is to watch a carver, who dissects the joints smoothly without slashing up and down the bone, wondering if they will ever hit the joint. When one carves with ease and grace, producing smoothly cut pieces, it immediately brings forth enthusiastic and favorable comment.

In some homes, I have experienced a let-down after the carving got under way. For instance, last winter, I visited some friends, where eight were to have dinner. The husband was to bring himself and three others, but a sudden wash-out of a bridge prevented their arrival. Present was the hostess, a couple, and myself. When the turkey was placed on the table, the hostess invited the gentleman to carve. He eagerly accepted—and what did he do? Well, he proceeded to hack off all the meat on one side of the turkey and then turned it over and did the same thing on the other side, yet only four persons were to be served. You can imagine what the hostess thought, and what her husband said when he returned home and observed what had happened.

Another case I encountered was a novice carver and a roast of beef. He judged his slices by his own appetite and cut them so thick there was not enough meat to serve all those present. Was he embarrassed? It is doubtful whether he has offered to carve since.

The other extreme is a person carving slices so thin you suspect he wanted the roast to last until next pay day.

Carving should be done at the table always, except when there are too many guests present, which makes this impractical.

Standing to carve is not necessary and certainly is not a graceful poise, as carving does not require unusual strength. The carver's chair should be high enough—if you are a short or long-waisted person, adjust your chair to a suitable height.

No matter how good a story-teller you are, save them until after the carving is done, because slow carving takes the zest out of an otherwise fine dinner. While the carving is being done, let someone else tell the stories.

Knowledge, thoughtful practice, and always a sharp knife (which should be sharpened before it is placed on the dinner table) are the essentials for good carving. Above all, do not hack, slash, or saw. Use a swinging, smooth stroke and cut across the grain whenever possible. If you cut parallel with the grain, the meat will be tougher. Also be sure that you inquire of your guests if they prefer rare, medium, or well done, light or dark meat, the oyster of a fowl, etc. Do not serve all the most delectable cuts to one person.

After starting to slice, do not change the angle of your knife, or you will get a jagged slice instead of a nice, smooth one.

You should make a mental note of how many guests you have at your table, and for the first serving, cut no more than is needed, as the second helping should be as savory as the first. However, keep an eye on your guests' plates and be ready to carve and serve second helpings promptly when desired.

I have noticed how some men with robust appetites cut hunks or slabs of meat or fowl when serving the ladies. Occasionally, you may encounter a woman who will hold her own in matching your eating capacity, but remember, it is better form to serve the ladies thinner slices. They will accept a second helping, if desired, just as readily as we men. No one relishes mountains of food on a plate.

After you have mastered the art of carvng, then strive for speed.

Guests should appear unconscious of the efforts of the carver. The thoughtful hostess will engage the attention of the others so there will not be a pall of silence over the assembled guests as the carving is being done.

The method of carving in public eating places is necessarily quite different from carving in the home.

### TO THE LADIES

In days gone by, so history records, ladies of royalty and others took weekly lessons from a Master Carver and became experts in the art of carving.

Later on, correct carving in the home became practically a lost art, but today, in America, many women are taking an active interest in carving, and what a thrill it is to watch a woman do an efficient and dainty job of it. I do not mean that their slices are skimpy, but as I have said before, heavy pressure or great strength is not required. We men had better be careful, or the first thing we know, we will be relegated to the kitchen to become experts in the realm of dishwashing. If so, I hope we learn to do a clean job of it.

Before meats or fowl are arranged on the platter, see that any skewers, thread, cord, toothpicks, steel pins, etc., used for trussing are removed, excepting those used on rolled roasts, etc., that are necessary to hold the meat together while being carved.

Clean-cut slicing is impossible if the meat or fowl is under or over-cooked. The most attractive slices are the ones cut just the right thickness for the particular kind of meat that is being carved. Too thin slicing is ungenerous and too thick slicing lacks appetite appeal.

All too often, the meat or fowl is placed on the table in the wrong position, making it impractical for the carver. In my home, to help overcome this unfortunate handicap, I drew a chart showing the correct position in which a roast, etc., should be placed on the table. This chart was hung in the kitchen so the maid or anyone else could offer no excuse for placing the platter on the table in the wrong position.

The platter holding the roast, etc., should be of ample size, with enough margin around the meat—say 2 inches to 4 inches.

When a large roast or turkey is carved, there should also be a small extra platter (preheated) on which to place drumsticks, wings, etc. Place the brown or most appetizing side of the meat up on this platter.

Many carvers forget to serve parsley, watercress, etc., and serving more than just a bit is a hindrance. Do not put too many garnishes or vegetables on the platter when a roast is served, as you may see some of it scattered over the table. Remember, the carver needs plenty of room on the platter to do the right kind of job.

Very often the carver's end of the table is cluttered up with water glasses, candlesticks, flower vases, and other do-dads, so that there is not sufficient room for him to maneuver efficiently or gracefully. Be sure there is plenty of elbow room at this end of the table.

The carving directions given are for right-handed people. Left-handed folks will naturally adjust the position of the roast, etc., to suit their particular needs.

Spoons for serving gravy, dressing, etc., are very often overlooked when placing the carving set on the table. These are always necessary.

The illustrations that follow are of cuts of meats that are most frequently served in American homes, and the majority of these illustrations clearly show the principal bone structure of the various cuts of meats. If you will keep their location in mind, it will greatly aid you in your carving efforts.

While the art of carving cannot be mastered overnight, let me again emphasize that it is not difficult to learn, and the reward of your efforts is the feeling of self-satisfaction, plus the praise of your guests which is a pleasure in itself, well worth striving for.

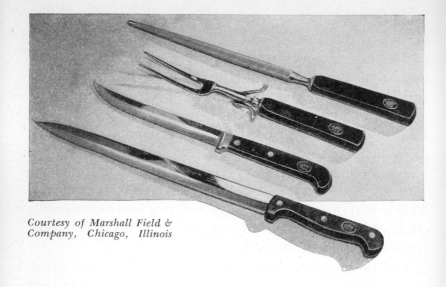

*Courtesy of Marshall Field &*
*Company, Chicago, Illinois*

# CARVING SETS

The knives illustrated above have a bevel blade similar to a straight razor. The entire line contains knives with blades of various lengths and shapes and they are not expensive.

When buying a carving set, select one with steel that will satisfactorily hold an edge and do not let beautiful handles mislead you.

The length of knives to be used for various cuts of meats and fowl is largely a matter of personal preference.

For broiled steaks, a 5½-inch to 6-inch stiff blade is used. The same type knife is also used for other broiled or fried meats.

For small game, use a knife with a 6-inch or 6½-inch stiff blade.

For a roast of beef and a leg of lamb, veal, etc., or for general carving, a knife with an 8-inch semi-flexible blade may be used.

For turkey or large roasts, use a knife with an 8½-inch to 10-inch semi-flexible blade.

All knives should be sharpened before they are brought to the table, as no one can carve satisfactorily without having a sharp knife. The same steel may be used for sharpening short and long blades.

The carving set should be kept separate from the rest of the cutlery as a matter of precaution in protecting the carving edge of the knives. It is a wise practice to wash the carving set separately and place the knife blades in leather cases to avoid dulling the edges by running against the steel or fork, which usually happens if loosely laid away.

For fish, use a silver knife with a broad 8-inch blade having a dull edge, and a wide fork.

There is also a larger, longer, and wider pronged fork named the "Carver's Helper" (not illustrated), which is often used to more securely hold large roasts firmly on the platter.

## HOW TO USE THE STEEL

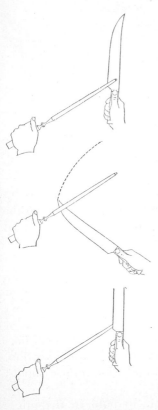

The steel is used to put a keen or sharp edge on the knife and there is a technique in handling it. The steel should be held firmly in the left hand, thumb parallel with fingers across and on top of handle. (See illustration.) Hold the point of the steel upward and slightly away from your body. Hold the knife in the right hand, as shown, place the heel of the blade (where the blade enters the handle) against the point of the steel on the side farthest from your body. With a quick swinging motion of the wrist and forearm, bring the blade down and across the steel toward the left hand, and continue this motion until the point of the blade has passed over the steel. Then the knife is again brought into position, but this time on the side of the steel nearest your body, and with the same motion, is drawn across the steel. This brings both sides of the blade in contact with the steel. As a rule, a half dozen strokes on each side will be sufficient. Do not bear too heavily on the knife, nor hold it at too great an angle. The edge of the knife should make about a 25-degree angle with the steel. The same steel may be used for short and long knives.

A PORTERHOUSE STEAK

The first step is to separate the meat from the bone as shown in illustration (on next page). The carver holds the steak steady by inserting the fork to the left of the large muscle and with the point of the steak knife severs the meat from around the bone, making the cut as close to the bone as possible. The bone should be removed to one side of the platter, so it will not interfere with making the slices.

With the fork still in position, and with the knife at right angles to the original position of the bone, the carver cuts slices about one inch in width, beginning at the bone end as illustrated (on next page). In this way the tenderloin and the large muscle are cut at the same time. It may be necessary, however, to cut thinner slices from this tenderloin section in order to serve each person a portion. (See drawing.) A slice of the tenderloin and wide muscle should be served each person.

In carving steaks, cut slices at an angle to hold in the juices and prevent the meat from drying out too quickly.

Unless the number of persons to be served makes it necessary, the flank end of the steak is not carved, but may be used in some attractive left-over dish at another meal. If it is to be served, it should be cut across the width. Thus the fibers that run lengthwise in this part of the steak are shortened and make a more desirable serving.

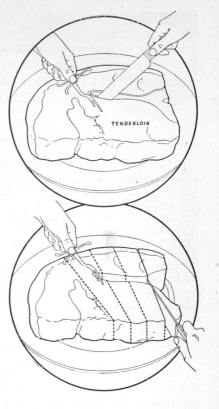

### SIRLOIN AND OTHER STEAKS

Carving a sirloin steak is essentially the same as carving a porterhouse steak. The bone is removed by cutting down close to it with the point of the knife. The steak is then cut into slices about one inch in width, cutting them on an angle to hold in the juices and prevent the meat from drying out too quickly. In carving any steak, the width of the slice is usually determined by the number of persons to be served. In sirloin steaks, the direction of the muscles change and the angle of the blade should be increased to cut the fibers as short as possible.

Carving a pin-bone sirloin steak is much easier if the pin bone is removed by the butcher and the flank end ground and inserted in the cavity left by removal of the bone. This not only makes carving easier, but it solves the problem of the flank end, because grinding this portion cuts the connective tissues and the flank end is made just as tender as the rest of the steak.

## ROUND STEAK

As a rule, the butcher cuts round steak much thinner than porterhouse or sirloin steaks and in carving round steak much wider portions are served. The individual portions usually are cut about 2 inches wide and 3 inches to 4 inches long. The natural divisions between the muscles may serve as a guide in carving round steak.

## SWISS STEAK

A swiss steak, being thicker than round steak, individual servings are carved thinner than a round steak.

## BEEF TENDERLOIN

Being boneless, beef tenderloin presents no problem in carving, except to cut even slices.

The carver holds the meat with the fork grasped in his left hand. Beginning at the large end, the tenderloin is cut across in slices a little less than ½ inch in thickness.

## BEEF BRISKET

Place boned beef brisket on the platter with the flat side down and with the largest end to the right of the carver. The general direction of the muscle fibers is parallel to the length of the platter. With the fork inserted in the thick part of the brisket, the carver begins at the small end and cuts straight down to the platter, making slices not more than ⅛ inch in thickness. These slices are cut across the grain of the meat.

## BEEF TONGUE

The tongue should be trimmed, removing the skin, etc., before bringing it to the table. It should be placed on the platter with the large end to the right and the rounded side away from the carver. The fork is inserted in the thick part and thin slices are cut straight down across the grain. About 2½ inches of the tip end should be severed and sliced lengthwise, so as to get the greatest number of good-sized slices.

STANDING RIB ROAST

Have the backbone separated from the ribs at the market, as this facilitates removing the backbone easily after roasting. With the backbone removed in the kitchen, carving is much easier because it leaves only the rib bones from which the slices must be loosened.

*Carving Instructions on next page.*

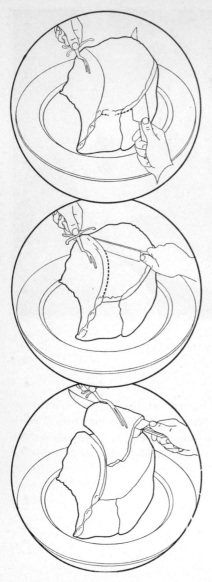

The roast is placed before the carver with the cut surface up and the rib side to his left. The carver firmly inserts the fork, with the guard up, between the two top ribs; beginning at the outside right edge at the large end of the roast, the knife is drawn through the roast to the rib side as shown in top drawing. A slice about ⅜ inch thick makes an attractive serving. It may be somewhat thicker or thinner according to personal preference.

The slice is loosened by cutting along the rib bone with the tip of the knife as shown in middle drawing.

As each slice is cut, it is steadied with the fork and lifted on the blade of the knife (as shown in bottom drawing) to one side of the platter, or if the platter is not large enough, to another hot smaller platter placed near the carver to receive the slices as they are made.

## ROLLED RIB ROAST

In carving a rolled rib roast, the important consideration is to make even slices which are uniform in thickness. To accomplish this, care should be taken not to alter the angle of the knife when making the slices.

The rolled rib roast is held together by cords, which obviously cannot be removed in the kitchen. If they were, the roast would fall apart. Good carving of a rolled rib roast, therefore, necessitates the cutting and disposition of cords in a neat manner. Only one cord is severed at a time as it is reached in making the slices. The cord is cut with the point of the knife, loosened with the fork, and removed to one side of the platter.

The roast is placed on the platter with the smaller cut side up and the larger side down so it will rest firmly. The carver holds the roast steady by inserting the fork at the extreme left side 1 inch or 2 inches below the top of the roast as illustrated. The guard on the fork should be up as it is in all cases when the carver is cutting toward his left hand. As the slices are made, the carving fork is taken out and moved downward from time to time as necessary.

In making the slice, the carver draws the knife from right to left through the roast. The thickness of the slice depends on personal preference and will vary from $\frac{1}{8}$ inch for a thin slice to $\frac{3}{8}$ inch for a thick slice. As each slice is carved, it is lifted on the blade of the knife and steadied with the fork as it is placed on one side of the platter, or to another hot platter provided for this purpose, or on the dinner plate.

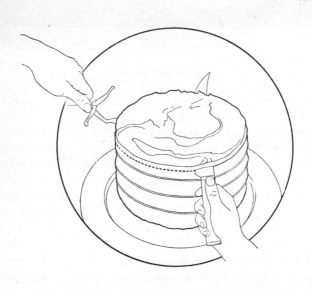

### BLADE POT ROAST

A blade pot roast contains at least a portion of one rib and a part of the blade bone. In the relatively long cooking period, the connective tissue, which binds the bones to the muscles, is softened to such an extent that these bones are loosened and may be slipped out easily, in which case it is just as well to remove them in the kitchen before the roast is brought to the table for carving. The carver then has only the task of making attractive servings from a boneless piece of meat. The chief problem in carving a blade pot roast, whether the bone is in or not, is to make attractive slices across the grain of the meat. There are several muscles, the fibers of which run in different directions and because of this, and because the bones may be in the roast, it is not possible to carve a slice parallel to the cut surface, such as one does in carving a rib roast. A very satisfactory method of carving a blade pot roast is illustrated on next page.

Holding the pot roast firmly with the fork inserted into the

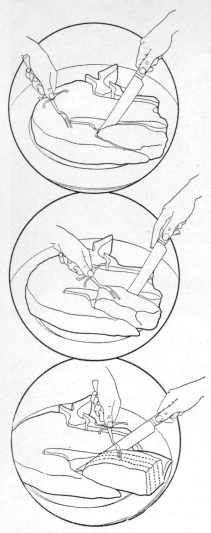

left, and following the natural dividing line between muscles, the carver removes a small section of the pot roast, separating the meat from the blade bone (if it has not been removed in the kitchen). The first drawing shows the carver cutting one section by running the knife along the division between two muscles and between the muscle and the bone. Next, the carver inserts the fork in the place just separated and with the knife on the top surface, he turns the meat so that the surface, which was in a horizontal position, is now in a vertical position, as shown in the second drawing. The grain of the meat is now parallel with the platter, and the carver can easily cut slices across the grain. With the fork inserted in this smaller portion of the roast (shown in the third drawing), the carver cuts slices down to the platter.

These slices should be cut ¼ inch to ⅜ inch in thickness. When one section of the pot roast is carved in this fashion, another section is carved in the same manner.

ROAST LOIN OF PORK

It is much easier to carve a roast loin of pork if the backbone has been separated from the ribs. This is done by the butcher sawing across the ribs close to and parallel to the backbone. The backbone becomes loosened during the roasting and is removed by cutting close to the backbone and parallel to the ribs as shown on the drawing. (On next page.)

The roast is placed on the platter so that the rib ends are up and the platter is placed before the carver so that the rib side is toward him. There are two good reasons for placing the roast before the carver in this fashion. First, the guests at the table see the more attractive side of the roast, and, second, it is much easier for the carver to follow the direction of the rib bones, which are his guide in making the slices, as all of the rib bones may not be absolutely perpendicular to the platter.

In carving a roast loin of pork, it should be born in mind that the servings are more tempting if the slices are cut fairly thin. A fork is inserted between the ribs to hold the roast firmly. The carver then draws the knife as close as possible to the left side of the first rib. In making the second slice, the knife is drawn as close as possible to the right side of the second rib. The third slice will be cut close to the left side of the second rib. Proceed in the same manner until there are enough slices to serve everyone at the table. One serving will contain a rib bone and the next will be boneless. It is not necessary to lift the slices to one side of the platter; instead they are allowed to fall back as they are cut off.

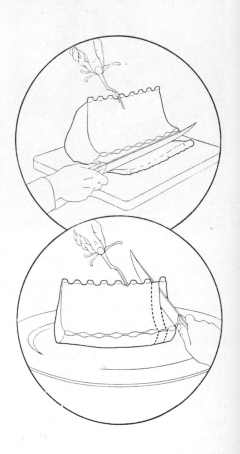

If personal preference indicates serving thicker slices than those previously outlined, then the cut is made between each two pairs of ribs; thus each serving contains a rib.

With a large roast loin of pork, it is possible to cut two boneless slices between each two ribs.

CROWN ROAST OF LAMB OR PORK

A crown roast of lamb or pork which has been prepared properly at the market is very easy to carve. In fact, the carver proceeds in much the same manner as in carving a pork loin roast.

*Carving Instructions on next page.*

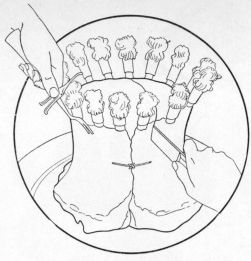

*Crown Roast*

The carver steadies the crown roast by inserting the fork to the left between the ribs. He then makes the slices by cutting through the center between each two ribs.

One chop and a portion of dressing or vegetables that may be used to fill the center of the crown are served to each person.

A crown roast of lamb or pork is suitable for special occasions, and it lends itself to many garnishes and may be served with a number of different accompaniments.

### BONED AND ROLLED SHOULDER ROASTS

Veal and lamb shoulders are boned and rolled for roasts and are placed on the platter with the cut surface at right angles to the platter. The carver makes the slices by cutting from the top of the roast down to the platter and allowing each slice to fall back as it is made. Boned and stuffed shoulder roasts are carved in the same manner, i.e., down through the meat and the dressing to the platter. These rolled shoulder roasts are held together with cords or skewers, which are removed by the carver as required.

ROAST *(left)* LEG OF LAMB

   Strange as it may seem, few carving instructions have ever taken
into consideration the fact that both right and left legs must be
carved, yet with the shank end always to the left of the carver, it is
obvious that there will be a difference in the position of the cushion
as it lies upon the platter.  If a left leg, the cushion will be toward,
and the thin side away from, the carver, as shown in illustration
above.  If a right leg, the reverse is true.   Behind the leg bone in
both a right or left leg is a large meaty section known as the cushion.
It is from this section that the most desirable servings are obtained.
In front of the leg bone in either leg is the thinner section.

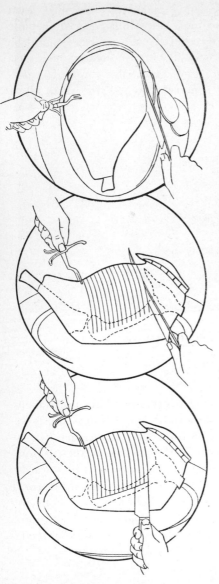

Drawings show a right leg.

Understanding the location of the bones will be a great help to the carver in making the most desirable servings. The two lower drawings indicate the bone structure and the lines on the chart represent the direction the knife will follow in making the slices. Note the relation of these lines (slices) to the bones.

If a large (right) leg, illustrated at left, the carver first inserts the fork firmly in the large end of the leg and carves two or three lengthwise slices from the thin side by turning the platter as shown in top drawing. This makes a flat surface on which the roast is then turned upright and rests firmly on this cut surface while the cushion is carved, as shown on two lower drawings. If it is a large left leg, the thin section will be away from the carver, in which case simply turn the platter in order to make these first few slices to form the base upon which the roast will rest while continuing the carving.

With the fork inserted in the left of the roast, and beginning at the shank end of the leg, the carver makes the first slice down to the leg bone and continues to make slices until the aitch bone is reached, if that many slices are required. These slices should be $\frac{1}{8}$ inch to $\frac{1}{4}$ inch in thickness to make the most attractive servings. With the fork still in place, the carver runs the knife parallel to the leg bone, right to left, in order to free the slices all at one time. These slices should be served on very hot plates with a little of the natural (mint-flavored) gravy.

A WHOLE HAM

There are many ways of carving hams; and while the method illustrated in the four drawings may appear to some as a decided departure from established procedure, it is not a departure from principles and has been carefully worked out to find the easiest way to secure the maximum number of servings, uniform in size and attractive in appearance.

Carving a whole ham presents some of the same problems encountered in carving a leg of lamb. It has the same bone and muscle structure, and right and left legs should also be considered. Since a baked ham is usually decorated in some way, it should be placed on the platter with the fat side up. The shank end should be to the carver's left, the same as a leg of lamb. If a right ham, the thin side of the ham will be nearest the carver, and if a left ham, be away from him. (The photograph shows a left ham, and the drawings show a right ham.)

In carving a right ham (see drawing), the first two or three slices are cut parallel to the length of the ham from the thin side, which is nearest the carver. The purpose of making these first few slices is to form a base upon which the ham may more firmly rest upright while the carving is being done. Next turn the ham so it rests upright on this flat-cut surface (see the two center drawings for bone structure of a ham). Hold the ham firmly with the fork and cut a small wedge-shaped piece near the shank end (note drawing); this facilitates making the slices and releasing them from the bone after they are made (note drawing). The carver then proceeds to cut thin vertical slices down to the leg bone until the aitch bone is reached. With the fork still in place to steady the ham, the slices are released from the bone by running the knife along the leg bone at right angles to the slices. If, after carving one side, more servings are desired, the ham is turned back to its original position on the platter with the fat side up, and slices are again cut at right angles to the bone. These slices are not as wide as those from the cushion section, but they do make attractive servings for second helpings.

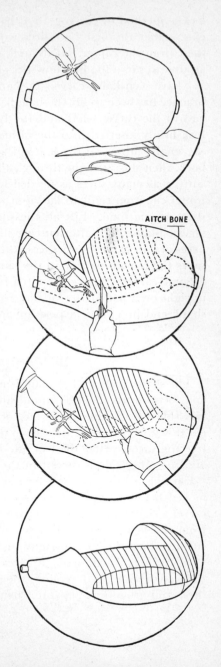

AITCH BONE

The method of carving a left ham is the same as for a right one, except that the first few slices will be removed from the side farthest from the carver. If desired, the carver may swing the platter around to carve the first few slices from the thin side.

I have seen hams carved in many different ways, and a common practice has been to lay the ham flat on the platter, fat side up, hock end to the carver's left and the butt end to the right. With the fork firmly inserted into the meat about $2\frac{1}{2}$ inches to the right of the small end, make the first cut a "V" about 3 inches right of the hock, then slice straight through the ham down to the bone. After cutting as many slices as needed for the first servings make a horizontal cut from right to left along the top of the bone to loosen all slices at one time. Lift all the slices at once and place them on a service platter. If, after cutting slices across to the aitch bone, it is necessary to carve more slices, turn the ham over and proceed to carve the remaining side in the same way.

Some carvers remove the aitch bone in the butt end and stand it upright on a flat platter or in a round deep dish, holding it by the shank end in a vertical position.

### CARVING A HALF HAM

The shank end of a half ham is not as difficult to carve as the butt end, because the bone is round and the carver can see it from the face side. Beginning at the face of the ham (cut surface), slices are cut down to the bone; then the knife is run parallel to the bone to free the slices. After the top side is carved, the ham is turned over and the other side is carved in the same way.

Carving a butt end will be much easier if the aitch bone is removed before carving. The face of the ham should be toward the carver's right, fat side up. Beginning at the top, thin slices are cut from the face of the ham down to the leg bone, and removed by cutting along the bone at right angles to the slices.

In carving a half ham, it is easier to carve only two or three slices at a time and remove them, rather than to make all the slices and attempt to separate them from the bone at one time.

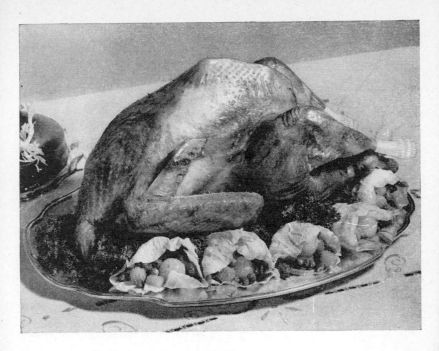

### A TURKEY

Again I emphasize the importance of having anything you carve placed in the correct position on the table. The turkey legs should be placed to the carver's right and the neck to his left. Usually the turkey comes to the table lying flat on its back.

In general, the muscles run lengthwise of the bird. Before starting to carve, tilt it a bit forward so the legs and wings are in a more accessible position to sever. Then remove the leg (both drumstick and thigh in one piece). To do this, only three cuts are necessary. Meanwhile the bird is held firmly by placing the fork astride the keel or breast bone. Make the first cut in front of the thigh and cut deep to the pinion or joint which holds it to the backbone. Second, cut back of the thigh to the pinion joint. These two cuts practically make a V. Third, cut the skin between the leg and body so it will not tear as the thigh is removed. All three cuts are shown in the top drawing (next page). Finally, grasp the frilled drumstick in your fingers, turn it toward you and the entire leg should easily

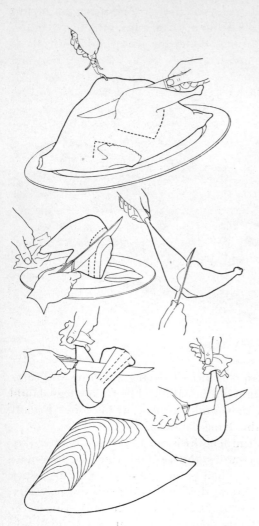

and quickly pull cleanly away from the socket joint. Of course, if the turkey is not thoroughly cooked, it may be necessary to force the leg away from the body with the knife to dislocate the joint. Lay the entire leg (drumstick and thigh) on the hot side platter. To separate the leg (drumstick) from the thigh, lay the browned side down, because the inside permits the joint to be more clearly seen and is an easier way to sever with one clean cut through the joint as shown on the drawing. If an attempt is made to sever this joint by cutting from the outside, you may be a bit embarrassed, because the joint is not so readily visible from that side. After the drumstick and thigh have been severed, place them upright on the platter, so the brown side is on top, which is more appetizing to your guests.

Next, remove the wing. Here some carvers encounter difficulties because they fail to observe the fact that the joint that holds the wing to the shoulder is much closer to the body than the joint that holds the thigh to the backbone. Therefore, in removing the wing, first make one cut on the outside a little in front of the shoulder joint. The second cut forms another V as shown on the top drawing. Then cut under the wing to sever it from the body, and as the joint is approached, turn the knife inward toward the front of the shoulder and cut deep enough so the blade will strike between the joint. Now place the fork under the end of the wing and push out and forward. It should disjoint easily. Place the wing on the side platter and, again, it is easy to sever the upper and lower part when cut from the inside. (The tips of the wings should be removed before roasting, as there is little meat on them to eat, and they are good for flavoring soups and gravies.)

A small piece of dark meat, the "oyster," is a choice morsel which lies in the cavity in the back, or on each side of the backbone just above the thigh, ahead of the tail. From the drumstick, slice the dark meat in ¼-inch slices. These slices are made by holding the end of the drumstick upright in the left hand and cutting from the inside down through the ligaments as shown on drawing. In slicing the thigh, hold it flat on the small platter with the fork and cut in ¼-inch slices. These lengthwise sections are then cut across the grain at a 45-degree angle into two, three, or four pieces, depending on the size of the bird. Do not stop to do a clean job of the bone.

Some carvers leave the drumstick and thigh in one piece. To carve in this manner, hold the drumstick as shown on drawing, slice the meat first from the thigh and then from the drumstick. It does not matter much which method you follow, but be sure to cut attractive-looking slices.

Some carvers place the dark meat at one end of the small platter and the white meat at the other end.

In carving the breast or white meat, hold the fork in the left hand and insert it firmly astride the keel or breast bone, just beyond its highest point. Another way is to insert the fork through the rib section. Some people carve the breast parallel to the breast bone, but many prefer the method shown on drawing, which is my favorite, because I can carve more uniform and appetizing slices by using this angle across the grain. Whether to carve enough white meat to serve all plates, or to cut the breast as each plate is served, depends on the preference of the carver, but in any case you should follow the method that will insure hot meat for all and be in keeping with the type of dinner service. Usually cutting slices as each plate is served is the better procedure.

Another method of carving a turkey is to remove only the drumstick portion of the leg, removing the wing as before, then tip the bird on its side, so the breast portion is away from the carver. This brings the thigh (still attached to the body) uppermost. Carve the dark meat from the thigh by slicing parallel to the bone, first on one side, then on the other side. This technique yields thick or thin slices as may be desired. The thigh is easily held in position with the fork placed astride the thigh bone.

Some carvers slice the breast upwards, but the majority prefer to carve the breast as outlined on the drawing.

A spoon is used for serving the dressing from the vent end, which usually has sufficient opening without further cutting. The vent end is more convenient for getting at the dressing until the bird needs turning around to carve the remaining side. Then, if need be, remove the dressing from the neck region, by cutting a section of skin and folding it back.

In serving, first place the dressing on the plate and on top of it, or to one side, the dark meat, and on top of the dark meat place slices of white meat. As some people prefer giblet gravy over the meat and dressing, others like it on the meat, and others on the dressing only, and some dislike it altogether, I believe the best procedure is to have the gravy served by someone else, or passed.

## CAPON OR ROAST CHICKEN

A capon or chicken is carved in practically the same manner as a turkey. The principal difference is in the smaller size of pieces served. However, some carvers, after removing the leg, thigh, and wing, prefer to have the position of the bird at right angles with the breast facing the carver.

The drumstick and thigh cannot be cut into as many pieces as a turkey and very often these pieces are served as full portions.

The back is smaller than a turkey, and for that reason the oyster may be too small to offer.

Broiled or fried chicken is usually served as it is cut for cooking.

These, or any other water fowl, are carved somewhat differently from a turkey or chicken, because the shape of the body is different. The greater portion of the meat is on the breast, consequently some carvers prefer slicing the breast before removing the legs or wings.

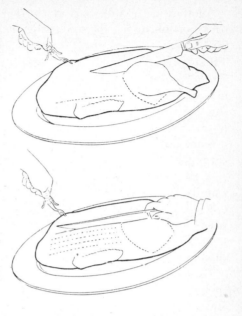

Although some epicures consider the wings a choice part, there is little meat on them, and many carvers make a cut parallel with the breast, just above the wing joint (see drawing), and do not remove or serve the wings.

The position of the bird on the table is the same as for a turkey or chicken.

To remove the leg and thigh in one piece, make a V cut, the same as for carving a turkey, but remember, the thigh joint lies closer to the backbone and is more difficult to remove from a small water fowl than from a chicken or turkey. You may need to use the knife blade to pry the thigh away from the back to dislocate the socket joint.

To carve the breast, leave the wing intact, insert the knife just above the wing joint parallel to the keel or breast bone, and push the knife straight down. As it hits the breast bone, turn the blade slightly to loosen the meat from the bone. Hold the bird by inserting the fork prongs deep and piercing the breast bone; one prong on each side. Do not carve the slices too thick. An average duck should yield four slices on each side of the breast, a larger duck, five or six slices. Some carvers prefer placing the duck or goose with the breast facing them, but, again, the position is a matter of personal preference.

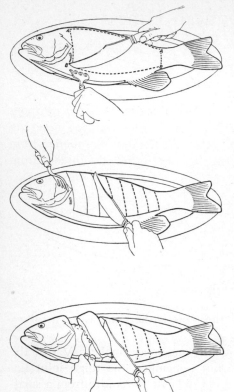

Place the whole fish on a platter, tail to the right and the backbone away from the carver. Use a broad 8-inch silver (not steel) blade knife with a blunt edge and a wide fork. Hold the fish firmly by placing the fork in the head, as shown on drawing. Sink the blade of the knife deep to the middle from "A" to "A" and from "B" to "B," also cut from "A" to "B" near the head and tail (see drawing), then cut in 1-inch to 1½-inch slices as indicated. Use the same procedure for carving the other side of the fish.

### SMALL PAN FISH

When serving small pan fish, first cut from "A" to "A" and from "B" to "B," also from "A" to "B" along the lines as shown on drawing. Then lift the entire filet away from the bone structure by first loosening and lifting along the top line "A" to "A" and then down to the bottom line "B" to "B." Each side or filet is served as one portion.

*Thanks to the National Live Stock and Meat Board, Chicago, for their aid in compiling these carving instructions.*

# Every Traveler Should Have
# These Books by Duncan Hines

Here is an unbiased directory of about 2,000 of the best eating places along the highways and in cities of America from Maine to California and Canada, from Minnesota to Florida and Mexico.

6th Edition (illust.)
9th printing
5"x7½", 296 pages
### $1.50

This book describes hotels, inviting cottages, modern auto courts and guest houses of refinement from Coast to Coast with accommodations appealing to discriminating guests.

2nd Edition (illust.)
5"x7½", 296 pages
### $1.50

**NEITHER BOOK CONTAINS ANY ADVERTISING AND NO FEE IS ACCEPTED FOR LISTINGS**

*These books make delightful gifts for bridge or party prizes, birthdays, anniversaries, vacationists, travelers, holidays, etc.*

# INDEX

---

*If you possess any recipes that are simple, easily prepared and which have always appeared on the table with exclamations of pleasure I shall be happy indeed if you will send them in for use in future editions.*

*PLEASE DO NOT ASK FOR ADVERTISING RATES in my books. For obvious reasons, I cannot accept any commercial advertising.*